Beads and Bead Makers

Cross-Cultural Perspectives on Women

General Editors: Shirley Ardener and Jackie Waldren,
for The Centre for Cross-Cultural Research on Women, University of Oxford

ISSN: 1068-8536

Beads and Bead Makers

Gender, Material Culture and Meaning

Edited by
*Lidia D. Sciama and
Joanne B. Eicher*

Oxford • New York

First published in 1998 by
Berg
Editorial offices:
150 Cowley Road, Oxford, OX4 1JJ, UK
70 Washington Square South, New York, NY 10012, USA

Berg is the imprint of Oxford International Publishers Ltd.

Library of Congress Cataloging-in-Publication Data

A catalogue record for this book is available from the Library of Congress.

British Library Cataloguing-in-Publication Data

A catalogue record for this book is available from the British Library.

ISBN 1 85973 990 3 (Cloth)
        1 85973 995 4 (Paper)

Typeset by JS Typesetting, Wellingborough, Northants.
Printed in the United Kingdom by Biddles Ltd, Guildford and King's Lynn.

Contents

Foreword

Lidia D. Sciama and Joanne B. Eicher

Most of the chapters in this volume were first presented at a workshop held at Queen Elizabeth House under the auspices of the Cross Cultural Centre for Research on Women at the University of Oxford (Sciama 1995). The intent was to continue earlier cross-cultural studies of women and crafts, covered in part in the volume on *Dress and Gender* (Barnes and Eicher 1992). Our initial plan was to examine the labour conditions of the women who make, thread, or otherwise work with beads and to analyse their activities as traders, entrepreneurs and employers of other women, in a number of different geographical and cultural areas. Other themes were the present-day uses of beads, as well as a broad historical overview of the processes and routes through which large quantities of glass beads, mainly made in Europe, were traded worldwide, while some eventually made their way back to Europe, their value much increased. The range of knowledge and variety of approaches of workshop participants and subsequent contributors, enlarged the scope of our book. Consequently, the papers presented a variety of subjects and emphasis shifted from the making to the exchange, the uses and the symbolic meanings of beads, and the enquiry partly turned from the makers to the objects, with gender the overall theme.

Although workshop contributions ranged in time from pre-history to the present, we have chosen to start *in medias res*. The Introductory Essay highlights different aspects and shows potential lines for future enquiries and studies of beads. Trivellato's paper on the making of glass beads and their worldwide export from Venice, covers the period from the Middle Ages to the nineteenth and early twentieth century, when the bead trade was most active.

Carey's Overview shows the importance of beads in African aesthetic and ritual culture, and Eicher shows that on the Kalabari island of Buguma, Nigeria, a hand-blown glass bead from Venice is the emblem of the Fubara, or Jackreece, family. The bead, as an exclusive and cherished property, is displayed with great dignity and pride at all ceremonial and festive occasions. For another part of Nigeria, the town of Ilorin, Kwara state, Ann O'Hear treats the topic of *lantana* beads and their more frequent use by women than by men in contemporary times. Such use contrasts to other areas of Yorubaland where both male and female title-holders wear beads as part of their regalia.

In the Americas, Laurie Wilkie analyses the cachet of men, who receive and wear the beads tossed to them by women, during Mardi Gras in New Orleans. Helen Bradley Foster opens the subject of beads worn by African Americans. The religious significance of a rosary as a string of beads and its modified interpretation among both Protestant and Catholic Aymara makers and wearers in Isluga, Chile, is the focus of Penny Dransart's paper. Lynn Meisch looks at beads and their gendered use in Ecuador, emphasizing the colour red as a critical aspect. Monica Janowski investigates a variety of factors related to gender and status in the wearing of beads by the Kelabit people of Sarawak on the island of Borneo. She indicates that value is related to age, and the most valued beads may go back over two thousand years, which raises archaeological questions.

While some scholars have considered the study of beads to be of little interest, archaeologists have shown otherwise. Indeed, beads, usually crafted from materials that outlast long-standing burial and are less subject to decay than other artefacts (such as textiles), are frequently found in archaeological sites. As we edited this volume, we continued to be surprised by the amount of archaeological knowledge that can be derived from careful interpretation of beads as found in the work of Spector (1976) and shown in the presence of extensive bibliographies, such as Karklins' and Sprague's (1972).

Several authors draw from this source for their chapters. For example, Foster finds that beads are generally ignored in discussions of African American dress, but she points out that archeological finds, paintings and portraits add a dimension to understanding the life and treasured objects of African descendants in America. Archaeological evidence also bears on Carey's discussion of several types of beads throughout Africa. Cecilia Braghin surveys evidence from China in Neolithic and early historic times with earliest dates of 3000 BC to a later date of 771 BC. Helen Hughes-Brock's chapter on Mycenaean beads from roughly 1650 BC to 1100 BC – a remarkable example of archaeological research methods – shows their relevance to understanding of contemporary material culture by anthropologists.

The Appendices by Stephanie Tomalin and Carol Wills acknowledge an important dimension to the topic of beads – the fact that the wearing of beads continues as a fashion among men and women in Europe and America. Tomalin, herself an active bead worker and entrepreneur, provides definitions for terms that she has found helpful in the course of her work and which could be of interest and value to bead collectors and wearers, while Wills describes numerous examples of the role of Oxfam in promoting bead production and distribution beyond the confines of isolated places.

A general point to be made from the chapters in this book concerns the closeness of craft objects to their makers and users, and indeed the nature of craft work itself. In the Venetian context, where experience and skill in different trades, such as building, glass blowing, weaving, restoration and carving are often upheld as among the best and most enduring traits of the local culture, the closeness between object and maker emerges with striking evidence. If therefore we ask why people are prepared to pay very high prices for slowly manufactured things, sometimes hardly superior to mass produced equivalents, we might answer in Maussian terms, that, compared with even the best of industrial products, handmade objects carry something of the spirit of the person who made them, or, in Derrida's words, who 'gave [them] their time' (Mauss 1950; Derrida 1991).

This is certainly true for objects strongly connoted as 'male', as for example, the elegant boats, patiently crafted in Venice's yards. But it may be even more apposite for those crafts such as lace making (Sciama 1992) and bead making or stringing to which women have traditionally given much of their time and attention, and which have been an integral basis of their livelihood, their self-image and sense of identity.

Acknowledgments

We are grateful to all the workshop participants who not only prepared their original papers, but willingly responded to our comments for final editing. We also thank the authors we found later who have contributed to the volume and added to its scope.

We thank Professor Glauco Sanga, Dr. Gianni Dore, Dr. Nadia Filippini, Dr. Alberta Basaglia, director of Venice's Centro Donna, and the 'Italian Society of Women Historians' for their invitation to hold an additional meeting in Venice, where we enjoyed a unique opportunity to meet local experts on the history and the technical aspects of bead-craft. We appreciate the invitation of the editors of *Ricerca Folklorica* to publish some of the papers, which Berg Publishers courteously permitted.

Several colleagues and friends need specific mention: professor Preston-Whyte kindly permitted us to reproduce some of her illustrations and Lois Dubin, her useful trade map. Robert Liu allowed us to print his picture of a Venetian glass bead of the type most prominent in Kalabari ceremonial. Professor Wendy James generously provided several of her own field photographs.

In addition we want to acknowledge the work of authors such as Lois Dubin, Peter Francis, John and Ruth Picard and Robert Liu whose books with excellent colour illustrations provide general coverage and display their knowledge of and passion for the study of beads. The Picards have also opened a museum dedicated to the history and aesthetic display of trade beads in Africa. Robert Liu and Carolyn Benesh serve as co-editors of the magazine *Ornament* which celebrated its 20th anniversary in 1997, contributing significantly through the years to documenting the history, production and use of beads throughout the world.

We would also like to thank the directors and staff of Venice's Museo Correr and of Oxford's Pitt-Rivers Museum for their assistance and their permission to reproduce valuable materials, Barbara Sumberg who carefully read through each chapter draft with her keen editorial eye, raising useful questions for the editors and the authors, Kathryn Earle, Sara Everett, Judy Mabro and Nigel Hope for their attention and their patience in the production of this volume. We are grateful to all members of the Centre for Cross-Cultural Research on Women; Lucy Butterwick for her invaluable activity in ensuring its smooth and orderly running. Professor Sandra Burman and Cecillie Swaisland provided interesting materials, while Professor Abner Cohen and Dr. Helen Callaway offered insightful comments on parts of the manuscript. Above all, thanks to Shirley Ardener, whose enthusiastic support of the idea of mounting a workshop on beads, invaluable advice and practical help made this work possible.

Lidia D. Sciama and Joanne B. Eicher

References

Derrida, J. (1991), *Donner le temps*, Paris: Galilie.

Dubin, L. (1987), *The History of Beads from 30,000 BC to the Present*, New York: Harry N. Abrams Incorporated.

Filippini, N.M. and Sciama, L.D. (eds) (1996), 'La vita sociale delle perle. Produzione materiale, usi simbolici e ruoli sessuali: da Murano all'Africa e al Borneo,' *La ricerca folklorica*, 34, 3–58. Brescia: Grafo edizioni.

Francis, P. (1954), *Beads of the World: A Collector's Guide with Price References*. Atglen, Pa: Schiffer Publishing, Ltd.

Karklins, K. and Sprague, R. (1972), 'Glass Trade Beads in North America: An Annotated Bibliography', *Historical Archaeology*, no. 6, 87–101.

Liu, R. (1995) *Collectable Beads: A Universal Aesthetic*, Visa, Ca: Ornament, Inc.

Mauss, M. (1923–4), 'Essai sur le don: forme et raison de l'échange dans les sociétés archaïques', *L'Année Sociologique* I, pp. 30–186. Available in English as *The Gift: Forms and Functions of exchange in Archaic Societies*. Translated by Ian Cunnison (1967), New York: Norton.

Picard, J. and R. (1986), *Chevrons from the West African Trade*, vol I, Carmel, CA: Picard African Imports.

—— (1986), *Tabular Beads from the West African Trade*, vol II, Carmel, CA: Picard African Imports.

—— (1987), *Fancy Beads from the West African Trade*, vol III, Carmel, CA: Picard African Imports.

—— (1988), *White Hearts, Feather and Eye Beads from the West African Trade*, vol IV, Carmel, CA: Picard African Imports.

—— (1989), *Russian Blues, Faceted and Fancy Beads from the West African Trade*, vol V, Carmel, CA: Picard African Imports.

—— (1991), *Millefiori Beads from the West African Trade*, vol VI, Carmel, CA: Picard African Imports.

—— (1993), *Chevron and Nueva Cad Beads*, vol VII, Carmel, CA: Picard African Imports.

Sciama, L.D. (1992), 'Lacemaking in Venetian Culture', in J. Eicher and R. Barnes, eds., *Dress and Gender: Making and Meaning*, Oxford: Berg.

—— (1995), Beads and gender, *Anthropology Today*, vol. II, no. 2, pp. 21–2.

Spector, J. (1976), 'The Interpretive Potential of Glass Trade Beads in Historic Archaeology', *Historical Archaeology*, no. 10, 17–27.

List of Figures

1

Gender in the Making, Trading and Uses of Beads: An Introductory Essay

Lidia D. Sciama

Introduction

Beads are among the most ancient and widespread of human ornaments. In parts of Africa, especially Libya and the Sudan, beads fashioned from ostrich shell were made as early as ten thousand years BC. Throughout the centuries materials used to make beads included stone, shell, clay, seeds, animals' teeth and bone, or metals such as tin, iron, copper and gold. The people of Benin, for example, have made elaborate beaded clothing and regalia since the fifteenth century, using coral brought mainly by the Portuguese. In Ilorin, throughout the nineteenth century, the Yoruba used agate, carnelian and red jasper, which they obtained through trans-Saharan trade, while in Bida and at Ife, the original home of the Yoruba people, beads were manufactured with glass obtained by melting down bottles imported from North Africa and Europe by a technique which recalls that of Venetian lamp work (O'Hear, this volume & Beier 1982: 4).

Glass beads found by archaeologists in coastal areas of Southern and Eastern Africa were imported from Egypt and Rome through the Sahara since the fourth century AD, while opaque Indian glass beads probably go back to the third century AD. However, most of the glass beads used in Africa since the fifteenth century were imported from Italy, Bohemia and the Netherlands – as Geary writes, 'by the million' (1994: 1–4, & Carey, this vol.). Indeed, most ethnographic museums have long been in possession of considerable collections of beads and beaded objects, largely gathered throughout the nineteenth and early part of the twentieth centuries.

An idea that a study of beads and their manufacture and trade might be interesting and timely occurred to me after a visit to Oxford's Pitt-Rivers Museum, where numerous samplers specify the Venetian origin of the beads (Figures 1.1, 1.2 and 1.3). But the popularity and diffusion of beads are not solely confined to history and to antiquity. On the contrary, over the last ten or fifteen years, beads have appeared in most markets throughout the world in great quantities and in a large variety of styles and materials. Numerous antique shops and exhibitions have shown

1

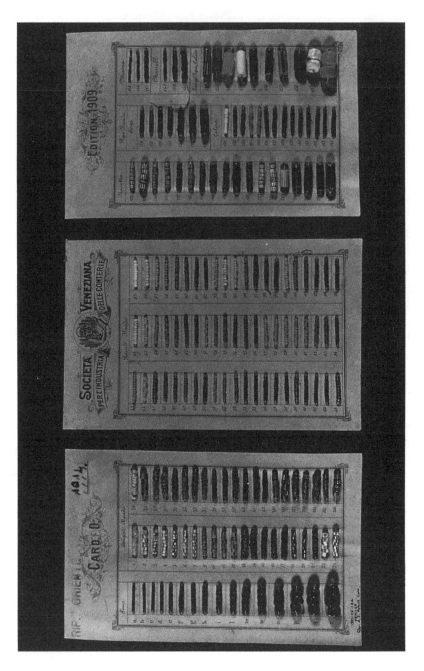

Figure 1.1 A sample card from the *Società Veneziana per l'Industria delle Conterie* (Oxford, Pitt Rivers Museum).

Figure 1.2 The Lion of Saint Mark (Oxford, Pitt-Rivers Museum. From a South African Mission c. 1890).

Figure 1.3 The Island of Saint George, Venice (Oxford, Pitt-Rivers Museum).

unprecedented quantities of beaded objects and necklaces, as well as loose beads, of the most varied and heterogeneous fashions. In Venice, where I have conducted my fieldwork, these are often described as 'African'. As was explained to me by the owner of a well-known glass factory, in the last century beads which proved particularly popular on the African or other extra-European markets were especially produced for export. Despite competition from factories now operating in various parts of the world, Venetian beads are still in demand and their production has enjoyed remarkable continuity.

Since the 1960s, when beads were first adopted as personal ornament by Californian 'flower children' and 'hippies', they started to appeal to the imagination of collectors and traders, and to be often worn, especially by the young. Such widespread use of beads, especially those bearing some mark of 'exoticism', clearly witnessed a new interest in and attraction towards 'other' cultures and a critique of the West; in the United States this was often associated with the Equal Rights movement and the Vietnam protest, as well as a disenchantment with the consumer society. The mere wearing of a token, commonly associated with Indian holy men, or with African and South-East Asian worlds, then imagined to have been happier and freer than Western societies, was at the same time a protest against and a rejection of too rigid a division of gender roles and control of sexuality.[1]

As some of the papers in this volume show, the use of beads is (or was) often tied to beliefs concerning both the social and the cosmological order, ritual cycles related to human production and reproduction, persons' progression through systems of age-sets, their position within status hierarchies, and, above all, distinctions of gender. Beads then clearly stand out as symbolic markers and their presence in conjunction with the most diverse styles of apparel stimulates anthropological questions concerning their meanings in different cultures.

Our aims in organizing a workshop on beads were both to examine some of their present-day uses, and to look back in time at the processes and the routes through which large quantities of glass beads, mainly made in Europe, were traded worldwide, while some eventually made their way back to Europe, their value much increased. As well as describing aspects of the social life and the social histories of different populations, our contributors also brought to light a number of general questions which I shall briefly sum up in the paragraphs to follow.

Bead Making and Material Culture

Gender is always a fundamental criterion in the organization of traditional crafts and early industries.[2] According to tradition, glass blowing in Venice is strongly connoted as masculine work (Sciama 1992: 122–3). The island of Murano where most glassworks are located, with its smoke-filled furnaces in low-ceilinged one-storey factories, darkened windows, large sparkling showrooms and noisy transport boats piled high with freshly packed cartons, clearly strikes one as a predominantly 'male space'. Indeed most of the glass-blowers and master-craftsmen I spoke with strongly emphasized that fashioning the hot molten glass, mainly by the force of one's lungs, was certainly not a woman's task: both the physical demands and the artistry required are viewed as exclusively masculine. It naturally follows that women are assigned tasks considered 'lighter', but in reality these too demand a very high degree of skill, precision and perseverance. It is the men's task to produce, cut and finish the multi-coloured glass canes from which are made all manner of beads and seed beads, while the women thread them and prepare them for shipping. There is, however, a completely different branch of production in which Venetian women excel, and which has traditionally been an essentially feminine craft: the making and decorating of beads one at a time, by the use of a small but intense flame (see Trivellato, this volume).

In many parts of Africa, as Margret Carey points out, the decisive criterion in determining whether beads should be made by women or men is the nature of the material used: it is usually women who create beads from substances deemed relatively 'soft', like clay, seeds or ostrich egg-shells, while the men cut hard stones, or they prepare the kiln and melt down the glass, which women have previously collected and reduced to powder, before they are recycled as beads. In Mali and Mauritania the women imitate the metal filigree jewellery made by men by using the supple blades of golden straw grass (Carey, this volume).

That men should do the stone cutting and drilling, leaving it to women to polish, finish and thread the beads, seems to have been an almost universal rule, but according to Ann O'Hear 'the division of labour is not invariable', since changes may have occurred through time. For example, in Bida, Nupe women may have been the principal bead makers. In her view, the industry there is less gender specific than is the norm, but genders are segregated in different stages of the process. What is more, as was the case in Venice, the women's participation may have been hidden and subject to male control.

An interesting feature of glass beads is that, unlike those made from materials found in nature, like shells, stones, seeds, and so forth, they were often made deliberately to imitate natural stones, through the chemical transformation of sand and soda.[3] In that respect they may truly be regarded as an early example of much in contemporary life that is (often negatively) viewed as the product of an all-pervasive artificiality, and a matter of reflection for anthropologists: synthetics, plastic, and, to make a leap to matters of deep current concern, artificial intelligence and artificial insemination (Leroi-Gourhan 1977, vol. II: 463–72; Strathern 1992: 47–55 & 198).

Also in their use as tokens of value, beads may be viewed as early signs of a progression towards disembedded, impersonal economic exchanges, increasingly divorced from the social contexts in which they take place. However, in as far as the economic power which beads symbolize is visible and often expresses aesthetic as well as purely economic aspirations, they are a far cry from present-day currencies and from 'invisible' plastic-card finance (Graeber 1996: 5).

It is worth adding that an abundant production and active worldwide distribution of glass beads has not in any way undermined the prior and much greater prices of genuine stones, but, on the contrary, it may have caused their value to rise, by emphasizing their authenticity and their relative scarcity. It is, however, of interest that old glass beads are eagerly sought out by collectors and dealers, since, thanks to their history and their supposed migrations, their value too has much increased. As Walter Benjamin observed, authenticity is itself created partly by time.

History and Long-distance Trade

Numerous historians have recently observed that, by creating systematic interaction between distant and separate societies, trade maintains 'transcultural' networks of relationships, with their own rules and conventions, which may be viewed as cultures in their own right. Their study sheds new light on the history of areas hitherto described under the generic label of 'Third World' and, in particular, on aspects of social groups or village communities that earlier ethnographies may have left in obscurity, conveying an exaggerated idea of their isolation (Cohen 1965; Wolf 1982; Curtin 1984 and Appadurai 1986).

Beads, along with textiles, are among the foremost items of long-distance trade. Moved from continent to continent since very early times, they were often used in conjunction with, or in place of, cowries which were brought to the east coast of Africa from the Pacific Ocean since the tenth century BC, as at a later stage were turquoise from Egypt and lapis lazuli from Afghanistan (Leroi-Gourhain 1977, vol. II: 96). Glass beads were made in Egypt and Mesopotamia as early as the middle of the second millennium BC and traded by Phoenicians in the first half of the first millennium, but their greatest diffusion dates back to the early Renaissance (Hughes-Brock, this volume).[4]

As Trivellato shows (this volume), beads were economically significant items in early Venetian exports. Indeed, although geographical expansion at the turn of the sixteenth century ironically worked to the detriment of Venice's economy, the importance of its international exchanges is fully illustrated in the city's iconography: the largest room in the Doge's apartments, which extends from the courtyard adjoining St Mark's Square to the canal at its back, and which was mainly used as a reception and audience room, is entirely decorated with maps, while two large globes represent respectively the earth and the celestial spheres. In other words, the whole is a *summa* of Renaissance geographical knowledge, and the aim is obviously to show the full extent of Venetian power, the range of the city's commerce and the daring of its travellers.[5]

The most interesting of the maps in this context is that which represents the coast of West Africa, 'from Morocco to Mandinga', with the islands of Cape Verde, Madeira and the Canaries (Figure 1.4a). Above the maps, and following the curvature of the windows, are the portraits of Venetian explorers, as well as the picture of a group of travellers receiving gifts or, as the art historian writes, 'tokens of submission' from African indigenes (Franzoi 1982: 2).[6] The main focus of the picture is on two princely figures standing proudly in the foreground (Figure 1.4b). Three Africans adorned with pendant earrings and feathers, held by a cloth band round the forehead and waist, kneel before them proffering precious stones and pearls, while another displays a large elephant's tusk which he is holding high over his shoulder.

Among the portraits is that of Alvise da Mosto, the first Venetian to have ventured down the West African coast and up the rivers Senegal and Gambia, and the author of a famous narrative of all he learnt and experienced in his travels (Figure 1.5).[7] As one of the earliest accounts of trade along the West African coast, da Mosto's

Figure 1.4a The Western Coast of Africa (Venice, the Doges' Palace).

Figure 1.4b Travellers receiving gifts (detail of 1.4a).

Figure 1.5 Alvise da Mosto (Venice, the Doges' Palace).

report would deserve greater attention than space and our focus on beads allows here, for, although he does not discuss beads in any detail, his narrative is nonetheless very informative on the manner in which trade was conducted.

As Frederic Lane writes, da Mosto first went to sea at fourteen when, in his position as a bowman of quarterdeck (a kind of apprenticeship generally reserved for young noblemen) he voyaged to various ports in the Mediterranean. 'He was hardly twenty when Andrea Barbarigo, a cousin, entrusted him with the bartering of some cloth and beads for gold in North African ports' (1973: 345). It is therefore not unlikely that he may have taken quantities of beads on his later journeys as well, and that bead exchanges may have followed some of the routes and conformed to the customs that regulated trade in general.

Without any false modesty, da Mosto describes himself as, at the age of twenty two,

> the first of our noble city of Venice who set out to navigate the Ocean seas outside the Straits of Gibraltar – not known either from memory or from writings to have ever been sailed before – toward the South and into the lands of the Negroes of lower Ethyopia (5).[8]

When he started on his expedition his course was really directed to Flanders, but, forced by contrary winds to stop at Cape St. Vincent in Portugal, he was eventually persuaded by Prince Henry's envoys to turn his course southwards to the West African coast and to navigate and trade for Portugal. He was quite determined 'to endeavour at any cost to earn some measure of means (*facultade*)', but he was at the same time very keen to see the world, and as well as 'utility' he hoped to 'attain also some perfection of honour'.

His human interest and his curiosity were 'just as strong as his search for profit', and his descriptions of different places, peoples and manners are always detailed and accurate. Indeed his testimony is particularly interesting in the light of recent studies of African trade, since it is now widely recognized that medieval or earlier caravan routes remained practically unchanged till the end of the nineteenth, and in some instances till the beginning of the present century (Vansina 1962; Cohen 1965; Meillassoux 1975).

As da Mosto repeatedly points out, and with that mixture and confusion of motives that so often characterized European expansion, Prince Henry's eager interest in exploration and trade also had a political and religious side, and that was the long-standing fight of the Portuguese against the Moors and their hope to find allies against Muslim infidels in sub-Saharan Africa. He therefore describes the religious customs of the peoples he visits and tries to assess the extent and the strength of their Islamization. He may be writing just what Henry wants to hear when, in his account of the Wolof, he adds, the faith of these first Negroes, who live just south of the desert, is Mohameddan, but they, and in particular the most humble people, are not as firm in their faith as are the 'white' Moors. The lords always keep in their households some Muslim priests called *Azaneghi*, (that is, clerics of the school of Al-Azhar), who tell them that it is immensely shameful to live without a faith. But when they come into contact with Christians and as trust and familiarity develops, they believe in Mohameddanism even less; because they like our customs and they see our riches and our intelligence in all things, . . . they say that that God who gave us so many good things shows signs of a very great love for us and must have given us very good laws. But, since also their laws were from God, they may be saved in them as we are saved in ours (44).

He first reaches Madeira, then the Canary Islands; continuing his southward journey, he passes the White Cape, where, getting closer to the coast, he navigates alongside the desert. His descriptions render with some amusement both his own and the Africans' sense of wonderment at their first encounters. As they see the sails of ships go down, they mistake them for some great birds. They imagine the white slavers who attack them in the darkness of night to be ghosts. All this, as he writes, shows 'how new they were to our things' (30).

From Taghaza, large quantities of salt are taken by Arab traders to various localities, especially to Timbuktu, then Mali. Mali, he explains, has a climate so adverse to animals that hardly a quarter of those taken there survive. If, after the trade in Mali is completed, any salt remains unsold, it is taken further south by caravans on foot. Da Mosto's description of the way salt is paid or bartered for with gold is an interesting example of invisible trade. This, he writes, is an ancient custom; he both heard about it from Arabs and he experienced it himself. Exchanges take place in a number of steps (31–6). Small piles of salt, or other goods, are left in a place established by convention. The receiving party will place beside them the goods they are prepared to give in exchange, but if the quantities offered are not satisfactory the whole process is repeated, and sometimes the exchange may fail altogether.

An attempt by the Emperor of Mali to break the silence and try to see 'what kind of people were those who wanted to remain invisible' had miserably failed, when a trader, captured to satisfy the Emperor's curiosity, had died in captivity after four days, having stubbornly refused to eat or to speak. As da Mosto openly warns his readers, his knowledge of the incident is mainly second-hand, but he heard it from so many sources, that he must and can believe it.[9] Some inhabitants of Mali, he writes, think that the traders must all be mute, or unwilling to speak through pride and disdain. At any rate, after the incident the people of Mali remained without salt for three years, because the merchants would not take their gold, but they eventually returned to their past habit. 'After all', as da Mosto comments with good-natured pragmatism, 'the trade is just as useful, whether they do or do not speak' (35–6).[10]

While da Mosto does imply that he personally witnessed instances of invisible trade in the vicinity of the Senegal river, and he thinks that the custom was prevalent especially in the areas of Mali and Timbuktu, he, on the contrary, developed good relations of friendship and trust with some trading partners; indeed he was their guest for about a month, and was even presented with a young slave girl 'for the service of his chamber (50)'.[11]

My reason for reporting his account of the tradition is that, unexpectedly, on a recent visit to Murano's glassworks, an instance of invisible trade was again reported to me by a glass manufacturer. He had heard it from an old man who had himself been in charge of delivering beads to a remote African settlement in the 1930s. Unfortunately the man could not recall in what part of Africa the trade had taken place, and my first reaction was naturally one of disbelief. Some details in his narrative, however, gave it a touch of plausibility and verisimilitude (and while these were certainly not likely to convince an historian, they were nonetheless of great interest for an anthropologist).

As the old man recalled, some large boxes full of beads were left at the boundaries of the area in question, but when, on the following day, he and his colleagues had approached to see what was offered in exchange, they were faced with an unexpected sight: large ants had eaten into the packing paper, they had got through the cardboard and the beads had all fallen out and collapsed to form a small mound crossed in all directions by the dark insects. Eventually it was found that the ants only liked and attacked paper of certain colours and not others and the trade could be resumed. Whether the old man had told the bead manufacturer something he had actually witnessed or whether, like da Mosto five centuries earlier, he was merely reporting received tradition, was in itself an interesting question. In either case, however, the repetition of the tale itself bore witness to a distinctive culture of trade, with its own traditions and myths, and to the old man's feeling of having participated and belonging in that culture.

Da Mosto describes the delta region of the river Senegal, and the way in which, on reaching the Atlantic sea, it forms two large mouths with an island between them. As he explains, the river, which forms a natural boundary between the desert and 'the fertile lands of the Negroes on the south', is one of four which spring from the Garden of Eden. It irrigates the whole of Ethyopia, while the Nile, which goes through Cairo, ends in the Mediterranean sea. As well as his refreshingly direct and naive descriptions, however, da Mosto also took pains to record geographical and economic data that might be useful to other traders: according to his estimate, it would take fifty to sixty days to cross the desert to the White Cape on horse. The distance from Taghaza to Timbuktu is a forty days' ride, it then takes between twenty and thirty days to reach Mali from Timbuktu.[12]

'In this land', he writes,

> there is no coined money, but it is the custom to barter things against other things . . . In inland areas, both Arabs and Negroes use white shells, or cowries . . . They say that gold is sold by the weight of a shell as is the custom also among Berbers, and such 'shell' is worth about one ducat' (37, 68).[13]

We learn that black Africans would give to the Arabs two to fifteen slaves in exchange for one horse, and salt was sold at a price of 200 or 300 shells per camel load. But, although he mentions some necklaces he offered to his trading partners as opening gifts, we do not find in his report any extended references to glass beads – a silence for which we can find several explanations: since his initial plan had been to direct his trading expedition to Flanders, and only on arriving in Portugal was he persuaded by Prince Henry to turn southwards to the west coast of Africa, he may not have brought beads in any significant quantity. Or, being Venetian, he may have taken glass beads for granted and included them in general terms like 'knick-knacks', 'fancy trifles', 'minimal things', or 'small things of little moment', phrases which often occur in his text, and which he sensitively qualifies 'according to our opinion'.

Exchanges which involve glass beads are repeatedly mentioned in a report by an anonymous Portuguese trader (roughly contemporary with da Mosto) who relates how

> infinite caravans of Negroes bring gold and slaves to sell. Some of them were captured in wars, but others are led by their fathers and mothers, to whom it seems to confer on them the greatest favour in the world to send them to countries where the living is more abundant. They take them entirely naked, as they were born . . . and in exchange they receive some glass *Paternosters* in diverse colours, and objects made of copper and brass, colourful cotton cloth and similar things, which they then spread throughout Ethyopia (220).[14]

Very often, however, as in da Mosto's report, and as is frequently the case for things associated by Western travellers with women and female vanity, glass beads are classified as 'minor' trade objects, and subsumed under the general description of 'other trifles' at the end of lists of more substantial goods, like salt, luxury goods, horses, embossed leather and textiles. Furthermore, when beads are mentioned, it is mainly to describe the supposed naïveté of buyers, who take them as payment for far more valuable items – often, as we have seen, even slaves. Emphasis on the asymmetry of exchanges is an almost inevitable topos in the narratives of European travellers – probably also due to a need to demonstrate the economically worthwhile nature of their extremely dangerous enterprise. As da Mosto relates, when during his stay in Portugal don Henry's envoys persuaded him to turn his course southwards to the African coast, they assured him that all those who had been there had made considerable earnings, 'from one coin there could be made seven and ten' (12).

An American anthropologist recalls how in the USA every schoolchild learns that Dutch settlers bought the island of Manhattan for the equivalent of 24 dollars in beads. And the story, which has become one the foundation myths of the United States, is told to show how the Indians were primitive and naïve (Graeber 1996: 4). The harshness and dishonesty of European traders have certainly not escaped the condemnation of anthropologists and early critics of colonialism. For example, Montaigne writes with sadness of 'cities destroyed, nations exterminated, millions of inhabitants killed by the sword, and the richest and most beautiful part of the world overturned by the pepper and bead trade!' (Cited in Todorov 1995: 68).

Or, to quote a more recent example, as Alberto Moravia writes in his essay on 'Beads and Tourism',

> In the beginning there were the Portuguese forts spread along the coast, with their squads of soldiers – their heads closed in iron helmets, which we now can see . . . in the sculptures of Benin. They were there to defend the first acts of European arrogance: knick-nacks, glass beads against gold, precious stones and rare spices. But Africans did not know that the beads were worth nothing and gold and precious stones [were worth] a great deal. Their scale of value was that of imagination; that of the Europeans, instead, was that of profit. Then in the following centuries came the slave merchants, dressed in velvets, silks and brocades, shorts over stockings, with swords at their side; and again, for beads and trifles, Africans gave them something far more precious: they gave them their brothers, with the complicity and the permission of their kings. Then they were chained and shipped off to be sold as chattel in America. Also then the Africans ignored the inestimable value of the human goods they were giving to the Europeans in exchange for beads. But the Europeans knew that value very well, Christianity had taught it them for centuries . . . (1972: 139 my translation).

However, in recent literature on trade there have been attempts to give greater consideration and understanding to the motives and rationales of both parties to such exchanges (Parry & Block 1989; Hugh-Jones & Humphrey 1992). As Graeber points out, and as research on different societies has abundantly shown, criticisms of the bead trade were sometimes quite ill-founded, since they entirely failed to take account of the fact that beads had been used in exchange for centuries before the arrival of Europeans (1996: 4). Their worth, like that of our money, was determined symbolically by social consensus. In that light Moravia's notion of *value* can be said to be an entirely Western and ethnocentric one. Furthermore, while most people today would view slavery as evil, they would also agree that its badness is absolute – whether the price paid for a human being is great or small, gold or glass beads. To understand that the people of America or Africa were not as naïve as some early travellers implied, does not in any case condone the iniquities of European colonialists and traders.

An example of how Africans sought to protect themselves from European fraudsters is mentioned in the report of the unknown Portuguese traveller I have quoted above. His description of the exchanges that took place at the Castle of La Mina, where the Portuguese king kept a severe monopoly over all trade, relates how Africans would arrive there in large numbers, bringing gold grains and powder with which they usually paid for a variety of goods. The *paternosters* offered by European traders were of two types: some were made of gold, others, of much greater value, were composed of thin canes made out of a blue stone they called 'coril' – not however lapis lazuli. 'For that kind of beads', he continues, 'they are prepared to pay with large quantities of gold', but they certainly do not accept them blindly, on the contrary, well aware that those offered are often inauthentic, 'they place them on fire to ensure that they should not be false imitations, because there are also brought some very similar ones that are made of glass, and which do not withstand the test of fire' (Ramusio 1837: 220).

Symbolic Uses of Beads[15]

While in Africa, as in Venice, women undoubtedly participated in the bead trade, international exchanges which involved long and adventurous journeys were wholly or predominantly conducted by men. Dimensions of gender, however, emerge as we turn to consider their uses and meanings. A fundamental question is: how do we explain, if at all, the human desire to beautify the body, and how do we account for differences in adornment and attire based on gender and for their changes through time and space? Indeed, although from an artistic viewpoint beads are certainly minimal objects, the mere fact of wearing them derives from a deep-seated aesthetic impulse and a need for self-expression which, as evidence shows, is almost universal. Among many groups it is often exercised through transformations of the body, and in particular the skin – our first canvas and art object. Such transformations (literally, such *dressing*) of the body are at the same time aesthetic expressions and ritual behaviour – they are in either case associated with culturally defined ideas of physical beauty, and with magical actions aimed at achieving or maintaining health and keeping away illness and other calamities.

Beads, like cowries, which, thanks to a subtle resemblance of openings and curved lines, symbolically represent the eye as well as the female genitals, and with which they are often joined to be used as ornaments, amulets or exchange media, are intimately associated with ideas of fertility both of the land and of women. As Elena Kingdon shows, throughout the ancient Mediterranean, beads shaped as eyes were (and in some areas still are) believed to prevent the ills caused by others' envy and malevolence, and to deflect those negative influences, which, it is feared, might damage the fertility of the soil or destroy women's generative power (unpublished workshop paper).[16]

Amulets thought to help avert illness, impotence, loss of breast milk, or the alienation of a husband's affection, often include 'eye beads' strung together with cowries. But, while such amulets are most commonly found throughout the Mediterranean – especially in North Africa, the south of Italy, and Asia – an association of beads and reproduction is present also in other radically different cultures: as Janowski shows, possession of ancient beads associated with particular ancestors determines both the status and the desired continuity of genealogical lines (this volume). Prestige, prosperity, and clan identity are also implied in the possession and the wearing of beads among the African Kalabari (Eicher, this volume).

One general feature that has emerged from our comparison of the uses of beads in different cultural contexts concerns the ways in which strings of beads, which on leaving Europe already had well-defined religious significance, after reaching their new destinations rapidly took on new meanings, in keeping with the most diverse cultures and symbolic systems. In particular those made up as rosaries, which were among the earliest exported from Venice in significant quantities by crusaders, were soon transformed to become secular ornaments or else were added to garments and objects related to entirely different belief systems and rituals (Trivellato, Dransart, this volume). They were often used as counters (or *numeraires*) in trade, or else, acquiring rarity value, they were removed from economic exchange cycles, to become ancestral property, only changing hands as bridewealth, or validating claims to royal and aristocratic status.[17]

As we learn from accounts of the development of Nilotic kingship, the possession of certain types of beads was an indispensable requirement to sanction royal status, and they would figure very prominently in early ethnographic descriptions of royal investitures. An example is Seligman's account of the mythical origins of the Anuak's dynasty and of their separation from the Shilluk. As he writes, the founder was Gila, a brother of Nyakang, who led the Anuaks northwards and eastwards from the area they previously inhabited with the Shilluks. According to Anuak legends, three brothers arrived to the neighbourhood of Lake No, where, at Wi Pan Dwong, there took place the quarrel that led to the splitting of Anuak and Shilluk. The Anuak regarded Cuway, Gila's grandson, as their first true sovereign. He was the second son of Gila's daughter, born from her union with a river man, who had first emerged in the guise of a large fish, then changed into a crocodile and then turned into a man. It appears from the narrative that the royal status of Cuway was fully established when Gila's daughter's first born, Ucoda, who had returned to his father in the river, had reappeared, bringing with him two necklaces, *Ucock* and *Gurmato*, to take Cuway's daughter, Koi Nyaru, as his wife.

The two bead necklaces, in addition to two four-legged stools and a small drum called *Udola Waracamu*, were subsequently the royal insignia; they were, 'of such mixed and dazzling colours that they were said to bring tears to the eyes' of those who beheld them (Colonel Bacon: SN&R, vii, 1924, quoted in Seligman 1932: 114–17). In yet another, somewhat different, account of the Anuaks' royal investiture, there also figures 'a three-legged stool, one leg being very weak'; if the king elect was able to balance on it without falling he was recognized as a true son of the king and rightful heir to the throne; but if he fell over he was held to be an impostor and killed. 'If he succeeded, a certain necklace made of large red beads, with one much larger ivory bead in the centre would of its own accord come crawling like a snake upon the ground and encircle him' (Heasty, quoted in Seligman).

As we have seen, the origin and the consolidation of Cuway's dynasty is also linked with the marriage of his daughter, Koy Nyaru, to his older brother Ucoda. Indeed, as well as part of the insignia that would validate Cuway's claim to royal status, the two necklaces brought by Ucoda from the river were a bridewealth payment. In that respect the myth may have served as an example and a foundation for all Anuaks' marital exchanges in which beads figure very prominently. As Seligman reports:

An average transfer of bridewealth might include: one bead necklace (*shauweir*), five waist-strings of *tet* beads, two waist-strings of *dumoy* beads, four cows, one bull, seventy spears of the *okwen* type, two spears of the *dem* type, one spear of the *jo* type, ten brass wrist bangles. The *dumoy* beads are of an opaque blue colour varying in shade between a watery blue to a dark blue. They are very unevenly cut at the edges – the Anuak say they were made by their own people in olden days. They are very scarce and none can be bought in any open market, but they are much in request and always form part of a marriage dowry. In consequence a single waist-string of about thirty inches long is worth one cow or thirty okwen spears . . . The *shauweir* bead is a largish red bead, and the *tet* bead is of a dark greenish colour (111).

Possession of beads is therefore of great significance at all levels of society and is closely associated both with individual and with group identity. As Francesca Declich recorded, the founding ancestress who led the Somali Zigula out of slavery, and who presides over women's initiation rituals, Wanankhucha, is believed to have been buried entirely covered in beads. Tiny white beads, like those said to be sometimes found by her grave, are required in all women's transition rituals. A beaded belt, or *usalu*, which Somali women wear round the waist under their traditional dress, is given to brides by their mother or mother's sister and is thought to be a source of attraction and pleasure. In later life it is associated with memories of important intimate moments and it symbolizes the enjoyment of full adult sexuality (1992: 212–17). As we learn from Eicher's paper, a bead given at birth is tied up with a person's subsequent history, while its loss may be the cause of a man's exclusion from his clan and his family.

Among the Uduk, beads figure prominently in ceremonies that celebrate the incorporation of new-born or adopted children into the parental kinship group: during a ritual that seems to underline the bond between the parents that is brought about at the birth or adoption of a child, the father is adorned with female beads. As Wendy James relates, he is decorated by the women of the village with the bead ornaments of a woman including head band, neck ring, and anklets. He is smeared with oily red ochre by his mother-in-law, his affinal relatives in turn offer him food and 'he is then led outside by his wife, in solemn mien and his "female" finery' (1988: 104) (Figure 1.6).

Contrary to a tendency in many societies to categorize women of authority and distinction as 'honorary men', the Uduk consider motherhood and childbearing as the highest of human achievements. The successful hunter, like the diviner at his investiture, is therefore symbolically associated with the newly-delivered mother and decorated with female bead ornaments (ibid.: 102–6) (Figures 1.7–1.10). However, at times of mourning, displacement and sorrow, the Uduk wear very little or no ornaments (Figures 1.11–1.12).

Like different national or regional costumes, beads, in their different colours, arrangements and styles, are important symbols of collective, as well as individual identity for many social groups. Ndebele women, uprooted from their original area by white South Africans around 1880, affirm their sense of continuity with the past by wearing bead garments woven according to typical geometrical patterns, which they also draw on the walls of their houses (Ama Ndebele 1991: 69–70, quoted in Geary 1994: 18–20). The Masai make distinctions between those groups which they consider to be 'true' pastoralists and semi-nomadic groups, whose members practise agriculture as well as herding, and who, from their point of view, are only marginally Masai, as can be seen also from the way in which they make and wear their bead ornaments (Klump & Kratz 1993: 195–221).

As well as showing ethnic and regional differences, however, wearing such garments and ornaments, now considered traditional costume, is viewed as an affirmation of a general black South African identity (Preston-Whyte 1994: 91; Carey, this volume).

Conclusion

Beads have been made since ancient times in the most diverse and distant societies; beads fashioned from ostrich egg shells, found in the Sudan, go back to the tenth century BC, while in Ife, the mythical place of origin of the Yoruba people, beads made by melting down pieces of glass bottles imported from Europe and the Middle East go back to the ninth century AD (Beier 1982: 3–4). But a truly large-scale worldwide diffusion of beads from Europe, and especially from Venice, where

Figure 1.6 Among the Uduk a woman's first child is born in her own village. The father's in-laws decorate him with red ochre and beads in the style of a woman for the procession which escorts the baby to the father's village (© Wendy James 1966).

Figure 1.7 As a result of a grave and dangerous illness the diviners have made this boy one of their own. Here he is wearing his first diviner's beads and cowrie shells (© Wendy James 1966).

Figure 1.8 Uduk women threshing grain (© Wendy James 1966).

Figure 1.9a Uduk women ready for the diviners' dance (© Wendy James 1969).

Figure 1.9b Uduk men ready for the diviners' dance (© Wendy James 1969).

Figure 1.10 Youths dressed for the dance (© Wendy James 1969).

Figure 1.11 At times of mourning, displacement and sorrow, the Uduk wear few or no ornaments. Children in a displaced people's camp in Nasir upper Nile province, Sudan (© Wendy James, October 1991).

Figure 1.12 Martha Ahmed, a prominent woman in the community. Her lack of ornament indicates separation and bereavement during displacement from her home area (© Wendy James 1991).

they could be produced in great plenty with relative facility and little capital investment, mainly took place in the fifteenth and sixteenth centuries (Trivellato this volume). Thanks to their durability and their vivid and luminous colours, Venetian beads proved particularly suitable for decorating garments and objects, like masks, royal vestments and crowns, and to render those strong contrasts and dichotomies which are intrinsic to many cultures, especially in Africa, with very striking dramatic effects (Turner 1963; Coote & Shelton 1982).

Historians agree that some of the techniques by which glass beads, especially those tiny ones often described as 'seed-beads' (or *conterie*), were threaded, embroidered or woven into cloth and applied to leather, followed the routes of colonial expansion. On the other hand, it is obvious that the objects produced, from the grand crowns of Yoruba kings to the simplest ornaments and garments, present a very wide range of fashions and styles.

To return briefly to our main theme, that of the work of women, a remarkable example of the extent to which the bead craft is now a natural part of life for many Africans is described in the writings of Eleanor Preston-Whyte on the works of some Kwa-Zulu women who live in an area known to whites as the Valley of Thousand Hills and to its inhabitants as Nyuswa, Suthumba and Ndwedwe (1991: 74–6). The Valley, about sixty miles away from Durban, now a prosperous industrial city, has suffered years of isolation and neglect; it has no paved roads, and till a few years ago it had no piped water and no electricity. Christianity is quite widespread, but most families continue to favour traditional modes of dress. Beaded garments are worn at all times in everyday attire, but in even greater plenty on ceremonial occasions, especially in the early years of marriage and during courtship. Young women make small bead jewels for their favourite boys, and since, by contrasting different colours and shapes, these can carry a variety of meanings, whites have described them as 'love letters'.

The men generally seek work in the city, but women are discouraged from taking salaried jobs and usually remain in the Valley with the children to cultivate their few fields. In order to earn a little money they sometimes conduct various types of informal trade. Partly responding to a demand for souvenirs, created by a developing tourist industry, some women started to make small figures, or dolls wearing beaded garments that recall ethnic costume, and sell them mainly to holiday makers in the vicinity of Durban; but stimulated by reasonable successes, they eventually developed their skills and their expressive capacities to the point of attracting the interest of collectors and antique dealers (Preston-White 1991: 64).

These beaded craft objects show the same accuracy and love of minute detail which we see in the more traditional works of European inspiration, but at the same time, as Eleanor Preston-White observes, they are strongly tied to local tradition: for example, that of African children who make toy cars, aeroplanes, or animal figures, by bending metal wire or coat hangers of the type used by dry cleaners, as well as an older local tradition, the making of small figures adorned or covered with beads, to be given to girls during the transition associated with puberty rituals, and which, as their name, 'fertility dolls', implies, would have supported their child-bearing capacities (1994: 54).

Similar figures are sometimes made by the girls themselves to play or to give to their boy friends who may hang them round their neck, like the 'love letters'. But recently, as Preston-Whyte writes, the production of beaded figures has been so varied and imaginative as to become quite significant both in economic and in artistic terms. Their charm is also due to the choice of subjects which often express keen social awareness and observation: they represent scenes of traditional African life, or they portray, often ironically, their view of the life of whites; one example is a small tableau of little boys playing football, the street game of the poor, in contrast to the figures of expensively equipped white girls, with long, blond, wind-blown hair, playing tennis (Figures 1.13 and 1.14), or the police helicopter – a sinister presence in the life of many a South African suburb – covered in shiny dark beads (Figure 1.15–1.19); or an explicit, yet moving, representation of child-birth, possibly the most important moment in the life of a Zulu woman (Figure 1.20).

The success of the craftswomen may be partly due to their capacity to bring together two different traditions: the painstaking and fastidious accuracy of European work, mainly introduced by missionaries, with the imaginative exuberance and the sense of colour of Zulu culture. This becomes altogether obvious if we compare the objects in Figures 1.2 and 1.3 with some of the works made by the craftswomen described by Preston-Whyte. The first clearly represent Venetian subjects embroidered on minute and detailed design patterns; their brief Museum description simply states that they came from a South African Mission and that they go back to the last years of the nineteenth century; it seems natural to imagine that an Italian missionary may have given her pupils some beads, and instructed them to embroider a view of Venice, following a precise design, possibly copied from a print or a postcard. The work is executed with impeccable precision and is in fact little different from objects made in similar institutions in Italy or elsewhere in Europe. On the contrary, the works freely conceived and carried out in recent years by Zulu craftswomen in the suburbs of Durban show a spontaneity and expressive vigour which, as Preston-Whyte observes, make strict distinctions between art and crafts somewhat irrelevant.

In conclusion, I should like to underline that both the organization of work, and the humble position and economic difficulties from which the South African women endeavour to break out, present interesting analogies with features of the domestic lives of Venice's bead makers and threaders and of their work – typically associated with underdevelopment, and, in some measure, with tourism; lacking any trade-union protection, but tied with networks of cooperating kinswomen, deeply rooted in local traditions and life-styles.

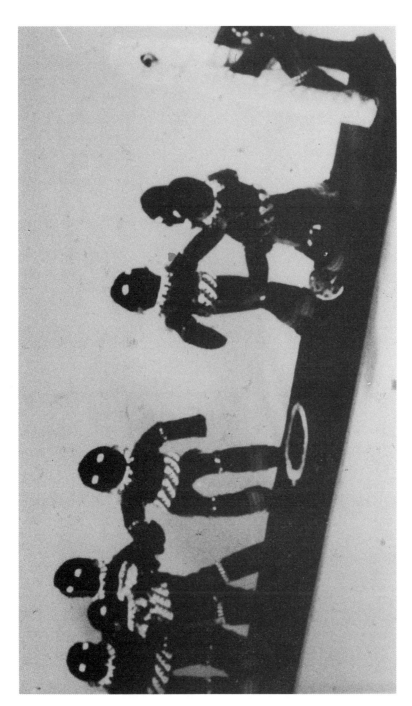

Figure 1.13 The Soccer Match, by Mavis Mchunu, 1985. Cloth, beads: length 70 cm. Thorpe Collection, Durban, photo: C. Wafer 1988 (Preston-Whyte, p. 72).

Figure 1.14 Girls Playing Tennis, by Mavis Mchunu, 1984. Cloth, beads, yarn, netting, board. Height 22 cm. Photo: C. Wafer 1988. Thorpe Collection, Durban (Preston-Whyte, p. 72).

Figure 1.15 Helicopter, by Gabi-Gabi Nzama, 1987. Cloth, Beads, Wire: Height 36 cm. Photo: C. Wafer 1988. Thorpe Collection, Durban. (Preston-Whyte, p. 70).

Figure 1.16a Woman grinding corn by Sizakhele Mchunu, 1987. Cloth, Beads, Yarn Stone. 5 cm. Photo: C. Wafer 1988. Author's Collection, Durban.

Figure 1.16b Wood carrier by Thandi Mchunu, 1987. Cloth, Beads, Wood. 29 cm. South African Museum, Cape Town. Acc. N. Sam 12294. Photo: C. Wafer 1988 (Preston-Whyte, p. 73).

Figure 1.17 The Culture Broker. By Sizakhele Mchunu, 1988. Cloth, Beads, Paper, Plastic. 28 cm. Photo: C. Wafer 1988. Thorpe Collection, Durban (Preston-Whyte, p. 71).

Figure 1.18 Thembi Mchunu in her Diviner's Costume, 1988. Photo: C. Wafer 1988 (Preston-Whyte, p. 69).

Figure 1.19 Young Zulu Girls in their Courting Finery, 1980. Photo: Robert Preston-Whyte (Preston-Whyte, p. 68).

Figure 1.20 The Birth of a Baby by Sizakhele Mchunu, 1985. Cloth, Beads, Yarn, Lace. Length 38 cm. Photo: C. Wafer 1988. Author's Collection, Durban (Preston-Whyte, p. 74).

Notes

1. About the time of Margaret Mead's greatest popularity.
2. The labour conditions and the social contexts in which Venice's bead makers and threaders exercised their crafts and entrepreneurial activities have been described by Italian historians. Their essays counter earlier representations of the city's bead workers as the prototypes of an industrious but leisurely female working class, eagerly photographed and described by travellers – almost stock characters in a repertoire of 'popolani', boatmen and artisans (Bellavitis, Filippini & Sega, 1990).
3. Early formulas, or 'recipes' for the making of glass would certainly satisfy a Levi-Straussian definition of culture as 'transformation'.
4. Early glass was always blue – not by choice, but because the ingredients used contained copper and cobalt (Hughes-Brock, personal communication).
5. The canal separates the dungeons from the Palace, but the two buildings are joined by the Bridge of Sighs. As well as maps of Canada, Terranova, Arabia, are those of Palestine, Egypt, France, Italy, Greece and Asia Minor, Ireland, Scotland, Scandinavia and Greenland; Northern and Southern America, the Islands of Green Cape, the East Indies, America and Asia. The maps were first drawn in about 1540 by the cosmographer Giovanni Battista Ramusio in collaboration with Gastaldi, but were replaced in 1762 by Francesco Grisellini and Giustino Menescardi, after the first ones were damaged by fire.
6. Among others, Josaphat Barbarus, Aloysius Amusto, Marcus Polo, and Marinus Sanutus, Andreas Grittus, Dominicus Trivisanus, Alexander Georgius and Peregrinus Brocardus.
7. Da Mosto sailed down the West African coast twice between 1454 and 1456 and is thought to have been the first European to have sighted the islands of Green Cape. As Lane writes, in the Venetian Republic, 'going to school was a relatively unimportant part of education, especially after the age of 16 . . . While there was no formal apprenticeship among the merchant nobles, young nobles went to sea at an early age, accompanying their parents or other relatives.' [Da Mosto was] 'an ideal example of how the institution of noble bowmen was to work in breeding seamen' (1973: 345). 'The adventure left him with a story to tell even if it did not prove a profitable search for the source of that Barbary gold which he and his cousin Andrea had bought in the Mediterranean ports of Africa. (1944: 30–1).

    His account of his travel has a complicated textual history: according to Almagiá it was written from memory in Venice, where da Mosto returned in 1463, and not in Lagos, as was maintained by his descendant, Andrea. According to Almagiá, the version printed under the title *Paesi Nuovamente Ritrovati* is better than the text edited by Ramusio, which would have been altered by a copier or by Ramusio himself (1927: 168–259).

    As the editor of a recent critical edition (Gasparrini Leporace 1966) writes, three reports, i.e., some notes by Pedro de Cintra, Alvise's notes and his nautical chart are in two codices at the Marciana library. The best is the 'Marciano Ital. class vi, 4554. It was partly translated into English by Crone in 1937 and published in 1948 by the Academia Portuguesa da Historia od Lisbon on the 500 years anniversary of Damiao Peres' discovery of Guinea.

Ramusio (1485–1557), a humanist and geographer, collected accounts of famous journeys from those of classical times to his contemporaries'. From his collections there derived those of Hakluyt, de Bry and St Purchas. He started editing *Delle Navigationi* in 1520 and the first volume, on Africa, was published in 1550 by Giunti. Translations of the works of Ramusio and Leo Africanus were also included in Thomas Astley's *New General Collection of Voyages*, vol. I, 1745. All passages from Da Mosto are based on the 1966 edition by Gasparrini Leporace. Translations are mine.

8. 'Ethyopia' was used to designate sub-Saharan Africa, with no distinction between east and west. The first time a European reached as far south as the Senegal river and sailed back to Europe was in 1444 (Vansina et al: 185). Before 1470 no European had ever sailed beyond the Sierra Leone. By 1490 there had been established regular relations with the Gold Coast and the expensive castle of El Mina had been built in 1481, mainly for protection against other Europeans. A new phase in sailing the Atlantic had begun in 1492 and ended in 1522 when Sebastian del Cano brought Magellan's fleet back to Spain.

9. Descriptions of invisible trade go back to Herodotus:

> The Carthaginians [possibly South of Morocco] also say that there is a place in Libya, and people living in it beyond the Pillars of Hercules. When they, the Carthaginians, come there and disembark their cargo, they range it along the seashore and go back again to their boats and light a smoke signal. The natives, as soon as they see the smoke, come down to the shore and then deposit gold to pay for the merchandise and retreat again away from the goods. The Carthaginians disembark and look; if they think that the price deposited is fair for the merchandise, they take it up and go home again. If not they go back to their boats and sit there. The natives approach and bring more gold in addition to what they have put there already, until such time as the Carthaginians are persuaded to accept what is offered. They say that thus neither party is ill-used; for the Carthaginians do not take the gold until they have the worth of their merchandise, nor do the natives touch the merchandise until the Carthaginians have taken the gold (Trans. David Green (1987): 352–3).

Cosmas Indicoplentes (mid-sixth century) describes caravans of Ethiopians who travelled towards the Ocean to purchase salt and gold. Ibn Battuta reports the same custom for Northern Russia and Siberia, where he used to purchase squirrel, sable and ermine furs (ibid.: 107). Medieval writers (Macondi, Al Hoisain, Al-Biruni, Al Zouhri, Yaqout, Ibn Al-Wardi, Ibn Said, Al-Harrani and Al-Bakourvi) reported the custom for Western Africa.

Fra Mauro in his famous globe appears to repeat da Mosto's description, 'they neither speak, nor see one another' for a place in the Sahara, between Elhoib, Avica and Zusda. But, as commentators pointed out, this is strange, since it is thought that Fra Mauro's map was earlier than da Mosto's report. George Francis Lyon implies this form of exchange was still practised by Pigmees in the nineteenth century (1821).

10. A recent hypothesis is that a reason for the silence was to ensure that the location of the gold mines should remain secret. As Fage writes, according to Al-Mas-Udi, gold

may have been mined in very distant places, for example, Ashanti. African traders would have had good commercial reasons to keep Arabs well away from any direct contact with the miners. That may have been the basis of reports of silent exchanges with 'primitive blacks', beyond the kingdom of Ghana (Fage 1995: 46).

11. Da Mosto's hosts were a king Bodumel, and his nephew Bisboror, who lived about twenty-five miles inland. According to Milanesi, *Bour* is the royal title of the Wolof and *Damel* that of the province of Cayor in Western Senegal (1978: 499). There, he writes, he was going to take Spanish horses, woollen cloths, Moresque silks and other things. In exchange for goods worth over 300 ducats Bodumel would give him 100 slaves (49–51).

12. In describing the 'first kingdom of Senegal' da Mosto offers his own account of its political system – of the way the king is supported thanks to the tribute of those lords who favour him, and the way he employs slaves captured in raids to cultivate his lands. What is more, since the king is allowed to have 'as many wives as he pleases', he has about thirty and

> holds some in greater esteem than others, according to their personality and to the position of the lords whose daughters they are. He keeps them in different villages; each has her own home with many young servant girls and also many slaves to work the land from which they produce the food they need. Each has some cows and goats. When the king visits those villages, he does not need to bring victuaries or other things, since it is his wives who are obliged to support him and those who are with him. In the early morning each wife has prepared three or four meals: some with meat, some with fish, or other moresque food. She sends her slaves to deliver them to his food store, so that in a short time he has forty to fifty meals. Thus he goes from place to place without worrying about food and when he wants to eat he chooses for himself what he desires and gives the rest to his people. But there is never enough; they are always hungry . . . (43–4).

13. His account of rates of exchange is not always coherent, since in another passage cowries are compared to small change, used to purchase small things. He uses the Venetian dialect terms, *porselete* (Italian *conchiglie cipree*) and *mitigal* (Italian *mitile*) respectively for cowries and shell. Comaroff's definition of glass beads in early nineteenth century Tswana as 'a widespread currency linking local and monetized economies' also applies to their uses in the mid-fifteenth century. Da Mosto's attempts to 'translate' African into Venetian values is a good illustration.

14. The passage is from a travel account entitled 'Navigatione da Lisbona all'Isola di San Tomé scritta per un Piloto Portoghese e Mandata al Magnifico Conte Raimondo della Torre, Gentiluomo Portoghese', included in the 1837 edition of Ramusio's *Delle Navigationi*.

15. As Ted Polhemus writes, 'There is a fine line between the artistic adornment of the human body medium . . . in many societies adornment and clothing are thought of as having an intimate association with the body of the person who wears them, such that they too should in some cases be accepted as part of the body set' (1978: 149).

16. Associations of beads with fertility, the evil eye and the sea are also present in the Bible. In the words of Jacob's blessing to the sons of Joseph, 'They will multiply like fish.' Fish symbolize offspring, as well as beings not exposed to the destructive influences of the evil eye, because they are protected by water.

17. Examples of the importance of beads in the early years of this century, and of the belief that they could be used as a prevention or cure against spirit possession can be found in Seligman's *Pagan Tribes of the Nilotic Sudan*. He writes,

> among the Shilluk, perhaps the commonest cause of sickness was the entrance into a person of the spirit of one of the divine kings, a cure being effected when the spirit could be persuaded to leave its involuntary host. We believe that only the early kings were thought to produce illness in this manner, and certainly the three or four cases into which we have inquired were all said to be possessed by Dag. One of these cases, a woman who recovered after two sheep had been sacrificed to Dag, wore bead anklets, and amidst the beads there were threaded small pieces of the conchae of the ears of goats. These anklets were considered protective against future possession by Dag (102).
>
> The Anuak (who inhabit the banks of the Baro, Gila and Akobo rivers extending into Abyssinia) . . . have an idea that they at some time separated from the Shilluk . . . they were driven northward and eastwards by Gila, a brother of Nyakang, whom they call Akango; indeed their legends bring the three brothers in amity to the neighbourhood of Lake No, where at Wi pan dwong – called by the Shilluk Wi Pac – they place the quarrel that led to the splitting of Shilluk and Anuak and the return of Dimo to the present country of the Luo, near Wau (Bacon, SN, v, 1922: 114, quoted in Seligman, 1932: 109).

In a footnote, the writer specifies that, as is seen on a photograph, a provisional king of Anuak, Agwa Akwon, is wearing five, and not two necklaces; *Okoc, Gumato, Wanklek, Gnalo, Gango* (Seligman, C.G. & B.Z. 1932).

References

Abiodun, R., *Understanding African Art and Aesthetics. The Concept of Ase*, Barbara Jean Jacobi Collection, UCLA, X86-1081, Los Angeles: Fowler Museum of Cultural History.

Allen, R. F. (1990), 'Tabwa Masks. An Old Trick of the Human Race', *African Arts*, vol. 23, no. 2, 37 & ff.

Allen, T. (1996), *In Search of Cool Ground: War, Flight and Homecoming in Northeast Africa*, London: Currey.

Almagiá, R. (1927), Riv. Geogr. Ital., XXXIX; 'Il Navigatore Alvise da Mosto', *Archivio Veneto* 2.

Appadurai A. (ed.) (1986), *The Social Life of Things: Commodities in Cultural Perspective*, Cambridge University Press.

Beier, U. (1982), *Yoruba Beaded Crowns: Sacred Regalia of the Olokuku of Okuku*, London:

Ethnographica in association with the National Museum, Lagos.

Bellavitis, A. (1994), 'Condizioni di lavoro e lotte operaie. La Manifattura Tabacchi di Venezia tra Otto e Novecento', *Venetica,* vol.11, no.3, 41–53.

——, Filippini, N. & Sega, M. T. (eds) (1990), *Perle e impiraperle: un lavoro di donne a Venezia tra '800 e '900,* Venezia: Arsenale Editrice.

Bohannan, P. (1956), 'Beauty and Scarification among the Tiv', *Man,* nos.129, 130.

Braudel, F. (1949), *La Méditerranée et le monde Méditerranéen à l'époque de Philippe II,* 2 vols, Paris: A. Colin.

Carey, M. (1986), *Beads and Beadwork of East and South Africa,* Aylesbury: Shire.

—— (1991), *Beads and Beadwork of West and Central Africa,* Aylesbury: Shire.

Cohen, A. (1965), 'The Social Organization of Credit in a West African Cattle Market', *Africa,* vol. 35, 8–19.

Coote, J. & Shelton, A. (eds) (1982), *Anthropology, Art and Aesthetics,* Oxford University Press.

Crone, G. R. (1937), *The Voyages of Cadamosto,* London: Hakluyt Society.

Curtin, P. D. (1984), *Cross-Cultural Trade in World History,* Cambridge University Press.

Curtin, P., Feierman, S., Thompson, L. & Vansina, J. (1978), *African History,* London: Longmans.

Declich, F. (1992), *Il processo di formazione della identitá culturale dei gruppi Bantu della Somalia meridionale,* Doctoral Thesis: Napoli: Istituto Universitario Orientale.

—— (1995), 'Gendered Narratives. History and Identity: Two Centuries along the Juba River among the Zigula and Shanbara', in *History in Africa,* Atlanta.

Derrida, J. (1991), *Donner le temps,* Paris: Galilie.

Douglas, M. (1970), *Witchcraft Confessions and Accusations,* London: Tavistock.

—— & Isherwood, B. (1978), *The World of Goods. Towards an Anthropology of Consumption,* London: Penguin Books.

Dubin, L.S. (1987), *The History of Beads from 30,000 to the Present,* London: Thames & Hudson.

Duby, G. & Perrot, M. (eds) (1991), *Histoire des femmes en Occident,* Paris: Plons, vol. 4, 169–97.

Dundes, A. (ed.) (1981), *The Evil Eye. A Folklore Casebook,* New York: Garland.

Fage, J.D. (1995), *A History of Africa* (3rd ed.), London: Routledge.

Filippini, N.M. & Sciama, L.D. (eds) (1996), 'La vita sociale delle perle. Produzione materiale, usi simbolici e ruoli sessuali: da Murano all'Africa e al Borneo', *La ricerca folklorica,* 34, 3–58, Brescia: Grafo edizioni.

Fischer, H. Th. (1978), 'The Clothes of the Naked Nuer', in T. Polhemus, *Social Aspects of the Human Body,* London: Penguin Books.

Franzoi, U. (1982), *Storia e Leggenda del Palazzo Ducale,* Storti.

Gasparetto, A. (1958), *Il vetro di Murano dalle origini ad oggi,* Venezia: Neri Pozza.

Gasparrini Leporace (1966), *Il Nuovo Ramusio. Raccolta di viaggi, testi e documenti relativi ai rapporti fra l'Europa e l'Oriente a cura dell'Istituto Italiano per il Medio ed Estremo Oriente,* Istituto Poligrafico dello Stato, Roma: Libreria dello Stato.

Geary, C. M. (1994), *Beaded Splendor,* Washington DC: National Museum of African Art, Smithsonian Institution.

Gimbutas, M. (1982), *The Goddesses and Gods of Old Europe, 6500–3500* BC. *Myths and Cult Images*, London: Thames and Hudson.

Graeber, D. (1996), 'Beads and Money: Notes towards Theory of Wealth and Power', *American Ethnologist*, vol. 23, no 1, February, 4–24.

Hamell, G. R. (1983), *Trading in Metaphors: The Magic of Beads. Proceedings of the 1982 Glass Trade Bead Conference*, C. F. Hayes (3rd ed.), Rochester Museum & Science Centre, Research Records no. 6, 5–28.

Harter, P. (1990), 'Beads in the Cameroon Grassfields', *African Arts*, 1993–4, vols 21 and 23, 4, 70 & ff.

Herlihy, D. (1990), *Opera Muliebria. Women and Work in Medieval Europe*, New York: McGraw-Hill.

Hodder, I. (1987), *The Archaeology of Contextual Meanings*, Cambridge University Press.

—— (1991), *The Meanings of Things. Material Culture and Symbolic Expression*, London: Harper Collins.

Hugh-Jones, S. & Humphrey, C. (1992), *Barter, Exchange and Value, An Anthropological Approach*, Cambridge University Press.

Israel, J.I. (1989), *Dutch Primacy in World Trade, 1585–1740*, Oxford: Clarendon Press.

James, W. (1988), *The Listening Ebony. Moral Knowledge, Religion and Power among the Uduk of Sudan*, Oxford: Clarendon Press.

—— (1993), 'Orphans of Passage', *Disappearing World: War*, Granada Television, Bruce MacDonald (Director).

—— (1996), 'Uduk Resettlement. Dreams and Realities', in T. Allen, *In Search of Cool Ground: War, Flight and Homecoming in Northeast Africa*, London: Currey.

Jones, M. (ed.) (1990), *Fake? The Art of Deception*, London: British Museum Publications.

Karklins, K. (1982), *Glass Beads*, Ottawa: National Historic Parks and Sites Branch. Environment, Canada.

—— (1985), *Glass Beads. The Levin Catalogue of Mid-19th Century Beads. A Sample Book of 19th Century Venetian Beads. Guide to the Description and Classificaion of Glass Beads*, 2nd edn, Ottawa: National Historic Parks and Sites Branch.

Kassam, A. & Megersa, G. (1991), 'Iron and Beads: Male and Female Symbols of Creation. A Study of Ornament among Booran Oromo (East Africa)', in I. Hodder (ed.), *The Meanings of Things. Material Culture and Symbolic Expression.*, London: Harper Collins.

Kingdon, E. (1984), 'The Bead as Eye. Symbolic Meaning in Ornament', Unpublished paper.

Klump, D. & Kratz, C. (1993), 'Aesthetics, Expertise and Ethnicity: Okiek and Masai Perspectives on Personal Ornament', in T. Spear and R. Waller, *Being Masai: Ethnicity and Identity in East Africa*. London: Currey.

Lane, F.C. (1944), *Andrea Barbarigo. Merchant of Venice, 1418–1449*, Baltimore: The Johns Hopkins University Press.

—— (1973), *Venice. A Maritime Republic,* Baltimore-London: The Johns Hopkins University Press.

Leroi-Gourhain, A. (1977), *Il Gesto e la Parola*, Torino: Einaudi. (First published in 1964, *Le geste e la parole. La mémoire et le rythme*. Editions Albin Michel.)

Luzzatto, G. (1979), 'L'economia veneziana dal 1797 al 1866', in *Storia della Civiltà Veneziana*, Firenze: Sansoni, vol. 3, 267–77.

Lyon, G. F. (1821), *A Narrative of Travels in Northern Africa in the years 1818, 19 & 20, accompanied by geographical notices of Soudan and the course of the Niger. With a chart of the route and a variety of coloured plates illustrative of the costumes of the several natives of Northern Africa*, London: John Murray.

Marin, C. A. (MDCCC), *Storia Civile e Politica del Commercio de' Veneziani*, Venezia.

Mauss, M. (1923–4), 'Essai sur le don: forme et raison de l'échange dans les sociétés archaïques', *L'Année Sociologique* I, 30–186. Available in English as *The Gift: Forms and Functions of Exchange in Archaic Societies*, Translated by Ian Cunnison (1967), New York: Norton.

Meillasoux, C. (ed.) (1971) *The Development of Indigenous Trade and Markets in West Africa*. Studies presented at the tenth African Seminar, 1969. Fourah Bay College, Freetown. Sierra Leone, London: International African Institute.

Milanesi, M. (ed.) (1978), *Giovanni Battista Ramusio. Navigazioni e Viaggi*, vol. 1, Torino: Einaudi.

M. de Montaigne (1967), 'Essais', in *Œvre Complete*, Paris: Gallimard.

Moravia, A. (1972), *A Quale Tribù Appartieni?* Milano: Bonpiani.

Da Mosto, A., *Le Navigazioni Atlantiche del Veneziano Alvise da Mosto,* A cura di Tullia Gasparrini Leporace (1966), in *Il Nuovo Ramusio. Raccolta di Viaggi, Testi e Documenti Relativi ai Rapporti fra l'Europa e l'Oriente* , a cura dell'Istituto Italiano per il Medio ed Estremo Oriente, vol V, Roma, Libreria dello Stato.

Ninni, I. (1873), *L'impiraressa*, Venezia: Tip. Longhi e Montanari.

Parry, J. & Block, M. (eds) (1989), *Money and the Morality of Exchange*, Cambridge University Press.

Picard, J. & R. (eds) (1986), *Beads from the West African Trade*, 6 vols, Carmel-CA: Private.

Polhemus, T. (1978), *Social Aspects of the Human Body*, London, Penguin Books.

Preston-Whyte, E. (1991), 'Zulu Bead Sculptors', *African Arts*, vol. 24, no. 1, 64–76.

—— (1994), *Speaking with Beads*, London: Thames and Hudson.

Ramusio, G. B. (1837), *Il Viaggio di Giovan Leone e le Navigationi di Alvise da Ca' da Mosto, di Pietro di Cintra, di [. . .] un Piloto Portoghese e di Vasco di Gama*. Quali si leggono nella raccolta di Giovan Battista Ramusio, Venezia: Giunti.

Roheim, G. (1981), 'The Evil Eye', in Dundes A. (ed.), New York: Garland. pp. 21–222.

Sahlins, M. (1985), *Islands of History*, London: Tavistock.

Sciama, L.D. (1992), 'Lacemaking in Venetian Culture', in R. Barnes & J.B. Eicher (eds), *Dress and Gender: Making and Meaning in Cultural Context*, Oxford: Berg.

Seligman, C.G. & B. Z. (1932), *Pagan Tribes of the Nilotic Sudan*, London: Routledge.

Spooner, B. (1970), 'The Evil Eye in the Middle East', in M. Douglas (ed.), pp.311–19.

Stewart, C. (1991), *Demons and the Devil*, Princeton University Press.

Strathern, M. (1992), *After Nature. English Kinship in the late Twentieth Century*, Cambridge University Press.

Tilly, L.A. & Scott, J.W. (1978), *Women, Work, and Family*, New York: Holt, Rinehart and Winston.

Todorov, T. (1995), *Le morali della storia*, Torino: Einaudi. (Original title (1991): *Les morales de l'histoire*, Paris: Éditions Grasset & Fasquelle.)

Turner, V. (1963), 'Colour Classification in Ndembu Ritual: a Problem in Primitive Classification', ASA Monograph 3, London: Tavistock.

—— (1970), *The Forest of Symbols*, Cornell University Press.

Vansina, J. (1962), 'Long-distance Trade Routes in Central Africa', *Journal of African History,* vol. 3, no. 3.

—— (1990), *Paths in the Rainforest: toward a history of political tradition in equatorial Africa*, London: Currey.

Vernant, J. P. (1985), 'La Mort dans les yeux', Textes du XXième Siècle, Paris: Hachette.

Westermack, E. (1926), *Ritual and Belief in Morocco*, vol.I, ch. VIII, London: Macmillan.

Williams, S. (1987), 'An Archaeology of Turkana Beads', in I. Hodder (ed.), *The Archaeology of Contextual Meanings*, Cambridge University Press.

Wolf, E. R. (1982), *Europe and the People without History*, Berkeley: University of California Press.

Zecchin, L. (1987–90), *Vetro e vetrai di Murano. Studi sulla storia del vetro*, 3 vols, Venezia: Arsenale Editrice.

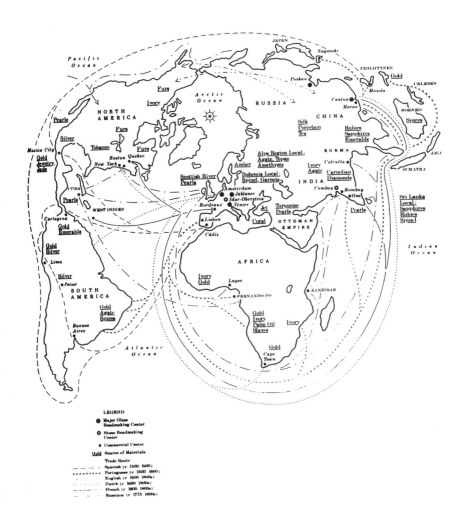

Bead Trade Routes in the Age of European Expansion. Courtesy of
Lois Dubin.

2

Out of Women's Hands: Notes on Venetian Glass Beads, Female Labour and International Trades

Francesca Trivellato

The Setting

One of the thousands of women employed in stringing glass beads in bunches of threads or making floral decorations tiptoes into a novel set in Venice during the early 1880s.

> This was a young lady with powdered face, a yellow cotton gown and *much leisure*, who used often to come to see him. She practised, *at her convenience*, the art of a stringer of beads (these ornaments are made in Venice, in profusion; she had her pocket full of them and I used to find them on the floor of my apartment) (James 1888: 93).

Henry James's idyllic sketch of an *impiraperle*, or *impiraressa*, as these women were called, echoes the voices of a variety of local and foreign observers – folklorists and journalists, social reformers and painters – who at that time portrayed this very characteristic figure of the Venetian popular classes, with more than a hint of paternalism in their eyes. Romanticization aside, notice how the American novelist epitomized the activity of stringing beads together: it leaves 'much leisure' and is carried out at one's 'convenience'. The two concepts are not entirely inaccurate of the essence of this domestic work, if one considers the uncertain professional status of a bead stringer. But the picture presented by Henry James and his contemporaries needs to be put in context and compared with different sources which take account of the living and working conditions of those women in the midst of the first industrial boom.

A comprehensive and accurate picture of the nineteenth- and twentieth-century world of bead stringers emerges from wide-ranging research conducted in the last decade by some women scholars in Venice.[1] In the first part of this article, starting from the issues raised by their studies, I shall extend the discussion of women's roles in the manufacturing of Venetian glass beads to the periods prior to the nineteenth century. The main assumption for my retrospective analysis is that the exploitation of female labour during European industrialization cannot be examined without taking into account the specific features of women's work under the patriarchal guild system of production.

The vast majority of studies concerning the history of working women focuses on the era of industrialization. This is rich in documentation and, as I hope to show, it is of crucial importance for the relationship (not always a parallel one) between the history of labour and those of women's liberation movements. Research on women's work in the combined family economy has led to a conclusive revision of the concept of industrialization itself. As appears from recent scholarship, cultural and economic changes associated with the development of industry, are now seen as complex and uneven processes, rather than a clear-cut and sudden break. The most common evidence for such a gradual transition is the output system in textile production – to which bead stringing was in some ways similar, as will appear in the course of its description.[2]

In Venice, making glass beads was part of a highly skilled urban craft whose origin can be traced back to the Middle Ages and whose guild organization was particularly strict. The severe limitations imposed by European medieval guilds were based on the principle of male heredity, by which craft skills were treated as property and passed down from man to man. Therefore, corporate systems shaped the nature of women's productive enterprises (Herelihy 1990: 185–91).

For this reason, my attempt to show the emergence of a gender specialization within Venetian glass bead manufacturing is not designed to relate women's biological destiny to the intrinsic characteristics of the jobs assigned to them; on the contrary, it is meant to show that women's confinement to the least skilled operations, their exclusion from career advancements and their often unofficial employment can be seen mainly as reflections of the tradition of the guilds in Venetian and Italian – or European – industrialization. Glass-bead factories were among the earliest established Venetian industries and their organization had a serious impact on female labour. Nevertheless, women working at home continued to outnumber those working in factories, and both groups remained largely immersed in a traditional society.

In the second part of this chapter I shall focus on the demand and distribution of beads – the most trade-oriented of all Venetian glass manufactures – and examine the steps and the routes which took them outside the Italian peninsula. Indeed, since the Middle Ages, glass beads, ignored in Europe as much as they were requested in the other continents, became a primary export good and in the period of European expansion they were transformed into a powerful currency.

We lack consistent statistical data for the history of the trade of such a small, fleeting commodity, itself often used as a means of exchange and, to a certain extent, part of an undeclared production. However, even the analysis of the flow of glass beads between producing and consuming countries in the changing international equilibrium indirectly touches on the problem of the position of women in the labour market in capitalist and developing economies, as is shown by the recent import of inexpensive Asian glassware into Venice. Thus, neglecting consumption in favour of production and distribution, my aim in the second part of this chapter is to provide a brief historical overview of the commercialization of Venetian glass beads from the Middle Ages to the present. I shall, at the same time, examine the dynamics of continuity and change, both in the role played by women in their manufacture and in the international relations established through foreign trades.

The data presented here are drawn partly from secondary sources (especially for the nineteenth century) and partly from archival records, consisting of both guilds' statutes and private documents. Almost all the literature on the history of glass in Venice and Murano is written in Italian, but reference will be made to material in English or French whenever available. Moreover, this case-study on Venetian glass beads, with its special emphasis on women's work before and during the first Italian industrialization, is conceived as a dialogue with those historians – mostly women scholars – currently debating this subject, especially in the United Kingdom, the United States and France.

From Guild System to Free Labour Market

Starting from the thirteenth century, Venetian manufacturing began to be organized in craft guilds, as was happening in the majority of Western European urban economies.[3] Each guild, under a government's approval, regulated the access to apprenticeship and mastership, thus clearly dividing licit from unofficial labour. Generally guilds did not give women full rights as enrolled members. As in most European cities, in the sectors of the economy controlled by guilds, Venetian women were allowed to work only under two restrictive conditions: first, they had to be wives or daughters of a master in the trade; second, they were excluded from the possibility, granted to male journeymen, of reaching the rank of master. Widows, as heads of the household, were often allowed to own a shop in order to keep the property within the family, but only until their oldest son had reached the age of adulthood. Not officially recognized as economic actors, women were hence confined to a subordinate and marginal position.

Venetian glass-bead production was no exception; on the contrary, it tests some hypotheses about the character of women's economic contribution in early modern Europe. The city's judicial and administrative records show that guild regulations were largely unattained, thereby generating a parallel informal economic organization which absorbed a large number of working women. Although it is difficult to estimate the size of the female labour force, there is much evidence that in the making of glass beads women not only played a major role as unaccounted labour working in family workshops, but also worked as wage-earners.

A brief description of the pre-industrial guild system which informed the various branches of Venetian glass manufacturing between the thirteenth and the eighteenth centuries can help to explain how women took part in making different kinds of glass beads. In 1291 the Venetian government ordered all glass furnaces to be moved away from the town centre to the nearby island of Murano, primarily for safety reasons connected with fire risk, but also to impose stricter control over the important glassblowers' guild.[4] However, very small furnaces were allowed to remain in Venice, provided that they stood at a certain distance from neighbouring houses. This provision (besides giving rise to a continuous set of conflicts between Murano and Venice) resulted in a geographical division of labour in the manufacturing of glass beads. On one side, Murano glass-blowers held the exclusive right to produce glass canes; on the other, smaller workshops in Venice were equipped to make beads starting from the semi-finished product prepared in Murano.

Glass canes made by Murano glass-blowers were of two kinds: hollow rods (*canna forata*) and solid rods (*canna massiccia*).[5] Depending on the kind of glass canes used, the methods of making glass beads varied greatly and in the corporate economy each corresponded to a separate guild. First to develop was the method of making beads from a hollow rod, which was performed by the guild of *paternostreri e margariteri*. It consisted of six different stages, which reached different technological levels in various epochs but remained substantially unchanged in their sequence:[6] glass canes bought in Murano had to be separated according to thickness, then cut into small pieces and given a round shape. This last operation could be accomplished in two ways: thicker beads (*paternostri*) were fired on a skewer (method called *a speo*), while thinner beads (*margarite*) were spread in a copper pan (method called *a ferrazza*) and then heated up to be rounded. Once ready, glass beads were sorted out by dimension, polished and the very small ones had to be strung together in bunches in order to be sold. Those 'seed-beads' or 'bugles' (well known under the general name of *conterie*) had various dimensions and were all monochrome. The so-called Chevron beads (the famous blue-red-white *rosetta*) were also produced from hollow rods.

When using a solid cane, a different method was applied, which involved the individual manufacture of each piece. The end of a rod was melted on an oil lamp (since the nineteenth century, the lamps have been stoked with gas) and wound around a piece of iron wire, which, once the bead had cooled off, was pulled out leaving the proper hole. The latter technique became exclusive to the guild of *perleri e suppialume*, which in 1647 split from the rival one of *paternostreri e margariteri*. Following this method, a great variety of wound- or lamp-beads (*a lume* or *alla lucerna*) was made – among the best-known were the red-and-white Cornaline of Aleppo, the Mosaic and *Millefiori* beads.

Some operations in each method could be performed by women without violating guilds' statutes. The guild of *paternostreri e margariteri* officially allowed the wives, daughters and widows of its masters to accomplish the first and last stages of bead production, the first one consisting in separating glass canes by thickness and the last one in stringing beads together.[7] The guild of *perleri e suppialume* let women who were relatives of male masters work at lamp-beads, a job of slightly higher reputation.[8]

These provisions gave birth to such female specialization within the manufacture of glass beads, as to shape the collective imagination. By the eighteenth century, both lamp-bead artisans and bead stringers were depicted as women in the watercolours of a foreign visitor who portrayed all typical Venetian characters. A hundred years later, women were the indispensable trustees of the activity of stringing beads together, given that the patriarchal ideology of guild organization, not biology, had excluded them from the secrets of glass recipes. This job became a sort of female counterpart of the male art of blowing glass, marked by considerably lower reputation and pay. In nineteenth-century Venice, bead-stringing was so common among poor women that it can be considered the local and peculiar version of the general tendency for women's work to concentrate predominantly, when not exclusively, in 'female' jobs (Scott & Tilly 1975: 39).

We have no consistent qualitative and quantitative data to follow in detail the progressive formation of such a strong tie between glass beads and women's work. Nor can we rely solely on isolated and extraordinary cases, such as the story which attributes to Maria Barovier, daughter of Angelo, the most famous Renaissance glass blower, the invention of Chevron-beads in the mid-fifteenth century – although it is disputed whether she participated in the actual making process or was just responsible for creating the motif of this successful type of bead (Zecchin 1989: vol. 2, 211–14). Still, from both direct and indirect evidence concerning the tasks that women performed in accordance with guilds' statutes in early modern times, we can assume that a sexual division of labour within Venetian glass production was realized long before industrialization and that women's work was not restricted to the domestic sphere of production, as would have been required by the corporate spirit and order.

The largely illegal nature of women's employment makes it virtually impossible to estimate, even by approximation, the size of the female labour force in pre-industrial Europe. The first aggregate data concerning guild membership in Venice date to the second half of the eighteenth century, when the government promoted a series of surveys into the state of craft guilds in order to support reforms inspired by new criteria of economic organization.[9] The most extensive of these surveys, compiled in 1773, did not count any woman working in the glass-bead sector, as it

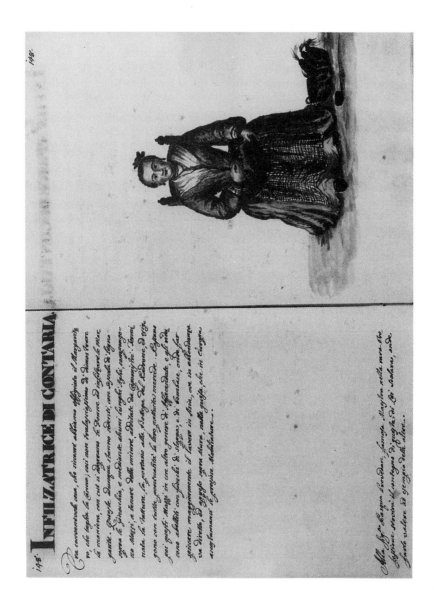

Figure 2.1 Watercolour of a bead stringer in Venice by G. Grevembroch, eighteenth century (Civico Museo Correr, Venice).

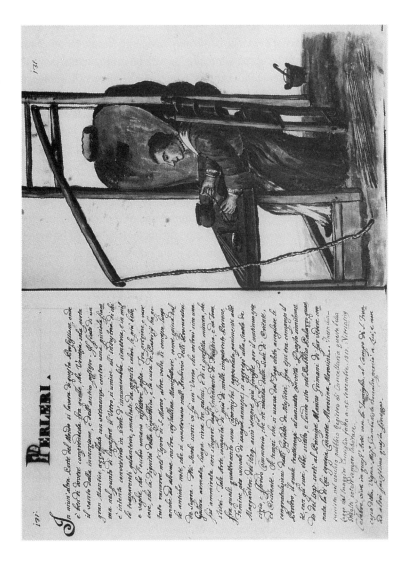

Figure 2.2 Watercolour of a woman working at lamp-beads in Venice by G. Grevembroch, eighteenth century (Civico Museo Correr, Venice).

probably ignored all illicit labour employed beyond guild membership.[10] In 1779, a governmental document listed 1,400 women among the *paternostreri e margariteri* specifically engaged in stringing beads together, masters and their sons being only 161: a disproportion in the women/men ratio which clearly demonstrates how this guild employed many women who were not necessarily related to male masters (Cecchetti 1874: 222).

Other scattered but significant evidence confirms that a large female labour force was involved in the activity of bead stringing outside official guild membership. A French traveller in the mid-seventeenth century described the streets of Venice as crowded with women of all social backgrounds engaged in stringing and making decorations with small bugles.[11] In those same years, a 1672 judicial sentence condemned the widespread practice of stringing beads outside masters' households (meaning by household both homes and families) and reinforced the order to preserve this activity within its legal boundaries.[12] But some clues from notarial records attest that bead masters were contracting out to women the stringing operation.[13]

What we know nothing about are the amount and forms of monetary or in-kind remuneration received by those women working outside their families; however, they were certainly considerably lower than the male masters' and apprentices' wage. Thus, in those duties carried out by cheap female labour in Venetian glass-bead manufacturing we can recognize a clear example of women's work in pre-industrial Europe. While peculiar in its forms, it was analogous in its substance to other women's contributions to the family budget in that 'economy of shiftmaking' dominated by precarious living conditions and sudden crisis, when women's earn-ings could ensure the family survival (Tilly & Scott 1978: chs 1–3). As noted for women's wages in eighteenth-century France, where income fell under the suffic-iency level, 'any holding at all represented a success story' (Hufton 1975: 10).

By 1806 all Venetian glass guilds were abolished and replaced by a free labour market.[14] The severe crisis which hit artistic and ordinary glass production did not affect the glass beads sector; in fact, this turning point coincided with the beginning of concentration in larger productive plants, extensive mechanization and output growth. In the nineteenth century, during the alternate vicissitudes of the Venetian economy, glass-bead manufacturing represented a major source of work and profit.[15] Seed-beads (*conterie*) in particular became the backbone of industrial development, with the glass cane factories mostly located in Murano.[16] One of these listed among its products: 'Venetian glass beads for trimming; chaplets and natives' ornaments; pound-, seed-, aleppo-beads; ceylon-, maccà-, lamp-, mosaic- and fancy-beads; gladstone; beaded articles: beaded flowers; fringes for lampshades; bags, necklaces'. At the same time, both bead stringers and lamp-bead workshops continued to be located in the town centre (with a fairly clear zoning, respectively concentrated in the neighbourhoods of *Castello* and *Cannaregio*). (Figure 2.3)

Figure 2.3 Bead stringers sitting outside their homes in Venice, about 1880 (Archivio Naya Böhm, Venice).

Bi-polarity between Venice and Murano was not the only legacy left by craft guilds to nineteenth-century glass production. Much more profound was the mark left on women's work. While Italian glass factories in general employed a smaller percentage of women than other countries, Venice was the exception.[17] In Murano, bead factories hired women to perform the same operations they had been in charge of under the guild system (namely that of separating glass canes and cutting them into pieces). Finished seed-beads were distributed to stringers working at home. Thus, industrialization did not alter significantly the tasks carried out by women in Venetian glass-bead manufacture, except for the discipline imposed in large factories. Moreover, as it was under the patriarchal corporate economy, women working in factories continued to be marginal to male skilled workers. Their wages, especially those of women working at home, often did not rise over the self-sufficiency level, since they were intended only to supplement poor family budgets.

As a guide to the world of the bead stringers who had captured the attention of Henry James, we can rely on a concise text written a few years earlier by one of them, Irene Ninni (1873). She collected oral poems transmitted by *impiraperle* and described with unprecedented detail the techniques and tools used by bead stringers, the various kinds of small glass beads and their different outputs, but also the general work organization (see Figures 2.1–2.3).

Women worked with a wood tray on their laps, from which they picked up the small beads by holding as many as forty to sixty needles in the first three fingers of their right hands; they strung beads on iron wire to make floral decorations and on cotton or silk threads to make common bunches. Often bead stringers sat on a chair in the street, sharing working time and space with their relatives and neighbours. Contrary to the common romanticized image and despite the cheerful tone of her booklet, Irene Ninni pointed out the difficulties faced by the women: a long day of work from dawn to dusk in exchange for miserable pay; a hard job which in the course of time could cause semi-blindness, as confirmed also by recent interviews and photographic material. And besides this occupational disease, the living conditions of the poorest social strata to which bead stringers belonged exposed them to all kinds of miseries.[18] (Figure 2.4)

Whether and how the increased opportunities for wage labour made available to women by industrialization contributed to their emancipation is a debated question. To be sure, in financial terms the pay of bead stringers was so ridiculously low as to make it impossible for a woman to support a nuclear family or even just herself. Women's work was primarily directed to improve the well-being of their present and future families, first as daughters, then as wives. Young unmarried women saved their earnings for a proper dowry. In the glass bead industry, the disparity between women's and men's wages was particularly marked if we compare the most and the least skilled labour.[19] A significant difference existed also between the wages of women employed in factory or in domestic industry, a general

Figure 2.4 Bead stringers at work in the neighbourhood of *Castello* in Venice, about 1929 (Archivio Filippi, Venice).

characteristic of all Venetian manufacturing (Bellavitis 1994: 43). The salary of a domestic bead stringer between 1830 and 1871 varied from 0.5 to 1 ITL per day,[20] while in 1869 the average wage in a factory producing *conterie* was ITL 1 for women and ITL 2.5 for men.[21] Bead stringers were paid on a piecework basis: in 1899 it was calculated that an expert and industrious *impiraperle* could make up to ITL 1 a day, but the majority of these labourers could earn just 60 cents. According to the same estimates, women working in glass-bead factories were paid from 70 cents to ITL 1.20 and a male blowing master – also paid by piece – could earn ITL 4 or 5.[22] Piece wages increased instability also in the lamp-bead sector, as larger laboratories were established next to independent household workshops where workers could rent gas-lamps by the day and be paid by piece, without having ensured any permanent agreement.[23]

As explained by Irene Ninni, not only was a bead stringer very poorly paid, but she received her pay from other women (called *mistre*) acting as brokers on behalf of the male owners. So relations among working women in their collective actions and experiences were not always cohesive and harmonious. In Venetian glass-bead manufacture the output system was organized so that the finished seed-beads were transported from factories to the houses of these *mistre*, who arranged to have them distributed among a number of bead stringers. Each labourer owned her nails only, while the *mistre* distributed suitable threads together with the glass beads. This organization engendered hierarchies among working women, but also implied reciprocal dependency: *mistre* could be paid as much as twice the wage of simple bead stringers (and being in the pay-roll of a factory – after 1922 – they could receive the benefit of a pension in their old age). They enjoyed a higher status within the local community, but were personally responsible for the return of the final product measured by weight and they had to rely on the work of other women.[24] In its daily practice the activity of bead stringing was characterized by a high rate of inter-generational transmission and a strong collective dimension, but conflicts broke out when the beads distributed by *mistre* were damaged, or when bead stringers did not return the exact amount of beads they had received.

The ambiguous nature of the situation became clear during the first strikes organized by socialist trade unions at the turn of the century. Many bead stringers participated, their protest was directed not against the male owners of bead enterprises, but always against the *mistre*.[25] The strikers' goal was to exclude all intermediations and deal directly with their employers. This objective could easily be appropriated by moderate social reformers, both men and women. In a speech delivered in Venice in 1911, the head of a Foundation for Female Work proved to be less concerned with women's low wages than with the moral virtues of domestic industry, which she encouraged against the disruptive forces of capitalism by advocating more independence for women's self-employment and access to the market (see Ferrari 1911).

Such propositions were rooted in the 'organicist' views expressed by most social scientists, philosophers and politicians during the nineteenth century, when the family was regarded as the atom of civil society and community life. This paradigm pervades most of the sources available today for historical analyses; as a consequence, once these encoded messages are disclosed, the data provided by statistical sources lose their value in terms of quantitative information. This is the conclusion reached by Joan Scott in her study of mid-nineteenth-century French labour statistics: in apparently neutral classifications, she identifies the projection of an idealized economic system centred on the family as the fundamental productive unit and reveals the hidden desire to describe a society dominated by paternalistic relations and free from any class conflict (Scott 1986: 335–63). Statistical surveys compiled in Venice during the age of Positivism show similar limitations. Nonetheless, a critical use of data drawn from those surveys can add important insights – from both a quantitative and qualitative point of view – to the literary images of Venetian bead stringers presented by Henry James and Irene Ninni.

Not all official statistics concerning Venice's industrial and manufacturing sectors in the nineteenth century accounted for female domestic labour, but some sources did try to estimate it. According to the Venetian Chamber of Commerce, the number of women stringing beads in their homes between 1830 and 1871 varied from 600 to 1,000;[26] the survey ordered by the prefect of Venice in 1879 reckoned 1,600 *impiraperle*;[27] and in 1880 about 1,500 were counted.[28] Indeed, the reliability of these numbers is very dubious, as they probably underestimated the female labour force. A distinguished historian of the Murano glass industry at that time ventured only a general figure and assessed that between Murano and Venice there were 'several thousands' of women employed in stringing beads (Zanetti 1866: 36). And the author of the 1879 statistic warned of possible errors due to the fact that glass-bead production varied greatly from year to year (if not from month to month) in response to fluctuations of foreign demand and fashion (a frequent complaint); as a consequence, employment was not continuous, especially in the bead stringing occupation (Sormani Moretta 1880–1: 250–1).

These comments, besides inducing us to handle data about domestic labourers in the glass-bead sector with extreme caution, indirectly raise a crucial question: what was the professional status of women working in their homes, seen from their own rather than an external point of view? Trying to answer this question, oral history shows how most of the poorest working women did not distinguish between their autonomous professional identity and their role within the family. If work was a never-ending experience in their lives, its intensity and forms varied with the needs of the family life-cycle, depending on women's marital status, on their child-bearing and -rearing occupations, and their husbands' employment stability.[29] Bead stringing suited these demands: it adjusted easily to the rhythm of daily chores within or outside the household since it could be carried out early in the morning or late at night. In interviews, bead stringers expressed a general tendency to consider this task complementary to other factory jobs or, more frequently, to domestic service.[30] (Figure 2.5)

In the self-representations of *impiraperle* it is sometimes difficult to disentangle the activity of bead stringing from other means of supplementing the poor family budget. However, the ample diffusion of this occupation in Venice gave it the characteristics of a profession from both an objective and subjective perspective. But was this also true for earlier times which memory cannot recall? Given the lack of direct documentation, that seems quite plausible as may be argued from the ways data were collected and from the implicit assumptions of the least 'subjective' of all sources, that is, statistics.

According to the sources listed above, the number of women working at home as bead stringers in the second half of the nineteenth century would not have exceeded 1,600. This estimate changes if we take into consideration the population census ordered by the Venetian City Council in 1869: it counted as many as 2,095 *impiraperle* in the Venice town centre alone, in a total female population of 65,939 women.[31] The difference with all other sources becomes even more striking if we compare the census with another survey dated the same year, which reckoned only 636 *impiraperle* between Venice and Murano (Errera 1870: vol. 1, 337–44). Rather than a coincidence, such a discrepancy is the result of the different methods adopted in collecting the data and the goals of the two surveys. The census registered professions along with other private data about the population; moreover, it was based on the forms filled out by each head of household collected through a door-to-door inquiry, in which they were asked to declare also the occupation of all members of the family, including women. On the other hand, the 1869 industrial statistic was a private survey devised by a local statistician, who was also an influential businessman and the owner of a major factory producing *conterie* in Murano.

If we argue that those 636 bead stringers were only the *mistre*, those women who distributed the work-load among a larger number of domestic labourers, this would indicate that *mistre* alone were given a professional identity. What about all the other working women? As an experiment, the population census attempted to record all cases of 'double professions' by allowing everyone to declare more than a single occupational qualification. Only one woman declared to be both *impiraperle* and retired. If we assume that women who occasionally worked as bead stringers but were also employed in factories or in other occupations considered those other jobs as prevailing in terms of professional qualification, even the number of 2,095 *impiraperle* would represent only a portion of the whole female population occupied in this activity and not recognized as official labour.

Two points can made on the basis of this comparison of the two statistical surveys dated 1869. First, the qualification of bead stringer determined the professional

Figure 2.5 Two bead stringers together with other women next to fishermen boats in the area of the *Arsenale* in Venice, about 1929 (*Il Gazzettino Illustrato*, 2 June 1929).

self-definition of more women than those recorded by economic statistics. Secondly, although for most women bead stringing was indeed a discontinuous activity over the course of the day and life cycle, the underestimation of female domestic labour in economic statistics was in fact deliberate. From an economic point of view, hiding this labour force enabled businessmen to keep women's salaries under the self-sufficiency level and from a moral point of view it did not disrupt the ideal of family life.

The rediscovery of medieval corporatism in the light of *laissez-faire* at the end of the nineteenth century, praised the moral and social values of guild organization. A mythical image of pre-industrial society in which women had supposedly been confined to their domestic realm was crystallized, while the development of small enterprises and domestic labour was openly encouraged. Through this economic model, largely approved by the 'social doctrine' of the Catholic Church, the bourgeois ideal came to embrace also the lower social classes, thereby concealing the degradation and exploitation of women in the domestic industry. In Venice, these directives could easily be enforced in bead and lace manufacturing, which appeared as part of a 'natural' domain of female labour: they required more patience than physical strength, more training than tools; above all, these occupations seemed apt to convey discipline and teach submission through meticulous exercises.[32]

Women working in domestic industry continued to receive a dubious recognition well into the twentieth century. As the Italian child labour law of 1886 remained largely unattained, the employment of female labourers in their homes eluded controls and failed to observe all protective measures fixed by the first national collective agreement signed in 1908. In the 1920s, Fascist ideology blessed a new model of motherhood, which strongly discouraged women from working outside the family, but not from carrying out piece work at home. As a result, women's working conditions worsened: in addition to bead stringers, during the first inter-war period many women under fifteen were still employed in Murano's bead factories.[33] Between 1930 and 1933, while employers' agreements with Fascist trade unions fired many male workers, wages of women employed in Murano bead factories suffered a 13–25 per cent reduction, which for bead stringers reached 50 per cent.[34]

However low, those returns represented for Venetian women an essential source of income, especially during the economic depression of the 1930s and in the recovery that followed the Second World War. In the 1950s and 1960s, the activity of bead stringing maintained much of its earlier character and continued to provide work for a consistently female labour force.[35] Things started to change in the late 1960s, in conjunction with a major occupational crisis which hit the whole glass industry of Murano. In 1967 one of the two factories producing *conterie* was shut down, followed in 1993 by the other. As a consequence, the formerly common job of bead stringing progressively disappeared. One of the few *impiraperle* still alive and working, in 1991 declared that while she earned ITL 2,000 for one-hour/one-hour-and-fifteen-minutes of work and over the years had lost much of her eye sight, this did not prevent her from liking her job so much as to refuse to sell her wood tray to a tourist shop in Venice which would have sold it as a souvenir.[36]

Female specialization in Murano's bead production has never been limited to the activity of bead stringing, and lamp-bead manufacture has remained its distinctive sign.[37] Today, together with isolated cases of women working in their homes, female specialization in this sector is witnessed by one of the largest and leading firms producing traditional Venetian lamp- and Chevron-beads in Murano.[38] The company, Ercole Moretti, employs thirteen women out of fifteen workers – five of them make various sorts of lamp-beads, one attends to the grinding-wheel to round off the ever popular Chevron-beads, three assemble the small pieces for the *murrine* and three select finished beads in storage and packing.[39]

Under the Impulse of Foreign Demand

In the past few decades historians have increasingly turned their attention to the development of mass consumption in pre-industrial European and North American societies.[40] From this perspective women ceased to appear only as producers within the integrated family economy and emerged as crucial actors in household consumption and marketing strategies. When discussing demand and distribution of Venetian glass beads, it must be remembered that only rather recently did these beads become fashionable and common ornaments in the Western world. Beads made of a material with no intrinsic value had long been disregarded in Europe, being considered mere imitations of pearls and gemstones. Indeed, glass-bead production was born out of this spirit; but as the sense of authenticity varies from culture to culture, what Europeans deemed 'fake' was held in the greatest esteem by other populations.[41]

A telling legend, created at the beginning of the nineteenth century by an imaginative scholar, strengthened the connection between the art of glass-bead making in Venice, a counterfeiting process and the exploration of Far Eastern countries.[42] Coming back to his native city at the end of the thirteenth century, Marco Polo allegedly told his fellow citizens some exotic stories concerning the precious stones that Western merchants traded in the Persian Gulf region. These stories presumably inspired two industrious Murano glass-blowers to use glass to reproduce various sorts of gems much appreciated by the populations Marco Polo had visited in the Orient and by the Africans he had heard about. Despite its unrealistic elements, including the questionable existence of Marco Polo and the suddenness of such an invention, this mythical projection into the past summed up the most peculiar features of this manufacture: as later studies have demonstrated,

Venetian glass beads resulted from imitation of rosary grains made of rock crystal, amber, ivory or other precious materials;[43] and since the beginning, their success has depended upon foreign demand.

In the Middle Ages, the religious values connected to glass beads could not be dissociated from their overseas trade. During the early fourteenth century, the same word, *paternostri*, was used in Venice to mean both smaller worry beads and beads made of glass.[44] At that time Venice was a major stop along the *iter hiero-solymitanum* and could profit from pilgrims' galleys to carry abundant and lucrative trades.[45] While rosaries responded to immediate pilgrims' needs, glass beads made for this specific purpose left Venice and were sold in the Levant, especially in Aleppo (the Syrian town that gave the name to a famous kind of glass bead, that is, the Cornaline of Aleppo) and in Alexandria. These were not the final destinations of Venetian glass beads: local dealers and Muslim traders distributed glass beads in Africa and sent them off to the East Indies.[46] Here, at the end of an involuntary process of secularization, worry beads made of glass entered non-Christian cultural patterns, acquiring meanings and values unknown to their producers. A few episodes of such 'commodity indigenization', in the words of Marshall Sahlins, are recorded also in the literature about Murano: Vasco de Gama, upon arriving in Calicut in 1498, allegedly found that some large beads made of Venetian glass paste were being used there as a monetary means of exchange (Cecchetti 1874: 186).

The diffusion of Venetian glass beads occurred long before the systematic European explorations and colonial expansion. In non-Western cultures these items performed two major functions, as attested also by the two different etymologies proposed for the word *conterie* (used in Venice first to indicate glass beads in general and later seed-beads in particular): the above mentioned monetary function and a variety of decorative and symbolic functions.[47] Beads – and glass beads in particular – have often been among the favourite commodities selected to bear material and symbolic values, also for their relative scarcity as durable objects. Thus, beads not only served strictly utilitarian purposes, but have also been repeatedly placed at the centre of social rituals and ceremonies, granted magical and apotropaic properties or considered as emblems of power and status.

Women did not play any active role in those long-distance trades which took Venetian glass beads around the world. Instead, they were active on the local level. Under the guild system, local distribution was as carefully regulated as was production; in the case of glass beads, sales were controlled by the same guilds which produced them. Legally, women could not be involved in those activities any more than in production, but their presence is nonetheless attested. In 1271, the first statutes of Venetian glassblowers forbade all members, men or women, to sell imperfect articles (Monticolo 1905: vol. 2.1, 73): a clear indication that women took part in retail selling. Much later, in his account book for the years 1642–9, a Venetian tradesman identified his suppliers of glass beads with different expressions, all meaning 'the bead woman from Murano'.[48] Certainly, selling was a common source of occupation and income for women in a pre-industrial urban economy.[49] In the case mentioned here, women from Murano could have been trading either their own or their families' products; Venetian shopkeepers bought glass beads from them, and then sold these articles to native and foreign merchants directly involved in overseas trade.

Venetian cargo ships loaded with export goods, glassware along with other luxury commodities, sailed from the Mediterranean routes to the interior of the Black Sea and to the Atlantic in order to reach Flemish and English ports.[50] While these European sea routes are fairly well known, the subsequent branches of bead trading are rather obscure. The inherent characteristics (small size) and uses (means of exchange) of glass beads make it even more difficult to calculate amounts and destinations of this merchandise: they passed through many hands and from place to place. In the first years of the seventeenth century, the Spanish governor in the Venezuelan lagoon of Cumanà asserted that foreign ships, mostly English and Dutch, were arriving every year, bringing in textiles and hardware and taking out tobacco and beads called *margarite* (Parry 1967: 167) – obviously made in Venice or by Venetian glassworkers in Europe and brought there by the Spaniards. This case alone is a sign of the endless cycles and the sequences of middlemen through which Venetian glass beads passed and from which result a major difficulty in mapping out their ceaseless itineraries.

Despite the lack of precise data, one cannot overemphasize the importance of glass beads in the European colonization of a vast portion of the inhabited world. From Lisbon and Seville, from Marseilles, London and Amsterdam, glass beads were transported to the respective colonial empires.[51] There, they acquired an exorbitant purchasing power and were given to native populations as tokens in exchange for their gold and silver, their ivory and spices, their natural products and even their fellow human beings. In an emblematic act when conquering Mexico City in 1519, Cortez is told to have offered Montezuma a necklace made of small Venetian glass beads as a present, in return for the red-shell necklace with eighteen golden scarabs he had received from the Aztec king (Gasparetto 1958: 185). (Figures 2.6–2.9)

In the 1720s, the author of an authoritative French dictionary of commerce demonstrated awareness of the inequality of exchange and even of the different tastes of African people, so much as to suggest how to make the largest profit from trading seed-beads in Senegal and Angola. After listing the Venetian *conterie* among the most useful commodities to be traded with the 'Savage people' of Africa and North America,[52] Savary patiently described the thirty-seven kinds of glass beads ('verrotteries') favoured by the Senegalese, no less sensitive to changes in fashion than the Europeans, and most useful to implement the slave trade;[53] he also informed all readers that in Angola they could exchange 3,000 French pounds of seed-beads

Figure 2.6 Trade marks of a Venetian lamp-bead manufacturer of the guild of *perleri e suppialume*, late eighteenth century (Civico Museo Correr, Venice).

Fabbrica di Contarie a Lume d'ogni sorte e perle Dorate di Nuova invenzione di Gio:Batta Beto di Lepo .

Entro' Negoziante 1799

Figure 2.7 Trade marks of a Venetian lamp-bead manufacturer of the guild of *perleri e suppialume*, emphasizing the importance of overseas trades, late eighteenth century (Civico Museo Correr, Venice).

Figure 2.8 Trade marks of a Venetian lamp-bead manufacturer and trader of the guild of *perleri e suppialume*, emphasizing the importance of overseas trades, late eighteenth century (Civico Museo Correr, Venice).

Figure 2.9 Trade marks of a Venetian lamp-bead manufacturer and trader of the guild of *perleri e suppialume*, emphasizing the importance of overseas trades, late eighteenth century (Civico Museo Correr, Venice).

for 612 'Negroes' (less than 2 kg for each black male!), provided they carefully chose among the preferred items.[54] On the other hemisphere, in the Canadian regions covered by the Hudson's Bay Company – itself nicknamed the 'Hudson's Bay Bead' after its use of glass beads as means of exchange – in most trading posts price lists expressed the value of beavers in bunches of seed-beads, with disproportionate equivalence (Orchard 1929: 87–9).

To establish with certainty the place of origin of all glass beads which reached non-European continents has often proved to be an arduous task. At the end of the seventeenth century, together with its undisputed dominion on the Mediterranean Sea, Venice lost its technological and artistic supremacy in the art of glass making. At that time, glass beads similar to those manufactured in Venice started to be made in large quantities especially in Amsterdam (where Italian glassblowers did migrate and settle) and in the Bohemian town of Jablonec (known for its typical faceted-beads).[55] However, the constant expansion of colonial markets also sustained the Venetian production of glass beads, so that in the eighteenth century they were the only sector to survive the general crisis of the glass industry. Failing precise evidence, travellers' and merchants' accounts appear as a chief source, recording both the progress in glass-bead production which occurred in western European capitals[56] and the consistent flow of glass beads out of Venice.[57]

All through the last century and until the outbreak of the Second World War, the story of Venetian glass beads has not been distinguishable from that of colonization. A sample card of glass beads manufactured mostly in Venice, but also in Bohemia and Germany, and traded between 1851 and 1861 in Africa, specifies the product exchanged for each kind of beads: gold, ivory, palm oil and 'slaves'.[58]

In the middle of the nineteenth century, the major importing countries of Venetian beads were England, Holland and France, which in turn shipped them to the respective colonies (mostly in India and Senegal);[59] direct export from Venice was directed to North Africa.[60] In the meantime, a major shift brought glass beads in the limelight as embroidery ornaments of women's dresses and interior decoration. Venetian production of *conterie* reached a peak in 1867 in connection with the boom of the black seed-beads, called Jet for their similarity to the mineral (but better known with their French name, *jais*), used in clothing and in making funeral wreaths.[61] France had been at first a major consumer of this kind of bead, but in the 1880s it became almost self-sufficient, worsening the general crisis of the Venetian glass-bead industry in the last decade of the nineteenth century.[62] Besides short-term trends, throughout the *Belle Epoque* and the first half of the twentieth century Venetian glass beads continued to be a significant export to both European and colonial markets.

In the period after the Second World War, production declined steadily.[63] But in the 1960s and 1970s a new phenomenon began: on the wave of the hippies' movement, various kinds of Venetian glass beads passed from Africa to the USA (especially Cornaline of Aleppo from Ethiopia, Mosaic and *Millefiori* beads from West Africa) (Picard 1989: vols 1, 3, 6); and old glass beads increasingly began to return to antique shops in Venice and Europe, acquiring unprecedented value in Western markets. In the last decade or so, a second inversion has occurred in the bead trade: while developing countries cease to attract high quality Venetian glass beads, low quality glass beads, mostly manufactured in India, but also in Taiwan and in East Asia in general, are imported into Venice to supplement the mass tourism demand for cheap goods.[64] Once again, just as it was at the beginning of our story, glass beads are intended to imitate luxury goods; this time, in the new international equilibrium, the target of this counterfeiting activity is the 'Murano glass' trademark, originally a deceptive brand, and today a controversial seal which is trying to find its final definition as the guarantee of a fine handicraft.

A Few Additional Remarks

In the Western imagination, the connection between women and glass beads lies mainly in the conspicuous consumption of these ornamental objects. However, I have shown how in Venice, since the Middle Ages, work rather than display has been the link between women and glass beads, and this has not been restricted to the task of stringing beads together. More important, I examined the features of women's economic contribution to a specific pre-industrial urban craft in which the female labour force was largely illicit and overshadowed by male mastership.

In my analysis, I departed from some recent perspectives in women's history, and especially from the post-structrualist approach to women's work presented by Joan Scott and others. As argued by this American scholar, during nineteenth-century European industrialization the sexual division of labour resulted from all those discourses which based the antithesis of domestic and waged activities on the 'natural' opposition of a female reproductive and a male productive function – discourses which informed the claims of trade unions and social reformers as much as those of industrialists and the political economy;[65] and to which the Catholic Church should be added in the Italian case.[66]

In many respects, Venetian glass-bead manufacturing could supply this theoretical assumption with a fitting example of its 'natural' association with the feminine realm. However, I have stressed the structural elements in the conditions of labour and the institutional framework more than the ideological construction of gender categories. The prevailing nineteenth-century model of family and womanhood certainly gave its tacit *imprimatur* to the inequality of treatment between sexes and helped to conceal the harshness of domestic jobs; but these in turn were primarily the outcome of a centuries-old sexual division of labour within Venetian glass production created by the guild system.

At the same time, the employment of a large female labour force in the making and local trading of Venetian glass beads during the late medieval and early modern period not only provided women with a factual and cultural meaning of work, but also left its mark on industrial labour organization. In the pre-capitalist 'moral economy', paternalistic relationships between masters and simple labourers granted guild members some protection in terms of material welfare and patronage.[67] In this context, women worked alongside men but lived at the margins of guild privileges: deprived of any official status as workers and considered an endless stock of cheap labour, they seem to have experienced a precocious proletarianization, finding themselves in the unstable condition of free labour earlier and more dramatically than adult men. With the coming of industrialization, these elements became more visible, while new ones were at stake.

The emphasis placed here on the long-lasting influence of corporate economy on Venetian labour relations can also help to explain how female domestic labour has become a chief trait of the Italian path and rate of industrialization, persisting even in the post-war economic boom and up to now in some economic sectors and regions. However, while in Venice women continue to be the large majority of anonymous workers employed in medium-size firms, the massive exploitation of under-paid female labour has ceased to be a predominant feature of local bead manufacturing. Meanwhile, new issues are on the agenda of Western feminists: control over the underground economy and gender discrimination at work, as well as the effective solution of problems connected with a changing relation between work and family in most women's lives.

Indeed, the evolution of women's roles and the sexual division of labour in the Venetian glass bead sector should be seen in parallel to the changes that have occurred in the northern Italian family structure, besides those which took place in the economic and institutional framework. In this regard, today's globalization of the world economy is a major challenge for women's studies, opening up possibilities for fertile cross-disciplinary exchanges and comparative perspectives in the history of women's positions in the family and labour market. The case of glass-bead manufacturing could then enter more directly the debates on non-Western ways to capitalism, in terms of both a diachronic comparison between European pre-industrial society and traditional societies which in these years are experiencing rapid industrialization, and a synchronic analysis of the present conditions of women employed as a cheap labour force, especially in India and the East Asian countries which are now exporting these commodities to the West.

Notes

1. The results are collected in the catalogue of a thorough exhibit on the topic (Bellavitis, Filippini & Sega 1990).
2. Women's economic contribution in early modern Europe was not limited to the textile manufactures nor to rural areas, as it also extended to some jobs in the urban guild economy. For a comprehensive overview of women's work in pre-industrial Europe, with a comparison between France and England, see Tilly and Scott 1978. On women's employment in early modern urban crafts, see the case-study on Lyon by Zemon Davis 1986. Among the vast literature on the history of female labour in pre-industrial Europe, see also: Charles and Duffin 1985; Howell 1986; Hudson and Lee 1990; Hafter 1995.
3. For an overview which focuses on Venice, see Mackenney 1987. For a synthesis about craft guilds in medieval Europe, see Thrupp 1965.
4. For the most accurate and updated studies about Murano glassblowers, particularly devoted to the pre-industrial epoch, see Gasparetto 1958 and Zecchin 1987–90. For an outline in English, see Tait 1979.
5. In today's technical terminology, all beads made out of hollow rods are called 'drawn beads', while all those made out of solid rods are called 'wound beads' (or less precisely, 'lamp-beads'). For a guide to the description and classification of glass beads, in particular Venetian beads, see Karklins 1985.
6. For the most detailed descriptions of the two methods of preparing glass canes and making beads, dating from the nineteenth century, see Bussolin 1842: 15–25 (also in its contemporary French translation; Bussolin 1846) and Zanetti 1866: 30–6.
7. Since 1319, the statutes of *paternostreri e margariteri* restricted the number of women allowed to work for a male master; Library of the Museum Correr, Venice, *Manoscritti IV*, n° 99, fol. 6. In response to a conjunctural increase in glass beads demand, in 1754 women of masters' families were temporarily allowed to carry out also the operation of cutting glass canes into pieces; *Tre documenti . . .*, 1884. This permission assumed that women had some experience in this job, or at least made it possible for them to acquire it.
8. In the second half of the seventeenth century, the wives of those masters who had migrated out of Murano and Venice in search of better jobs obtained from the State the right to work for the guild; State Archives of Venice (hereafter abbreviated as A.S.V.), *Inquisitori di Stato*, busta 821. *Post mortem* inventories describing the belongings of some eighteenth-century bead makers confirm the presence of women in small family workshops in the Venice town centre; A.S.V., *Giudici di Petizion. Inventari*, busta 404.28 and busta 467.27.
9. For the projects to reform Venetian manufacturing in the Enlightenment period, see Venturi 1990: 136–41.
10. The survey has been entirely reprinted; for the parts concerning the two guilds of *paternostreri* and *perleri*, see Sagredo 1856: 255, 269. Two years before, in 1771, the guild of *perleri* had listed 98 women – between masters' widows and daughters – with a total of 822 persons (Bellavitis, Filippini & Sega 1990: 19n). In 1783 they were 340 out of 352 male workers, including children and apprentices (Cecchetti 1874: 222).

11. In Venice 'on voit dans toutes les rues les femmes, tant publiques que les pauvres, occupées à l'infilement, où à l'ornament de ces bagatelles' (Poullet 1668: 442).

12. *Statutes of the Perleri and Suppialume*, fol. 66v in A.S.V., *Arti*, busta 437. At the end of the eighteenth century, a rule approved in 1793 recognized the changes that had occurred: it allowed only masters' widows or female orphans to make beads, but all other women to string beads (Miani, Resini & Lamon 1984: 158).

13. A bead producer (*margariter*) died in 1740 leaving among his debts a sum due to 'women who strung beads in Murano'; A.S.V., *Giudici di Petizion. Inventari*, busta 437.23.

14. On this period, see Costantini 1987.

15. Excluding domestic labour, in the period 1834–45 Venetian factories producing *conterie* employed about 1,000 workers (Zalin 1969: 141). In 1845, the glass-bead sector as a whole was the most important of all Venetian manufacturing, second only to the naval industry (Romanelli 1977: 269). For an overview of Venice's economy during the nineteenth century, see Luzzatto 1979: 267–77.

16. The first factory to concentrate all stages of seed-bead production – except bead stringing – opened in 1817 (Dalmistro, Errera & Co.). In 1848 the first producers' association was created (Società Anonima Fabbriche Unite di Canna, di Vetri e Smalti per Conterie), a second one in 1898 (Società Veneziana per l'Industria delle Conterie), and the largest one in 1906 (Società Veneziana Conterie e Cristallerie, ex Franchetti). Various smaller units producing *conterie* were located in Venice town centre (for a map of the 27 units working in 1867–8, see Bellavitis, Filippini & Sega 1990: 26–7; for a description of some of them, see also the catalogue of an exhibit about Venice industrial archaeology, *Venezia città industriale . . .*, 1980).

17. An industrial statistic of 1903 calculated that women represented 28.8 per cent of the total labour force employed in Italian glass industry, but 25.1 per cent of them worked in the province of Venice (Marianelli 1983: 108).

18. A survey of the housing problem in Venice registered that between 1882 and 1901, out of 100 women who died of tuberculosis, 26 were bead stringers (Bellavitis 1994: 44, 52n).

19. In Turin, in one of the largest Italian dark-glass bottle factories, the highest wage of a male glass blower in 1893 was ITL 8 a day, while women employed in covering flasks and demijohns with straw were paid ITL 1.50 a day (Marianelli 1983: 111). The table of coefficients to calculate today's cost of living at retail prices and wholesale prices in any year since 1861 can be found in the most recent Italian statistical yearbook. According to the 1994 publication, 1893 ITL 8 corresponded to about ITL 42,000 in 1993 and ITL 1.5 to less than ITL 8,000 (ISTAT 1994: 452).

20. Data drawn from the Chamber of Commerce of Venice (Cecchetti 1874: 194). The value of ITL 1 in 1861 was equivalent to ITL 5,800 in 1993, while in 1871 fell to ITL 5,500 (ISTAT 1994: 452).

21. Data presented in an inquiry by the jury for the Second National Glass Exhibit (Errera 1870: vol. 1, 349).

22. In the factory, women were paid from 0.7 to 1 ITL for separating glass canes and from 1 to 1.20 ITL for cutting them (Richetti 1899: 986–7).

23. For a description of one of these large laboratories located in *Cannaregio*, see (Richetti 1899: 988).
24. For the relationships between *mistre* and simple bead stringers as collected through interviews, see Bellavitis, Filippini and Sega 1990: 28–32.
25. Some bead stringers joined a first strike in 1872 and about 2,000 of them took part in the general strike of 1904; on these aspects, see Bellavitis, Filippini and Sega 1990: 16.
26. At the same time, in 1851 and 1866 women employed in factories producing *conterie* exceeded men in a ratio of 4 to 1 (Cecchetti 1874: 192–4).
27. This survey also registered 149 women, 364 men and 58 children employed in factories producing *conterie* between Venice and Murano; 174 women, 116 men and 93 children in factories preparing solid canes. It calculated that in Venice there were about 400 gas-lamps to make wound-beads and more than 700 men and women working at them (Sormani Moretta 1880–1: 250–1).
28. The glass production as a whole employed a total of 3,900 individuals, among whom 2,300 worked at home and the rest in factories (Reberschack 1986: 239).
29. For a methodological discussion of these issues and research on nineteenth-century North America, see Hareven 1978: chap. 6.
30. Many of the bead stringers who have been interviewed work also as laundresses or domestic servants (Bellavitis, Filippini & Sega 1990: 35).
31. Murano and the other islands of the lagoon were excluded from the classification by profession. In Venice, 23 per cent of bead stringers were aged between fifteen and twenty and 10 per cent between forty and fifty; the large majority of them lived in the neighbourhood of *Castello*. In addition to those women, also ten men were classified under the category of *impiraperle*. No specific information is given about them, but being all under thirty-five or over sixty years old, they were probably just helping women in various ways. 787 women and 1,046 men were registered as working in the glass-bead production in general (*Rilievo degli abitanti . . .*, 1871: 6–7, 34–5).
32. Various records testify that bead work was taught and practised in religious convents and schools. At the Second Italian Glass Exhibit, organized in Murano in 1869, bead embroideries made by the young girls of a Catholic school were displayed (Errera 1869: 11–12). Ten years later, it was acknowledged that many religious school teachers were in contact with glass producers and traders to have female students stringing beads (Sormani Moretta 1880–1: 251). Also Irene Ninni (1873: 11–13) mentioned the custom of practising the art of stringing beads in prison, schools and convents as leisure.
33. In 1925, the major factory producing *conterie* in Murano hired 603 male workers and 349 female workers, while 355 *mistre* working at home were employed together with 1,900 bead stringers (Bellavitis, Filippini & Sega 1990: 18). According to the declarations to the Police authority given by the owners of two main beads factories in Murano, in 1923 the Fabbrica Conterie employed 422 women, only 109 of them were older than twenty-one, 102 were between fifteen- and twenty-one-years old and forty-three were under fifteen-years old; the firm Cristallerie Murano hired 131 women on a total of 643 workers, forty-eight of them were over twenty-one, sixty-four were between fifteen and twenty-one and nineteen under fifteen (Tosi 1992/93: 148).

34. Bellavitis, Filippini and Sega 1990: 18. It has been calculated that in 1928 bead stringers could not earn more than ITL 4 for a eight-hour working day and that women working in factories received an average salary of ITL 9 (Ibid.: 31). Considering that ITL 4 in 1928 were equivalent to ITL 4,400 in 1993 and ITL 9 to ITL 9,800 (ISTAT, 1994: 452), the monthly wage of a women working in a bead factory could be inferior to ITL 300,000 in 1993 and that of bead stringer to ITL 130,000.

35. On this period see the photographic documentation in Bellavitis, Filippini and Sega 1990.

36. The interview of a seventy-eight year-old woman who had worked in the bead factory until she got married and then as an *impiraperle* at home, is reported in Tosi 1992/93: 235.

37. In 1955 between Venice and Murano there were 50 lamp-beads workshops, employing about 500 women (Gasparetto 1958: 202–3).

38. According to a general survey on economic and labour organization of Murano artistic glass industry, in 1993 only three out of the sixty-five firms producing lamp-beads hired more than ten persons – the smallest ones working for local tourist markets and the largest ones mostly on orders (Crestanello 1995: 181).

39. A visit to this firm during a working day was made possible thanks to the courtesy of the present owner, Mr. Gianni Moretti. The Ercole Moretti & Co. was established in 1911 for the production of Chevron and *Millefiori* beads; samples of all types of glass beads produced by the company throughout the decades are displayed in a private collection.

40. For a collection of essays which covers a large spectrum of approaches to the history of consumption, see Brewer and Porter 1993.

41. Although usually not mentioned in this connection, the relativistic evaluation of glass beads can be seen in this perspective. For an exhibition at the British Museum of London which address these issues, see Jones 1990. For a classical anthropological approach to social and cultural values of consumption, see Douglas and Isherwood 1979.

42. The unpublished history of Murano by Carlo Neijmann Rizzi (*L'isola di Murano, ossia memoria storica e scientifica del vetro, anno 1811*) is preserved in two copies – one at the Glass Museum of Murano and one in the library of the Museum Correr in Venice. For the subsequent objections to Rizzi's hypothesis on the subject, see Gasparetto 1958: 182–3 and Zecchin 1987: vol. 1, 71–6.

43. The expansion of this counterfeiting activity is testified by the conflicts which arose in the fourteenth century between the guild of glassblowers and the guild holding the monopoly of crystal-made items (Zecchin 1989: vol. 2, 239–44).

44. The English word 'bead' itself is etymologically associated to devotional and religious functions: it derives from the noun *bede* – that means 'prayer' – and from the verb *bidden* – 'to pray' (see the entry 'bead' in *The Oxford Dictionary . . .*, 1966).

45. See for example Casola 1907: 161.

46. For the itineraries of sub-Saharan and Arabic caravans in the fifteenth and sixteenth centuries, see Braudel 1949: vol. 1, 176–81. For the trade routes through the Levant to China and the Indies, mostly controlled by the Mamluks, see Lane 1973: 71.

47. One hypothesis links the word *conterie* to the Latin term *comptus* and the local dialect noun *contigia*, both meaning 'ornament' (see the entry 'contaria' in Boerio 1856).

Another hypothesis suggests it descends from the Portuguese *cuenta*, that is 'account' or 'calculation' (Bussolin 1842: 56). The first written testimony of the word *conterie* dates back to 1603 and is recorded in a letter addressed by Emmanuele Ximenes, a Portuguese living in Antwerp, to Antonio Neri – author of the first printed treatise entirely dedicated to the art of glass making (Zecchin 1987: vol. 1, 87).

48. A.S.V., *Giudici di Petizion. Rendimenti di conto*, busta 978.

49. In Paris, in 1767 it was ordered to register all non-guild members employed in selling retail: 1,263 women were listed and only 486 men (Tilly & Scott 1978: 20, 50).

50. For all of the fifteenth century, the Venetian mercantile marine was organized in a system of convoys following prescribed routes and seasonal departures under state supervision and protection. Even when free navigation became more common during the sixteenth century, private ships maintained almost the same courses. For a detailed illustration of these routes, see Vivanti and Tenenti 1961: 83–6. For Venetian maritime trades in general, see the comprehensive work by Lane 1973.

51. Glass-bead trade is not discussed in detail by any of the many studies on European colonies. Among a vast bibliography, see Parry 1966; Scammel 1981; Israel 1989; Tracy 1990.

52. '. . . à traitter avec les Sauvages du Canada & les Nègres de Guinée'; Savary des Bruslons 1723: vol. 1, cols. 1481–2.

53. Ibid.: vol. 3, cols. 1288–90.

54. 'Dans une cargaison pour traitter six cents douze Nègres, principalement entre la rivière de Sestre & la rivière d'Ardres, il faut environ trois mille livres de rassade; sçavoir douze cents livres de contre-bordé, huit cents livre de rassade noir, & mille livres des toutes les autres couleurs'; ibid.: vol. 2, col. 1273. A French pound in the eighteenth century was about 0.4 kg (Martini 1976).

55. At the end of the eighteenth century, the so-called Russian blue beads were traded in the north-western Pacific for furs (Picard 1986: vol. 5).

56. In 1776, a Venetian merchant – Giorgio Barbaria (see figure 7) – wrote a report concerning the commerce of *conterie* in Spain, Portugal and England and denounced the growth of lamp-bead manufacturing in Paris (A.S.V., *Cinque Savi alla Mercanzia*, busta 358). In 1766–7 the Venetian ambassador in London alarmingly informed his government of the smuggling of Dutch glass beads along the English coasts, which was seriously damaging the direct importation from Venice (*Alcuni dispacci . . .* 1884).

57. From travellers' accounts we learn that at the end of the seventeenth century shipments of *conterie* reached Egypt and then were distributed along the Nile river in Abyssinia or brought to India (Sella 1961: 66). In 1765 a Venetian merchant observed that the Dutch demand for glass beads had significantly increased (A.S.V., *Cinque Savi alla Mercanzia*, busta 463). And in 1766 a French traveller in Venice noted that a vast export of 'perles fausses et verroteries' was sent to Lisbon and Cadiz to supplement the slave trade and to Alexandria and the Levant (Cecchetti 1874: 85). Extremely florid pictures of Venetian glass-bead production were given in 1752 by the French consul in Venice (Georgelin 1978: 182) and in 1761 by an officer charged by the Venetian government to report on this manufacture, which indicated western European nations as its primary buyer, followed by Egypt and Portugal (Zanetti 1869: 12–13).

58. The reference is to the sample card of the London businessmen Moses Lewin Levin, active between 1830 and 1913 (it presently belongs to the Museum of Mankind in London and has been analysed by Karklins, 1985). Incidentally, the dates proposed for these beads used in slave trading are very late and postdate the abolishment of slavery in both Spanish and British colonies.

59. In the early 1840s, France traded seed-beads in Senegal for gold sand, hides, precious wood and gum arabic (Bussolin 1842: 54–5).

60. In 1845, the whole glass-bead production, with its 50 per cent share of Venetian manufacturing, represented the first export item (Romanelli 1977: 269). In that year, the production of lamp-beads amounted to 320,000 kg against 1,959,000 kg of *conterie* (Bussolin 1846: 85–6).

61. According to the data of the Venetian Chamber of Commerce (Cecchetti 1874: 194–5), in 1867 6,015,200 kg of glass beads (for a value of more than ITL 15 million) were exported from Venice, while in the second half of the nineteenth century this export generally amounted to an average of 1,505,000 kg (ITL 4–5 million). The value of ITL 15 million at wholesale prices in 1867 corresponded to about ITL 53 million in 1993 (ISTAT, 1994: 452). A major increase in this export occurred in the second half of the century, considering that between 1818 and 1823 the export of *conterie* from Venice varied from 976,200 to 1,23,500 kg (Zalin 1969: 116).

62. For some export figures and a discussion about the measures taken to address the problem, see Richetti 1899: 988–90. Between 1870 and 1880 annual shipments of Venetian glass beads to the United States totalled 2,700,000 kg (Dubin 1987: 111).

63. According to the Chamber of Commerce, between 1955 and 1960 the monetary value of glass bead exports represented about 2 per cent of the total exports from the province of Venice (*Compendio statistico . . .* 1961: 285).

64. No detailed records document this import. It can be noticed that all activities related to tourism represent today the main resource of the Venetian economy. The forecast of about 7.8–8.6 million visitors for the year 2000 (Costa 1994: 247–50) has already been overtaken. In response to the needs of this mass consumption, some Venetian dealers import Asian products and some producers even establish branches of their own firms in developing countries – this is the case of a 900-worker plant started in Morocco by a Venetian businessmen to produce *murrine*.

65. Scott 1991a: 419–41. For a theoretical discussion of the post-structuralist concept of power as a discursive process which produces differences, see the updated overview of women's studies and feminist historiography in the United States by the same scholar: Idem 1991. The evolution in Scott's positions can be followed through her works: trained as a social historian (Wallach Scott 1974), her book with Tilly (Tilly & Scott 1978) was an open statement in favour of what she would now label as the 'social science approach' in opposition to post-structuralism; more recently, she repudiated her own previous writings for their confident reliance on statistical sources (Scott 1986: 337n).

66. For the position of women according to the Catholic doctrine at the end of the nineteenth century, see De Giorgio 1991: 169–97.

67. I borrow the expression from the model outlined by Thompson 1993.

References

Alcuni dispacci di Cesare Vignola residente in Londra per la Repubblica Veneta sull'argomento delle conterie (1884), Venezia: Tip. Cordella.

Bellavitis, A. (1994), 'Condizioni di lavoro e lotte operaie. La Manifattura Tabacchi di Venezia tra Otto e Novecento', *Venetica*, vol. 11, no. 3, 41–53.

——, Filippini, N., & Sega, M.T. (eds) (1990), *Perle e impiraperle: un lavoro di donne a Venezia tra '800 e '900*, Venezia: Arsenale Editrice.

Boerio, G. (1856), *Dizionario del dialetto veneto*, Venezia: Tip. G. Cecchini.

Braudel, F. (1949), *La Méditerranée et le monde Méditerranéen à l'époque de Philippe II*, 2 vols, Paris: A. Colin.

Brewer, J. & Porter, R. (eds) (1993), *Consumption and the World of Goods*, London-New York: Routledge.

Bussolin, D. (1842), *Guida alle fabbriche vetrarie di Murano e Venezia*, Venezia: Tip. A. Santini.

—— (1846), *Les célèbres verreries de Venise et de Murano*, Venise: Tip. G. Cecchini.

Casola, P. (1907), *Canon Pietro Casola's Pilgrimage to Jerusalem in the year 1494*, Manchester: Manchester University Press.

Cecchetti, B. (1874), *Monografia della vetraria veneziana e muranese*, Venezia: Tip. Antonelli.

Charles, L. & Duffin, L. (eds) (1985), *Women and Work in Pre-industrial England*, London: Croom Helm.

Compendio statistico della provincia di Venezia 1955–1960 (1961), Venezia: Camera di Commercio Industria e Agricoltura.

Costa, P. (1994), *Venezia. Economia e analisi urbana*, Milano: Etas Libri.

Costantini, M. (1987), *L'albero della libertà economica. Il processo di scioglimento delle corporazioni veneziane*, Venezia: Arsenale Editrice.

Crestanello, P. (1995), 'L'industria del vetro artistico di Murano', *Oltre il ponte*, no. 49, 179–96.

De Giorgio, M. (1991), '*La Bonne Catholique*', in G. Duby and M. Perrot (eds), *Histoire des femmes en Occident*, Paris: Plon, vol. 4, 169–97.

Douglas, M. & Isherwood, B. (1979), *The World of Goods*, New York: Basic Books.

Dubin, L.S. (1987), *The History of Beads from 30,000 to the Present*, London: Thames & Hudson.

Errera, A. (1869), *L'industria vetraria nel 1869*, Venezia.

—— (1870), *Storia e statistica delle industrie venete*, 2 vols, Venezia: Tip. Antonelli.

Ferrari, P. (1911), *Conferenza sull'industria privata femminile veneziana*, Venezia: Officine grafiche di C. Ferrari.

Gasparetto, A. (1958), *Il vetro di Murano dalle origini ad oggi*, Venezia: Neri Pozza.

Georgelin, J. (1978), *Venise au siècle des lumières*, Paris-Le Havre: Mouton-Ecole des Hautes Etudes en Sciences Sociales.

Hafter, D.M. (ed.) (1995), *European Women and Preindustrial Craft*, Bloomington: Indiana University Press.

Hareven, T.K. (ed.) (1978), *Transitions: The Family and Life Course in Historical Perspective*, New York: Academic Press.

Herelihy, D. (1990), *Opera Muliebria. Women and Work in Medieval Europe*, New York: McGraw-Hill Publishing Co.

Howell, M.C. (1986), *Women, Production and Patriarchy in Late Medieval Cities*, Chicago: University of Chicago Press.

Hudson, P. & Lee, W.R. (eds) (1990), *Women's Work and the Family Economy in Historical Perspective*, Manchester: Manchester University Press.

Hufton, O. (1975), 'Women and the Family Economy in Eighteenth-Century France', *French Historical Studies*, no. 9, 1–22.

Israel, J.I. (1989), *Dutch Primacy in World Trade, 1585–1740*, Oxford: Clarendon Press.

ISTAT-Istituto Nazionale di Statistica (1994), *Compendio statistico italiano*, Roma.

James, H. (1888), *The Aspern Papers. Louisa Pallant. The Modern Warning*, London-New York: Macmillan Co.

Jones, M. (ed.) (1990), *Fake? The Art of Deception*, London: British Museum Publications.

Karklins, K. (1985), *Glass Beads. The Levin Catalogue of Mid-19th Century Beads. A Sample Book of 19th Century Ventian Beads. Guide to the Description and Classification of Glass Beads*, 2nd edn, Ottawa: National Historic Parks and Sites Branch.

—— (1990), 'Dominique Bussolin on the Glass-Bead Industry of Murano and Venice (1847)', *Beads*, vol. 2, 69–84.

Lane, F.C. (1973), *Venice. A Maritime Republic*, Baltimore-London: Johns Hopkins University Press.

Luzzatto, G. (1979), *L'economia veneziana dal 1797 al 1866*, in *Storia della civiltà veneziana*, Firenze: Sansoni, vol. 3, 267–77.

Mackenney, R. (1987), *Tradesmen and Traders. The World of the Guilds in Venice and Europe, c.1250–c.1650*, London-Sydney: Croom Helm.

Marianelli, A. (1983), *Proletariato di fabbrica e organizzazione sindacale in Italia: il caso dei lavoratori del vetro*, Milano: Franco Angeli.

Martini, A. (1976), *Manuale di metrologia*, Roma: Editrice REA.

Miani, M., Resini, D. & Lamon, F. (1984), *L'arte dei maestri vetrai di Murano*, Treviso: Matteo Editore.

Monticolo, G. (1905–14), *I capitolari delle arti veneziane sottoposte alla Giustizia e poi alla Giustizia Vecchia dalle origini al MCCCXXX*, 3 vols, Roma: Istituto Storico Italiano.

Ninni, I. (1873), *L'impiraressa*, Venezia: Tip. Longhi e Montanari.

Orchard, W.C. (1929), *Beads and Beadwork of the American Indians*, New York: Museum of the American Indian-Heye Foundation.

(The) Oxford Dictionary of English Etymology (1966), C.T. Onions (ed.), Oxford: Clarendon Press.

Parry, J.H. (1966), *The Spanish Seaborne Empire*, Berkeley-Los Angeles-Oxford: University of California Press.

—— (1967), '*Transport and Trade Routes*', in *The Cambridge Economic History of Europe*, Cambridge: Cambridge University Press, vol. 4, 155–219.

Picard, J. & R. (eds) (1986), *Beads from the West African Trade*, 6 vols, Carmel-CA.

Poullet, le Sieur (1668), *Nouvelles relations du Levant*, Paris: chez Louis Billaine.

Reberschack, M. (1986), '*L'economia*', in Emilio Franzina, *Venezia*, Roma-Bari: Laterza, 227–98.

Richetti, C. (1899), 'L'industria delle conterie a Venezia', *Riforma sociale*, vol. 9, 984–93.

Rilievo degli abitanti di Venezia 1869 per religione, condizioni, professioni, arti e mestieri (1871), Venezia: Comune di Venezia.

Romanelli, G. (1977), *Venezia Ottocento. Materiali per una storia architettonica e urbanistica della città nel XIX secolo*, Roma: Officina Edizioni.

Sagredo, A. (1856), *Sulle consorterie delle arti edificatorie in Venezia*, Venezia: Tip. Naratovich.

Savary des Bruslons, J. (1723), *Dictionnaire universel du commerce*, 3 vols, Paris: chez Jacques Estienne.

Scammel, G.V. (1981), *The World Encompassed. The First European Maritime Empires c. 800–1650*, London-New York: Methuen.

Scott, J. (1986), '*Statistical Representation of Work: The Politics of the Chamber of Commerce's Statistique de l'industrie à Paris, 1847–1848*', in S. L. Kaplan and C. J. Koepp (eds), *Work in France: Representations, Meaning, Organization, and Practice*, Ithaca-London: Cornell University Press, 335–63.

—— (1991a), '*La travailleuse*', in G. Duby and M. Perrot (eds), *Histoire des femmes en Occident*, Paris: Plons, vol. 4, 419–41.

—— (1991b), '*Women's History*', in Peter Burke (ed.), *New Perspectives on Historical Writing*, University Park-PA: Pennsylvania State University, 42–66.

——, & Tilly, L.A. (1975), 'Women's Work and the Family in Nineteenth-Century Europe', *Comparative Studies in Society and History*, vol. 17, no. 1, 36–64.

Segatti, L. (1991), 'L'impiraressa: The Venetian Bead Stringer', *Beads*, vol. 3, 73–82.

Sella, D. (1961), *Commerci e industrie a Venezia nel secolo XVII*, Venezia-Roma: Istituto per la Collaborazione Culturale.

Sormani Moretta, L. (1880–1), *La provincia di Venezia. Monografia statistica-economica-amministrativa*, Venezia: Tip. Antonelli.

Tait, H. (1979), *The Golden Age of Venetian Glass*, London: The Trustees of the British Museum.

Thompson, E.P. (1993), 'The Moral Economy of the English Crowd in the Eighteenth Century', in Idem, *Customs in Common*, Harmondsworth: Penguin Books, 185–351 (first ed. 1971).

Thrupp, S. (1965), '*The Guilds*', in *The Cambridge Economic History of Europe*, Cambridge: Cambridge University Press, vol. 3, 230–80.

Tilly, L.A. & Scott, J.W. (1978), *Women, Work, and Family*, New York: Holt, Rinehart and Winston.

Tosi, A. (1992/93), 'I vetrai di Murano: condizioni di vita e di lavoro', unpublished thesis, University of Venice-Ca' Foscari.

Tracy, J.D. (1990), *The Rise of Merchant Empires. Long-distance trade in the Early Modern World, 1350–1750*, Cambridge: Cambridge University Press.

Tre documenti del secolo scorso relativi alle conterie (1884), Venezia: Tip. G. Cecchini.

Venezia città industriale. Gli insediamenti produttivi del 19° secolo (1980), Venezia: Marsilio Editore.

Venturi, F. (1990), *Settecento riformatore*, vol.5.2: *La Repubblica di Venezia (1761–1797)*, Torino: Einaudi.

Vivanti, C., & Tenenti, A. (1961), 'Le film d'un grand système de navigation: les galères marchandes vénitiennes XIVe–XVIe siècles', *Annales.E.S.C.*, vol. 16, no. 1, 83–6.

Wallach Scott, J. (1974), *The Glassworkers of Carmeaux. French Craftsmen and Political Action in a Nineteenth-Century City*, Cambridge-London: Harvard University Press.

Zalin, G. (1969), *Aspetti e problemi dell'economia veneta dalla caduta della Repubblica all'annessione*, Vicenza.

Zanetti, V. (1866), *Guida di Murano e delle sue celebri fornaci*, Venezia: Tip. Antonelli.

—— (ed.) (1869), *Scrittura di Gasparo Gozzi intorno ai mezzi di far rifiorire il commercio delle conterie in Venezia*, Venezia: Tip. Naratovich.

Zecchin, L. (1987–90), *Vetro e vetrai di Murano. Studi sulla storia del vetro*, 3 vols, Venezia: Arsenale Editrice.

Zemon Davis, N. (1986), 'Women in the Crafts in Sixteenth-Century Lyon,' in Barbara Hanawalt (ed.), *Women and Work in Preindustrial Europe*, Bloomington: Indiana University Press, 167–97

3

Gender in African Beadwork: An Overview

Margret Carey

Introduction

Before embarking on a review of gender and African beadwork, there are some points to make. The subject will be discussed under three broad headings: beadmaking; beadworking; and the uses of beadwork, whether to wear or for any other purpose. Beads are made of natural materials such as seeds, shells, stone and wood; out of metal, especially brass and iron; while most imported beads are made out of glass.

Beadwork needs to be defined. In its simplest form, it may be no more than a string of beads, even a single bead, worn on almost any part of the body, or added to a carved figure as decoration or as an offering. Beadwork can be more elaborate, with beads strung into complex ropes, sewn into fabric-like panels, applied as covering to figures, clothing and masks, or used to embellish everyday items, to make them more special. Bead-working is the act of making such beadwork, while bead making is self-explanatory and has to be part of my subject.

Africa is a vast continent, with numerous ethnic groups, cultures and styles, and while it is possible to generalize to some extent, there are many exceptions which cannot be covered due to lack of space. We know little of African beadwork before the mass import of trade beads from Europe from about AD 1480 onwards. Where beads were not available, personal ornament tended to manifest itself in body paint, scarification (i.e. raised tattoo designs on the skin), elaborate hairdressing, ear, nose and lip plugs (to protect body openings). Arm, leg and body ornaments might be made from elaborately plaited or knotted grass, split palm leaf and fibres, with the addition of fur and feathers. From the first millennium AD, Indian-made stone beads and glass beads from India and the Near East came into Africa via the trans-Saharan and the eastern coastal trade. Before Venetian glass beads became widely available, from about the beginning of the nineteenth century, most beads were made from metal, wood, seeds, ivory, bone and shell. The earliest beadwork that we know of is shown on some terracottas from Nok in northern Nigeria, dated to between the mid-first millennium BC and the mid-first millennium AD. Some of these depict human figures or busts wearing heavy collars and body ropes made up of multiple strands of beads (Eyo & Willett 1982: nos. 9, 12). It seems likely that these beads were made of some perishable substance such as seeds, wood or clay. Terracotta figures from Mali and Chad, dated to the mid-second millennium AD, provide similar beadwork evidence; as do some bronzes from Ife, southern Nigeria (Eyo & Willett 1982: no. 44). At Igbo-Ukwu in southern Nigeria, dated to the late first millennium AD, we find imported glass beads in quantity, especially in the burial of someone identified as a priest-king (Shaw 1977). These beads may have been imported ultimately from India and the Near East, and, as costly imports, their use was restricted to royalty, their families and their courts. A similar pattern can be seen in the use of beads in Great Benin, in southern Nigeria, and in the accounts given by early traders in southern Africa.[1]

In what we often describe as traditional African society (though this is in fact a sort of Utopian definition), gender plays its part in setting rules about the things that are 'men's work' and 'women's work', the clothes and ornaments they wear, and so forth. Some of these arise out of practical considerations such as the need for women to be home-based to look after the children which are so vitally important to the family and the ethnic group. Generally speaking, a woman will not do a man's work, and vice versa, though when the occasion demands, these 'rules' will be set aside. Differences arising out of gender play quite a large part in African beadwork. Some of these are documented by missionaries, travellers and researchers, while others can be inferred through intelligent guesswork. I plan to describe some of them, and try to analyse how they come about.

Bead Making

The earliest sort of social life found in Africa is that known as a 'hunting-gathering' economy, which comes before people settle down to a more stable pastoral or agricultural way of life. This is the 'traditional' way of life for San (Bushmen) women who go out with their children to gather various roots, melons, vegetables and small animals such as grubs and tortoises as food, while the men may be away for days at a time hunting larger game. Among the things women collect are ostrich eggshells, whether the entire egg which makes an outsize omelette (carefully saving the shell for use as a water container), or the broken fragments from a nest. So it is reasonable to find that women make ostrich eggshell beads by trimming the pieces into small rounds with their teeth, piercing them with a needle or a sharp thorn, then threading them on a sinew string, and filing and polishing them with a stone into smooth disks (Bannister & Lewis-Williams 1991: 12).[2] A needle or thorn is a 'woman's tool', which she may use in sewing skins together or in making a basket.

Making beads this way is a lengthy process, and a woman might take some weeks to make a two-foot long string of ostrich eggshell beads. This sort of thing is done between other tasks, in much the same way as we might pick up a newspaper or some knitting. Beads made from pierced and threaded sea shells, roots or tubers, all things that women might gather, are also surely made by women.

This is not to say that all ostrich eggshell beads were made by women. Arkell (1936: 307–10), described how men in the Sudan made disc beads from ostrich eggshell or land snail shell (*Achatina sp.*), although by then it was a dying craft. A man from western Darfur province demonstrated how he broke the egg shells or snail shell into pieces about 1 cm. square, and then chipped them into rough circles using a small axe. The discs were then soaked in water to prevent them splitting during the final operation of perforating them with an iron hand awl. After stringing them the beads were often rubbed on a grooved piece of sandstone to make them round and the same size. A man could make about one hundred beads in a day, and sell them by the string of approximately 130 cm. A bead string of snail shell, which is harder and thinner, used to cost about twice that of a string of ostrich eggshell. Men from other ethnic groups, such as the Shilluk and the Pokot[3] also made ostrich eggshell beads in this way. The large white beads made from the hinge of giant clams, and those made from *conus* shells, are probably made by men, since getting these shells involves some risk, and they are prestige beads.

Metal beads are a different matter. Women, especially if they are of child-bearing age, must stay clear of metal-smelting – in fact, men must also abstain from sexual relations during that time. In African thought, the ability to extract metal from ore was so mysterious that it was hedged around with taboos and rituals designed to ensure a successful smelting. Women's bodies, with their ability to conceive, menstruate and bear children are also mysterious and powerful, and if the two came together, there might be a risk of the smelting going wrong due to the forces in a woman's body. So, whether it was iron-smithing, brass-casting by the lost-wax process, or wire-drawing, the metal-working procedure is regarded as a man's preserve. We therefore find that iron, brass, silver or gold beads are made by men, whether he is a village blacksmith or a specialist worker in brass, gold or silver.

Making stone beads is a subject that is quite fully covered by Ann O'Hear in this volume, so I shall skip bead making in Ilorin, Nigeria, but will touch upon the rather different bauxite bead making practised in Ghana (Shaw 1945: 45–50). Bauxite, a reddish-pink mottled stone, is aluminium ore, and is usually got by digging in pits. Men do this work, but women share in all the other operations, such as carrying the excavated stone to the villages, making the beads, and marketing them. The beads are perforated by using a bow-drill and mounted on a bicycle-wheel spoke for grinding and polishing. In 1945 there were perhaps 500 people, men and women, making them; there was no apprenticeship system. The industry was then declining from a peak in about 1920, but the present-day interest in beads and improved equipment may well mean a revival of the craft. They were traded all over Ghana and were especially popular in the Ivory Coast. These beads were worn only for ornament, and only by women and children.

There are two sorts of glass bead making in Africa, both involving the use of recycled glass. The first sort, practised at Bida, in Nigeria, a Muslim community, involves melting down glass cullet in kilns heated with charcoal and manually-operated bellows. This highly strenuous work is done by men, organized into a guild, who are specialists, handing down their skills from father to son. The process and glasshouses have hardly changed since they were described in the early years of this century.[4] Women are not involved except to collect together glass cullet, coloured if possible, and to thread the beads made by their menfolk onto raffia for sale.

The other sort of glass bead made especially in Ghana, West Africa is called 'powder-glass', which is a pretty apt description of the raw material (Francis 1993a: 10–11; 1993b: 96–7, 100–101). Making these beads is very much shared between men and women; it is interesting to see how the 'woman's work' of gathering and preparing food is adapted to the female share in the bead making process. Women collect the glass cullet from the neighbouring town or village, and pound it into powder in a heavy metal tube mortar using a pestle in much the same way as they pound grain or yams for food, and sift the glass powder like flour. The master bead maker's job is to build and prepare the kiln, to make the moulds for the beads, and to dribble the powder into the moulds which are then fired for about fifteen to twenty minutes. This glass does not fuse completely; it is sintered, which gives powder-glass beads their characteristic granular surface. Women and children join in such jobs as fitting the moulds with the cassava stalks which make the bead perforations, polishing the beads when they have cooled down after firing, and stringing them on raffia for sale. This type of bead, generally called 'Krobo' may well have been made as long ago as AD 1700 in Ghana, and even the tenth to twelfth centuries in Mauritania, to judge from excavated moulds. Marketing is very much a woman's activity in Ghana and western Africa generally, so they do much of the bead selling, even coming to Great Britain, with a few strong sons as porters, to do so.[5] While the actual making and firing of these beads is usually done by men, some women are recorded as makers of powder-glass beads in Ghana. Women too, are involved in a form of bead making, or rather, bead modification, in which beads are 'boiled', in fact heated in a pot with layers of organic matter for about an hour, just as a stew might be put on the fire while the woman get on with other things. This 'boiling' will make a clear blue tubular bead opaque, with a striated surface. Women in general are the ones who grind down the sides or ends of beads imported from Europe or Egypt and the Sudan to suit local taste (Francis 1993a: 4).

There are two sorts of bead made in Mali and Mauritania by women only, and which are very interesting. One seems like an encroachment into a masculine preserve, that of making filigree golden jewellery, including beads. But this jewellery is made of fine golden grass or straw, bent and twisted to look like filigree gold, and set on a base of beeswax. These beads are made in the area of Timbuktu, Mali (Gabus 1982: 303–17). The other sort of bead is made of powder-glass. But while Krobo beads are almost mass-produced, these lovely 'Kiffa' beads are made one at a time, with meticulous detail. The glass cullet is collected, finely pounded, washed and dried. The powder, mixed with saliva, is gradually moulded over a tiny grass frame, incorporating the perforation, till it is the right size and shape. Then minute amounts of coloured paste, made by preparing pounded-up coloured glass mixed with saliva, are painstakingly tipped onto the bead form, using the point of a needle to get the desired effect. The beads are then fired in a rudimentary kiln made of a small piece of flat tin, with a fine layer of moist sand on it, covered with a potsherd and then all over with hot embers and baked for about fifteen minutes. As a bead maker can only make up to three beads a day, this means that Kiffa beads are scarce and expensive, and a researcher found that in about 1975, there was only one old woman surviving who had the skill to make them (Gabus 1982: 121–46, 207–14). The growing interest in beads and the demand for Kiffa beads has led to a small revival, and in 1994 there were six women, five of them apprentices, making them.[6]

At Ife, the holy city of the Yoruba, in southern Nigeria, glass beads from the Muslim world and Europe seem to have been reworked between about AD 1000 and 1500, and crucibles and glass waste have been found there, some during archaeological excavations (Willett 1967: 24–5). Obviously there is no information about any gender role played there – apart from the naming of a crucible 'Oduduwa's drum', thus linking it with a male god!

Beadworking

In most of eastern and southern Africa, beadworking is done by women and is, with a few exceptions, very much defined by gender. In southern Africa, for instance among the Zulu, if a young man wants to give a beaded message to his fiancée, he has to get a sister or other female relative to make it for him, as the rule is so strong that women do beadwork. In parts of eastern Africa, things may be a little different. Among the Pokot of northern Kenya, men may make ostrich eggshell beads and even beadwork; and some Maasai beadwork is made by men for their own use. When women do beadworking, it tends to be a social group activity, with gossip and skill-sharing going on. There are some recent photographs (e.g. Saitoti & Beckwith 1980: 222–3) showing women making beadwork, but unfortunately this was not a subject that interested early travellers, missionaries and collectors. An exception is a Victorian lady traveller, Helen Caddick, who published an account of her travels in 1900; she described how at Domasi in present-day Malawi she saw women making beadwork:

> the making of these bead ornaments was an interesting process to watch; it was almost as intricate as lace-making. The women make [spin] the cotton they use as thread. They have no needles, but make a fine point to the cotton and thread each bead separately; most of the patterns they invent themselves, but they are delighted to be shown new ones (Caddick 1900: 72).

In West Africa, ceremonial beadwork is found especially in Nigeria and Cameroon. In southern Nigeria, and adjacent areas of the country of Bénin (formerly Dahomey), beaded crowns of different sorts, beaded robes, footstools, slippers, fans and flywhisks are among the regalia used by Yoruba royalty. These are made by male professional beaders, who use the small glass seed beads imported from Venice to make their wares (Fagg 1980). Many of them come from the southern Ekiti region in eastern Yorubaland, and are members of the Adeshina family of Efon-Alaiye, who make crowns for most of the *obas* (kings) of central and eastern Yorubaland, often travelling to quite distant places to do so. Other beaded regalia include royal footstools, slippers and tunics, the bags worn by divinatory Ifa priests, and the beaded coats worn by *ibeji* twin figures, if they belong to a royal lineage. Benin City, also in southern Nigeria, has an *oba* who wears a heavy ceremonial costume made of coral or jasper beads; both beads and regalia are made by men. There is a special annual ceremony to 'fortify' the coral beads worn by the *oba* and his court, who are all men, apart from the royal wives and princesses. In Cameroon, royal regalia includes beaded stools, life-size statues, calabashes, flywhisks and scabbards. These too are beaded by male professionals (Perrois 1993: 89); the stools and figures are carved out of wood, then covered with a cloth foundation and beaded. While I have not been able to find confirmation to date, I think it very probable that the beaded clothing and masks found among the Kuba of Zaire, and the beaded crowns worn by royalty of the Pende and Yaka of Zaire were also beaded by men. In all these cases the reasoning may be that since royal or religious regalia are things of such power, they can only be made by men, because the power in women's bodies might have a bad effect on them, and hence on the divinity of the kingship or cult. On the other hand, women's bodies and their all-important fertility might be harmed. Even so, it is most probable that the everyday strings of beads worn by women and children in this area were strung by women.

Uses of Beads

Bead using is the last section of this chapter and I shall select some key examples to illustrate how gender affects African beadwork. In Africa, variation occurs naturally between ethnic groups. Even within one group, such as the Zulu of Natal, there are differing styles and local colour codes; bead colours change with the passage of time and fashion, and it is often possible to give approximate dating.

With men, beads and beadwork usually constitute a status marker in one way or another. In the early days of European contact, the local king or chief kept external trade, diplomatic gifts, tolls and payments including beads, firmly in his own control, and doled them out to his courtiers, wives and family as he saw fit. The insignia worn by royalty and the priesthood in Nigeria, Cameroon and Zaire show clearly how an important man's status is marked and enhanced by his official beadwork. The king of the Kuba, when fully dressed, wears a staggering 84 kg of regalia costume which is mostly beads and cowrie shells on raffia. A Cameroonian king's treasury of bead-covered stools, ancestor figures, ceremonial pipes, calabashes and other objects, underlines the fact that he is a great man. On a different level, a young man among the Zulu or Xhosa of southern Africa will receive beadwork ornaments from the girls who fancy him. The more of these he has and wears, the more of a lady-killer he looks! A married man among the Tembu of South Africa might have as many as seventy-five beadwork elements in his full dress outfit, showing that he has a devoted and skilful wife or wives and mistresses to make him stand out from the rest.

Small children normally wear little beadwork beyond a waist-string that is lengthened to show how they are growing. As a girl grows up, her beadwork will increase in quantity and change its nature as she goes from one stage of life to the next. Among eastern African peoples such as the Samburu of Kenya, when a girl's breasts start to grow, she begins to collect beads strung on a hoop, formerly of giraffe hair, nowadays of wire or doum palm fibre, which she wears in increasing quantity round her neck, so that her chin is almost resting on the top layer, and the lower ones almost cover her breasts. The first beads come from her father; as she grows up, any young men who admire her will add to them. The more of these she has, the better, and it will make a good show when she marries. A young bride wears a cloth 'toga'; later on, after the birth of her first child, she wears different beadwork which changes according to her status as her children grow up, become adult, and have children of their own. When she is widowed, she normally stops wearing any beads at all.

In Africa generally, an important time in a girl's life is her first menstruation, which is the outward sign that she is of child-bearing age, the whole reason for her being alive. Very often the first menstruation is followed by a period of seclusion, in which the girl is instructed in her womanly duties, after which she is considered ready for marriage. Formerly, among the Iraqw of Tanzania, it seems that the secluded girls beaded the leather cloaks that they wore before puberty to make the beaded skirts that are among the most spectacular examples of eastern African beadwork, and which they afterwards wore on special occasions (Wada 1984: 195).[7]

The Kalabari, who live around the eastern Niger Delta in southern Nigeria, mark progressive stages in a girl's life by five festivals during which she wears clothing and beads appropriate to each, and families vie with one another for the best display (Daly 1987: 58–61). *Iria Bo* (first motherhood) is an occasion for wearing many large coral beads and coral-beaded accessories.

Beads also feature in pregnancy and childbirth. A childless woman among the Sotho, Ndebele or Zulu of southern Africa may carry around a beaded 'doll', which has been 'doctored' by a diviner, as a form of sympathetic magic to cause pregnancy. Zulu women wear 'pregnancy aprons' of a skin with bead decoration to protect the child within (Morris & Preston-Whyte 1994: 40); this is later used to carry the newborn child. Women among the Kamba of Kenya and the Zulu of Natal use long strips of beadwork as stomach binders to reduce the bulge after childbirth. Such long strips are hardly ever sold, but may be handed down from mother to daughter, or between sisters.[8]

Beads and beadwork are a vehicle in social intercourse, such as in courtship, giving presents at weddings or naming ceremonies. Among the Zulu and Swazi of southern Africa, a girl who fancies a young man will make him a simple string of beads, while she will make and wear similar ones for herself. Such beadwork will be added to as the engagement progresses. The 'love letters' that she makes for him may include messages which can in fact be decoded by others in the community, and may sometimes be a means of social control, since such beadwork must be worn openly at least once. A man who received a string of black beads from the age-group of the girl he has jilted, must wear it at least once, or be named a coward (Schoeman 1968: 66). Likewise, a young man who does not like the way that his fiancée is behaving, might persuade his sister or another woman in his family to make a suitably beaded rebuke (Twala 1951: 120). A widow normally stops wearing her beads at the time of her husband's death, and passes them on to her daughters. If a piece of beadwork breaks, the beads will be carefully collected together and re-strung.

Beadwork in southern Africa clearly identifies one group, that of the diviner, often misleadingly called witch doctor. Both men and women may be diviners, and are called to be diviners through dreams. They combine herbal medicine and divination, and are important people, clearly recognizable as they wear white beads in quantity, since white is the colour of purity and the ancestral spirits. There is perhaps a small element of cross-dressing since the male diviner often wears a short beaded kilt rather than trousers, while the female wears a longer beaded skirt. The white beads are the significant element of the costume.

Beadwork is also a vehicle for socio-political statement and protest. A striking example of protest was given by Nelson Mandela, when he appeared for trial in South Africa in Tembu dress including a wide beadwork collar (South African National Gallery 1993: 76). The photograph, taken in the early 1960s, was not published till 1990, when the ANC was unbanned. Africans in South Africa are increasingly wearing beadwork as an affirmation of their identity and freedom to be African. I have read that among the northern and southern Transvaal groups, a meeting was held to agree upon suitable 'traditional' dress for older women, including beadwork, as they did not have any of their own and felt the need for it. In 1993, an exhibition in the South African National Gallery was devoted to the beadwork of South Africa, and the accompanying publication included a dozen short essays, four of them written by black Africans, and most of them written by women.

Beadwork enables a woman to become a wage-earner, by making and wearing massive quantities of personal beadwork and posing for photographs (for a fee). Well-known examples are the Ndebele of southern Africa or the Maasai of Kenya; while another option for women is to make beadwork ornaments for sale, as among the Maasai (necklets and bracelets), the Ndebele (dolls), the Zulu (cascade necklaces and beaded figures), to give just a few examples (Morris & Preston-Whyte 1994: 80–7). Thus beadwork, 'a woman's work' is giving house-bound African women increasing financial independence, a chance to contribute to the family budget, and a sense of worth through the quality of her beadwork. This work may be encouraged by Oxfam and other charitable or commercial enterprises, or the impetus may come from within, as in KwaZulu, where women members of the Nazareth Baptist Church, often called the Shembe Church, are encouraged to make beadwork in their own highly distinctive style to wear and to sell (ibid.: 72–3).

There is a tendency to dismiss beads as trivial, the sort of thing that men do not bother themselves with, 'a suitable job for a woman' as I myself found when, as the only woman in the Department of Ethnography in the British Museum, I was landed with responsibility for the African bead collections. That was in the early 1950s. At that time there was very little published material to draw on. Now there is almost too much to take in, and ongoing research is providing a growing body of evidence to show that beads play an important part in African women's self-perception, activities and self-expression as well as in indicating wealth and status among both genders.

Notes

A great deal of the source material is gathered from studying beadwork collections in museums; other information is scattered about in books and periodicals, sometimes only a few sentences at a time. The references include some of the more useful titles for general reading, as well as those cited in the text.

1. See Ryder (1969) where appendix VIII lists cargo manifests including bulk bead imports. Such bead imports were, on the whole, restricted to western Africa and its kingdoms.
2. The woman is suckling her baby while grinding and polishing a string of ostrich eggshell beads.
3. Personal information from E. J. Brown; Arkell 1936: 310.
4. See L. Frobenius, *The Voice of Africa*, pp. 444–5, written in 1911, and compare with e.g. R. Gardi (1969), *African Crafts and Craftsmen*, pp. 85 f.
5. Personal observation in Portobello Road.
6. There is now considerable interest in Kiffa beads and this has generated several publications such as those of the Oppers (1989); dealers also visit the area. Information on the increased number of bead makers was given by the Oppers in a paper presented at Santa Fe, 26 March 1994.
7. I am grateful to J. Coote for drawing my attention to this article.
8. Personal information from M. Wood and E. J. Brown.

References

Adamson, J. (1967), *The Peoples of Kenya*, London: Collins.

Arkell, A.J. (1936), 'Cambay and the Bead Trade', *Antiquity*, 10: 292–305.

Bannister, A. & Lewis-Williams, D. (1991), *Bushmen: A Changing Way of Life*, Cape Town: Struik.

Caddick, H. (1900), *A White Woman in Central Africa*, London: Fisher Unwin.

Carey, M. (1986), *Beads and Beadwork of East and South Africa*, Aylesbury: Shire.

—— (1991), *Beads and Beadwork of West and Central Africa*, Aylesbury: Shire.

Daly, M. C. (1987), 'Iria Bo Appearance at Kalabari Funerals', *African Arts*, vol. 21, part 1: 58–61, 86.

Eyo, E. & Willett, F. (1982), *Treasures of Ancient Nigeria*, London: Royal Academy of Arts/Collins.

Fagg, W. (1980), *Yoruba Beadwork: Art of Nigeria*, London: Lund Humphries.

Francis, Jr., P. (1993a), *Where Beads are Loved: Ghana, West Africa*, Beads and People Series 2, Lapis Route, Lake Placid, N.Y.

—— (1993b), 'West African Powder Glass Beads', *Ornament*, vol. 16, no. 4, 96–7, 100–1.

Frobenius, L. (1913), *The Voice of Africa*, trans. Rudolf Blind, New York: Blom.

Gabus, J. (1982), *Au Sahara*, vol. 3. Neuchâtel: La Baconnière.

Gardi, R. (1971), *African Crafts and Craftsmen*, trans. S. Macrae. Original title (1969), *Unter Africanischen Handwerken*, New York: Van Nostrand Reinhold.

Morris, J. & Preston-White, E. (1994), *Speaking with Beads*, London: Thames & Hudson.

Opper, M.-J. & Opper, H. (1989), *Kiffa Beads: Mauritanian Powdered Glass Beads*, Washington: Private.

Perrois, L. (1993), *Les Rois sculpteurs: legs Pierre Harter*, Paris: Musée National des Arts d'Afrique et d'Océanie.

Saitoti, T. O. & Beckwith, C. (1980), *Maasai*, London: Elm Tree Books.

Shaw, C. T. (1945), 'Bead-making with a Bow-drill in the Gold Coast', *Journal of the Royal Anthropological Institute*, vol. 75: 45–50.

—— (1977), *Unearthing Igbo-Ukwu*, Ibadan: Oxford University Press.

Schoeman, H. S. (1968), 'A Preliminary Report on Traditional Beadwork in the Mkhwanazi area of the Mtunzini District, Zululand' (Part one), *African Studies*, vol. 27, part 2: 57–81.

South African National Gallery (1993), *Ezakwantu: Beadwork from the Eastern Cape*, Cape Town: South African National Gallery.

Ryder, A. F. C. (1969), *Benin and the Europeans, 1485–1897*, London: Longmans.

Twala, R. G. (1951), 'Beads as Regulating the Social life of the Zulu and Swazi', *African Studies*, vol. 10, part 3: 113–23.

Tyrrell, B. (1968), *Tribal Peoples of Southern Africa*, Cape Town: Books of Africa.

Wada, S. (1984), 'Female Initiation Rites of the Iraqw and the Gorowa', *Senri Ethnological Studies*, vol. 15 (Africa 3): 187–96.

Willett, F. (1967), *Ife in the History of West African Sculpture*, London, Thames & Hudson.

4

Beaded and Bedecked Kalabari of Nigeria[1]

Joanne B. Eicher

Introduction

For several hundred years the Kalabari Ijo of Nigeria who live on islands near the
equator in the Niger Delta, have imported foreign textiles and other artefacts,
overland and by sea. Prestigious possessions include a variety of fabrics obtained
through trade from West Africa, England and India as well as canes, hats and
jewellery (often Italian coral). They use these imports to differentiate themselves
from other Nigerian ethnic groups (Eicher and Erekosima 1995) and to make
distinctions in age and gender within their own society (Daly, Eicher and Erekosima
1986; Michelman and Erekosima 1992). In addition, some textiles (which they
refer to as 'named' cloth) and certain accessories are visual markers of lineage
(Petgrave 1992).

Because of the interrelation of cloth and beads, I begin with a summary of
Kalabari gender and age hierarchies for dress, followed by a discussion of the
hierarchies of imported textiles and beads used with their dress ensembles. Next I
turn to the story of a specific glass bead that is the exclusive property of only one
lineage and analyse how this bead, said to come from Venice, relates to gender.

The Kalabari people today number less than one million in the Nigerian population of eighty-eight million. The Kalabari have occupied a strategic position in
the Niger Delta trade for several hundred years (Dike 1956; Jones 1963; Horton
1969; Alagoa 1972). Delta peoples traded with neighbouring groups as far north
as Aboh and Onitsha and as far east as Lagos. Salt and dried fish from the delta
were exchanged for foodstuffs such as yam, cocoyam and plantain, none of which
grew in the saltwater environment of the Kalabari, and for canoes (Alagoa 1970).
When Portuguese ships arrived in the Niger Delta in the late 1400s they used these
existing trade routes and networks to establish their own trade. They sought
foodstuffs to provision their crews as well as slaves and, from the mid-nineteenth
century, palm oil from the hinterlands of Nigeria in exchange for beads, iron bars
and vast quantities of cloth from Europe, India and elsewhere in West Africa.
Historical records indicate well-established trading stations at New Calabar (the

home of the Kalabari people) by 1588. In 1676 Olfert Dapper described New Calabar on the New Calabar River as one of the three chief ports on the Nigerian coast (Talbot 1926). In 1823, Captain John Adams reported detailed lists of textiles preferred by Kalabari traders (Adams 1823).

In the eighteenth and nineteenth centuries, the Kalabari strengthened their societal structure based on lineages (known as *wari* in Kalabari or as a War-Canoe House in English) by expanding the lineage to incorporate as family members those slaves who had served the *wari* and had become successful traders. This structural change was made in response to internal rivalries arising among the Atlantic coastal societies of the Niger Delta, and because of inroads made by the seafaring European traders (Eicher and Erekosima 1993).[2] Within Kalabari society, lineage rivalries extended to claims of 'ownership' of specific textile patterns and other items of dress, including beads. These textiles and accessories were obtained historically through world trade as they still are today since the Kalabari do not manufacture any cloth. Among the Kalabari, imported textiles, sometimes 'named', along with many accessories including beads, mark gender and lineage prestige.

The Hierarchy of Dress

Men's dress indicates position in the sociopolitical hierarchy of Kalabari society based on the earlier structural changes noted above. The public dress of men covers the body from neck to feet; formal dress demands that a hat be worn and that hand-held items of a walking stick, cane, umbrella or fan also be used. At the bottom of the male hierarchy are young adults, the *asawo*, glossed as 'the young men that matter', who wear a long shirt called *etibo* over a wrapper or trousers. *Opu asawo*, or 'the gentlemen of substance', are next in the hierarchy. They wear an outfit called *woko*, a tailored garment for the upper torso also worn with either trousers or a wrapper. Fedoras, caps or derby hats with a cane, walking stick or umbrella complete the *woko* ensemble. The *alapu*, the chiefs, wear a gown called *doni* with a wrapper and shirt underneath. Another gown, called *ebu*, with a matching wrapper underneath, is the ensemble for the *amanyanabo*, the king (Erekosima 1989; Erekosima and Eicher 1994). Each rank carries the expectation that the man holding the position wears an appropriate dress ensemble. Little or no tolerance exists that allows a man to wear the dress of a higher rank except during a funeral occasion when youthful relatives, distinguished as chief mourners, carry out their responsibilities wearing varieties of chiefly dress. Men of higher ranks, however, are free to wear the dress of a lower rank as casual or everyday dress.[3]

The *etibo* outfit of the young men, a long shirt and wrapper, warrants no strings of beads. At the neckband, a single stud of silver, gold or perhaps a coral bead, is used for closure and is deemed sufficient. Gentlemen, in wearing the ensemble called *woko*, fasten the top garment with three studs (usually gold, silver or coral). The chief's gown called *doni* has four studs for closure and the highest ranking gown, *ebu*, of Indian madras is worn with little jewellery, perhaps only a simple, long strand of coral beads.

One elaborate gown for men, called *attigra*, falls outside the male ranking system. Men wear this gown, ordinarily made of heavy velvet embroidered with metallic threads, for ceremonial and special occasions. These events include attaining chieftaincy, participating in the stately dance called *ada seki* at the end of a masquerade or when dancing as a chief mourner in the final hours of funeral ceremonies. This particular gown is usually worn with strings of coral beads of impressive size to convey opulence and with an enormous hat called *ajibulu*, decorated with a ram's beard, feathers, tinsel, Christmas balls and other shiny materials. (Figure 4.1) Accompanying this outfit are two hand-held objects: a fan and elephant tusk or an item shaped like one.

In contrast to the dress of men, the dress of women emphasizes sociobiological development, beginning with childhood (Iyalla 1968; Daly 1984). The first stage for females starts with premenstrual girls and is called *ikuta de*, glossed as 'bead display'. Next is *bite pakri iwain*, 'tying of a small bit of cloth', which allows modesty in covering the genitals as a girl approaches puberty. *Konju fina*, a 'half a wrapper tied around the waist' (or 'mini' wrapper), follows puberty. Full woman-hood involves wearing *bite sara*, meaning 'full-length cloth'. An *iriabo* is a person going through *iria*, and *iria* refers to the process of being sequestered after childbirth. An *iriabo* ensemble refers to the outfit of a woman who parades before relatives and the community after being sequestered. Her ensemble includes a knee-length wrapper emphasizing girth, with breast-covering an option.[4]

In these hierarchies of dress, young girls, adolescent girls and the postpartum women who celebrate the birth of a child expose more of their bodies than adult men at any stage or other adult women who are usually covered from neck to feet. The expectation and celebration of fertility are the focus of female dress. Four of the five stages of their dress are named in relationship to items worn on the lower torso. For men, dress ensembles indicate age grade and social accomplishment. The title for each male rank is accompanied by an appropriate ensemble of men's dress that carries the name of the garment covering the upper torso or whole body.[5]

The Hierarchy of Textiles

The hierarchy of dress for men and women, as well as a flamboyant system of dressing funeral rooms and funeral beds, involves another hierarchy, one of textile types (Eicher 1988). This system rests on prestige relating to price, opulence and aspects of Kalabari identity.[6] At the bottom of the textile hierarchy, but a staple of

Figure 4.1 Chief wearing an *ajibulu* with an *ebu* during the 'Parade of the Water Spirits' masquerade event on the island of Buguma, Nigeria in 1991. (Photo: Carolyn J. Eicher.)

Kalabari life, is the handwoven textile from India called 'real india' or *injiri* by the Kalabari (generally referred to as Indian madras in Britain and America). Kalabari people identify Indian madras as 'their cloth', for they select it to wear when they want to display being Kalabari.

Also in the hierarchical order is 'named' cloth. Among the Kalabari, this term refers to textiles with names that are connected to a specific lineage. A name may be either a proper name, an individual's nickname or a name that is said to characterize the textile pattern. If the name is that of an individual, it is usually because one person from the lineage is associated with the cloth, such as the first trader acknowledged as its distributor.

These named cloths are symbols of pride for each *wari* and are brought out to wear during events when the emphasis is on War-Canoe House achievements. Such events include a chieftaincy installation when the accomplishments of one man, who will now sit on the Council of Chiefs with the King, symbolize the glory of the House that he represents. Women often exhibit similar lineage pride by wearing the named textile that symbolizes their House when they dance in the town square as their men present the lineage masquerade.

A proper Kalabari man or woman knows which cloth to select from this hierarchy and which to use for everyday wear or special occasions. During the week, men and women working in the metropolitan city of Port Harcourt wear contemporary fashions found throughout the global world in the 1990s, items more appropriately called world fashion or cosmopolitan dress (Eicher 1995; Eicher and Sumberg 1995). On the islands and in Port Harcourt, children wear school uniforms daily. On weekdays, men and women on the islands wear either cosmopolitan dress or wrappers with shirts or blouses.[7] The textile hierarchy is most often invoked on the weekends when the social activities of the island focus on chieftaincy installations, funeral celebrations which occur throughout the year, annual masquerades after the new year turns, and during those occasions when an *iriabo* displays herself to the community.

Selections from the hierarchy of textiles move upward from Indian madras worn for everyday wrappers into the highest levels of the order, sometimes only one specific type is worn, sometimes the whole hierarchy is incorporated from top to bottom. For at least two occasions, celebrating motherhood and funerals, all are incorporated with appropriate sequencing (Daly 1987). Women celebrating mother-hood parade themselves to relatives and to the community with a series of ensembles beginning with Indian madras and ending with the striped silk or embroidered velvet wrappers. Men's dress is also ranked according to the system. Both men and women in the funeral celebrations draw from the hierarchy of textiles for their apparel throughout the eight-day ceremony. They begin with Indian madras as they escort the body from the mortuary to lie in state in the family home and they end with velvet and silk for the final dance.

The Hierarchy of Beads

Females wear a larger variety of beads than do men, and women's dress ensembles include beads at all stages of life. (Boys do not wear beads on an everyday basis, but tiny girls often wear a string of beads around their waist).[8] The first stage, 'bead display' usually involves several varieties of beads, but small in size whether agate, glass or coral. They hang as necklaces and also circle a girl's waist and hips, and are worn symmetrically on wrists, ankles and knees. As she matures to wear ensembles that include cloth, she continues to don the same type of beads, but with increasing size, and she often bedecks her hair with beads.

Beads are an optional item for a woman wearing a full-length wrapper, but if beads are worn when dressing for church or parties, they are not a focus of attention. The notable exceptions occur when a woman wears a velvet full-length wrapper to accompany her husband during his chieftaincy installation or a silk or velvet wrapper to attend a thanksgiving service as chief mourner or new mother. At that time, large coral beads are displayed just as they are when women dress to dance for the community as members of a women's society (Figure 4.2). On an *iriabo*, the ultimate outfit includes big chunks of coral around the neck worn with a beaded hat, a coral-beaded walking stick, coral upper armlets and a special necklace with symmetrical pendants fashioned of coral beads that hang in the middle of her chest and upper back. Women's hats worn for ceremonial purposes exhibit a wider variety of beads than do men's, as seen in the ensembles for an *iyi iriabo* (a new mother), *aseki iriabo* (masquerade dancer) or an *ede iriabo* (chief mourner).

As with textiles and garments, both Kalabari men and women during their lifetimes claim individual ownership of beads which they purchase or receive as gifts. At death, socially significant and prestigious strings of beads and other important jewellery and accessories of the deceased pass into the lineage holdings to be kept as joint or shared family property. As heirlooms, beads are stored in the 'strong room' (usually an inner, locked room) in containers called 'cloth boxes' along with the prized family textile inheritance. The eldest woman in each lineage supervises the care and lending of these treasures to lineage members for specified occasions. She is knowledgeable about the items as part of extended family genealogy and identity.

Beads worn by Kalabari men and women have some similarities. Both men and women cherish coral strings and accessories. Red-orange coral is used most often, although deeper red and white are also selected to wear depending on the colours found in the total ensemble. Both men and women display strands of coral beads when dressed as chief mourners. As well, a corpse may wear coral before burial (Figure 4.3) and coral is laid on the funeral beds which are decorated with textiles and accessories after the burial (Figure 4.4). Prominent men and women frequently wear necklaces of huge coral beads to complement the prestige of the men's

Figure 4.2 Members of a women's group dressed for dancing at the 'Feasting of the Chiefs' event during the Buguma Centenary in 1984. (Photo: J.B. Eicher.)

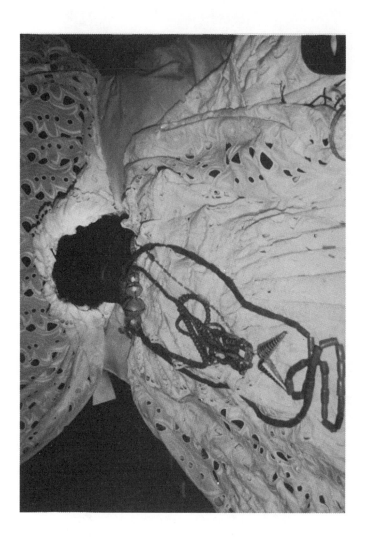

Figure 4.3 Corpse lying on funeral bed. (Photo: J.B. Eicher.)

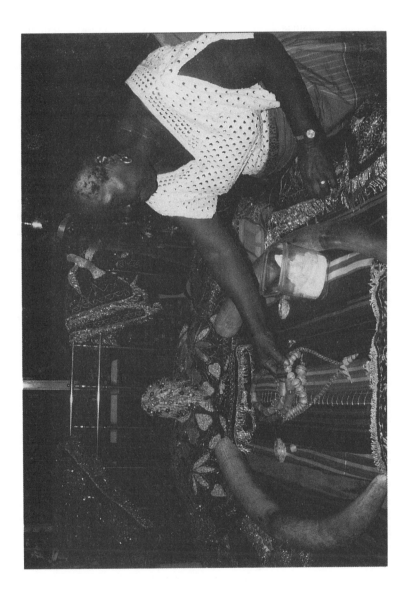

Figure 4.4 Funeral bed decorated with textiles, elephant tusks and a hat and gold and coral beads placed where the corpse has lain. (Photo: J.B. Eicher.)

embroidered velvet gown or the women's velvet or silk wrappers. For a chieftaincy installation, the chief wears as much coral as possible along with flamboyant accessories to demonstrate his wealth and extravagance.

In addition to coral, adults wear gold beads. Many beads, especially those used by young girls, are of agate and glass. A wide range of beads decorate ceremonial hats for both men and women. Bead use differs for men and women when they dress for special occasions. Women's dress generally allows for more beads than does men's dress, with the exception of the men's velvet ceremonial gown that emphasizes economic and social achievement and encourages extensive personal display of textiles and strings of massive coral beads. As with dress and textiles, beads reinforce the hierarchical patterns of Kalabari life.

The Seleye Fubara or Jackreece Bead

In general, the wearing of coral indicates wealth and prestige of individuals, but one Kalabari lineage distinguishes itself further by its ownership and display of a clear, fragile glass bead, about four inches in length. The hollow bead is hand-blown with spiral stripes of colour. Because the glass is clear, the spirals appear as a lattice design (Figure 4.5).

Seleye Fubara, the founder of a prominent Kalabari lineage, is credited with making the bead exclusive to his lineage. He is also known as Seleye Jackreece or Seleye Jack Rich. English traders, generally unwilling to learn the pronunciation of indigenous names, gave him the name of 'Jack Rich' because he was a wealthy and prosperous trader. The Kalabari alliterated Jack Rich to Jackreece, and Seleye Fubara is referred to by all three names.

The story shared among community members about his bead begins shortly after his birth. As a baby, Seleye was given one of the glass beads described above, called *ila*, to wear when his first tooth appeared. However, the bead fell into a crab hole and was lost. The story continues, according to my source:

> Because he had no *ila*, his family was going to have to give him away to another family. The day he was to go to the other family, the crab threw up the mud from his hole and the *ila* showed a little and was finally seen. The *ila* bead was given to Seleye, and the other family couldn't take him. When he grew up and was the richest man (among the Kalabari), he went where the *ila* were made and brought many, many, many back to Kalabari land. He brought so many he stamped on them and crushed them and when they were used, more were crushed. He [still] showed he had many and that *ila* belong only to the Jackreece compound.

The bead's connection to the Fubara lineage is reinforced by Data Ine Akobo's (1985: 52–3) description of how the female descendants of Seleye Fubara dress as *iriabo*:

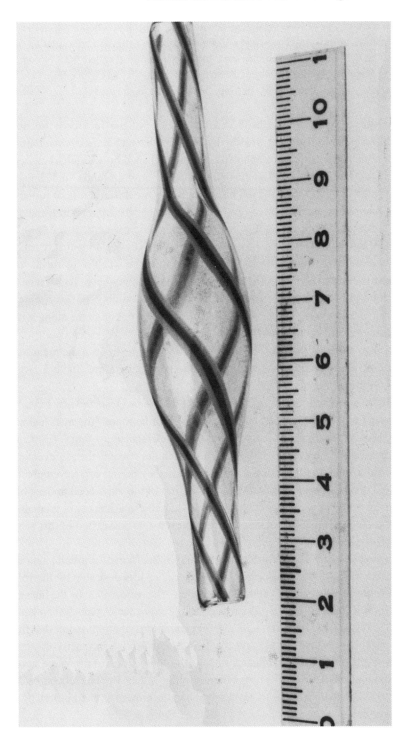

Figure 4.5 Hollow, clear glass bead from Venice (Courtesy of Robert K. Liu, Ornament, Inc.).

There is another type of [body] painting which is done only by the chieftaincy house of Seleye Fubara in Buguma. They paint red camwood on the hair. Also after wearing the *Iriabo* with the big coral beads, they have to add another bead called '*ila*'. No other family in Buguma can add '*ila*' except the Seleye Fubara family. Any *Iriabo* from Seleye Fubara house will be identified by these special features. (Figure 4.6)

Why is this story about the bead and the founder of the Jackreece lineage significant? Seleye Fubara was wealthy by both English and Kalabari standards. The importance of wealth in Kalabari society is established by a Kalabari author, Alate Fubara-Manuel (nd, 38–9), who reports that the word for 'chief' in Kalabari 'can be broken into two parts: "*ala*" means riches or wealth in terms of money, property, manpower and character, "*bo*" means a person. An "*alabo*" in Kalabari in the past was, therefore, a person who possessed riches or wealth.'

Fubara-Manuel (p. 41) stresses the importance of wealth by declaring that 'wealth, it must be pointed out, never hides', for a chief must be wealthy to fulfill his obligations to himself, his people, his town and his national deity. To become a chief, an individual must go through an *alate* or installation ceremony which includes an exhibition of followers and most notably, his possessions, along with feasting, singing and dancing and the swearing in.

And so it is equally clear that if a man is not wealthy, he has not the means to make himself and his premises attractive and cannot, therefore, have a large following (Fubara-Manuel, p. 45).

Among his duties to himself, a chief must take care to be clean and tidy in body and character and look dignified and respectable. Furthermore, 'the man history extols is he who, by dint of hard work, rises from obscurity to fame' (Fubara-Manuel, p. vii). In Kalabari terms, this obviously includes not only the achievement of great wealth, but also the display of possessions. In the example of Seleye Fubara, he flaunted his wealth through exclusive ownership of the glass bead and by his boast that he would obtain so many that he could literally smash many of them and still have more to display to the community. His exclusive possession of this bead epitomizes the ideal chief in Kalabari terms.

Alfred Gell (1986: 110) claims that 'consumption is a form of symbolic action' with consumption goods being 'objects made more or less desirable by the role they play in a symbolic system'. Thus, consumption of a precious item by the lineage founder furthers the entire lineage's prestige and prominence. As his descendants continue to display the bead through several generations, the reputation that the founder established for himself and his War-Canoe House in earlier days is constantly reaffirmed. Within Kalabari society, the competition of the War-Canoe Houses continues to flourish, and ostentatious display of luxury goods reflects pride of family achievements both from the past and into the present as exemplified by a fragile glass bead.

Figure 4.6 A new mother dressed as *iriabo,* celebrates the birth of her child by parading through town wearing a silk wrapper, beaded hat, coral necklaces and pendants and a girdle of Jackreece beads. (Photo courtesy of Mrs Dumo Jackreece.)

The story of the Seleye Fubara bead was recounted during my fieldwork on the significance of textiles in Kalabari life. At a final funeral dance in 1983 for a venerated elder of a prominent family in Buguma, one woman, a chief mourner, wore a striped silk wrapper and a distinctive pillbox-style hat decorated with the lattice-design, glass beads (Figure 4.7). Several days later, I observed a younger woman preparing to dance in the town square in support of her lineage masquerade[9] dressed as an *iriabo*, in a short silk wrapper with large coral beads around her neck and wearing the same hat (Figure 4.8). Her companion, Mrs Nume Taiwo West, a prominent business woman, had invited me to photograph her. I expressed surprise at seeing the same hat on another person. Mrs West explained that she owned the hat and loaned it to relatives of her mother's lineage at appropriate times. She originally made the hat with glass beads for her mother's funeral in 1978. For that same occasion, she had made the hat of branch coral she was wearing the day of our conversation (Figure 4.9). The woman at the funeral I had seen previously wearing the hat with glass beads was Mrs West's sister, born of the same mother but different father. Her sister displayed affiliation with Seleye Fubara, their mother's lineage, by wearing the hat with the distinctive glass beads at a funeral of a relative of her father.

Mrs West said that the distinctive beads on the hat were called *ila* and could only be worn by members of the Jackreece family. She then related the story of the baby, the bead, the crabhole and Seleye Fubara's pledge to show his wealth by obtaining a seemingly unlimited number of the beads which became so important in bonding him with his lineage.

At the time, my research centred on textiles, not beads, and I assessed the information as supplementary to data collected on named textiles used to underscore the importance of lineage distinction and rivalry in Kalabari life. Later, when analysing beads, I focused on their place in the hierarchy of dress and gender, emphasizing the frequent use and prestige of coral. In revising that paper (Eicher 1996), I discovered a photograph of beads identical to those worn by members of the Fubara family in two general books on beads (Francis 1994: 6; Liu 1995: 31). Francis (ibid.) states that the beads are 'apparently Venetian, late 1800s.' Liu (ibid.) provides additional data: 'Venetian blown glass beads, probably from Nigeria . . . thin white and blue cane are twisted; the thin cylinders are blown in the center, 9.3–10.0 cm long . . . It is remarkable that these survive both transit to Africa and being worn.' The additional evidence about these glass beads adds to our knowledge about world trade into the Niger Delta[10] and supports Seleye Fubara's claim that his beads came from afar, or as we know now, from Venice.

My field observations, photographs and fieldnotes from eight fieldtrips made since 1980 identify hats and girdles decorated with these glass beads as an exclusive possession of the Fubara family worn primarily by women at funeral celebrations, dancing at a masquerade (Figure 4.10), or dressing in the ensemble of a new mother.

Figure 4.7 A chief mourner at a funeral in 1983 wearing glass beads decorating a pill-box style hat to show her Seleye Fubara kinship affiliation. (Photo: J.B. Eicher.)

Figure 4.8 Woman with glass-beaded hat and coral strands. (Photo: J.B. Eicher.)

Figure 4.9 Young woman wearing the beaded hat (shown in Figure 4.7) with her *iriabo* ensemble for the Seleye Fubara masquerade performance with her companion, Mrs. West, who wears a branch coral hat with an embroidered velvet wrapper, lace blouse and coral beads (Photo: J.B. Eicher 1983).

Figure 4.10 Young woman dressed for the 'Parade of the Water Spirits' masquerade event on the island of Buguma, Nigeria in 1991 wearing another hat decorated with the glass beads of the Seleye Fubara lineage. (Photo: Carolyn J. Eicher.)

Seleye Fubara, as founding male of the lineage, provided the prominence and reputation for himself and his heirs through obtaining and displaying an exotic trade bead that continues to reinforce this lineage image, particularly through the dress of family members in celebratory occasions.

These data reinforce the importance of world trade in Kalabari life and expand our knowledge about global sources for material goods entering the Kalabari world. Evidence about the beads supplements the documentation on imported madras and velvet textiles from India (Evenson 1994; Sumberg and Eicher 1995; Lutz and Eicher 1996). Beads are an integral part of the hierarchy of dress and textiles among the Kalabari. The hierarchies of beads and textiles are intertwined in the age and gender hierarchies of dress. Each signifies importance of occasion as well as the prestige and reputation of individuals and their lineage.

Notes

1. Revision of Eicher (1996) with the emphasis shifted from a concern of local and global issues to gender. Thank you to Barbara Sumberg and Helen Bradley Foster for helpful comments in reorienting the article.
2. This point of structural readjustment to shifting societal conditions is fully developed by Erekosima (1989).
3. See Erekosima (1989) and Erekosima and Eicher (1994) for an elaborated discussion of the ranking system, types of dress and variations allowed.
4. This is a sketchy summary of a complex sequence of events related to *iria*, for the *iriabo* has special wear before her parade through the community and a series of outfits for the days of parading. In the 1990s, only two stages of women's dress are found with any frequency: the *iriabo* and the *bite sara*. Since the advent of universal primary education, girls and boys are in school full-time and the first three stages for females are acknowledged by dressing little girls and adolescent girls in this manner only for special festivities. Daly (1984) describes in detail the process of going through *iria* after childbirth and the ensembles associated with the coming-out display at the end of sequestering.
5. In another paper on the 'display of skin', I have analysed this difference more fully (Eicher 1993).
6. There are handwoven textiles imported from elsewhere in West Africa as well as from England and India. In Nigeria, textiles originate from an Igbo area north of the Kalabari and others from Yorubaland. Still another comes from Ghana. The names for these cloths largely indicate locations where the cloth is woven. Printed woollens come from England and handwoven madras and hand-embroidered velvets come from India, originally via British traders.

7. In the case of men, it may also be Kalabari-style shirts with trousers. Also of note is that the cotton 'print' textile known as *printi* by the Kalabari and elsewhere in West Africa as 'Dutch wax', 'Dumas' or 'wax' is not considered an appropriate cloth for a Kalabari person to wear when intending to dress 'as a Kalabari'. These textiles are identified in Kalabari lore as the cloth of the tutelary goddess Owamekaso, who also has within her possession tableware of vines and flowers, the motifs that identify wax prints to the Kalabari. These cloths are taboo wear during a masquerade festival, they do not adorn the walls or bed of a funeral room and are not within the hierarchy of cloth. One Kalabari woman told me, 'That cloth is not for we'.

8. Kalabari friends said that many women continue wearing these into adulthood under their clothing, for beads are considered sexually enticing and attractive to their male partners.

9. Women dance in a troupe in support of the men to display lineage wealth and prestige.

10. Skimpy evidence exists on the bead trade into the Niger Delta. Only descriptions, particularly about coral in Kalabari life, were noted by observers such as Talbot (1926: 395) who stated that coral was a principal ornament among the Edo and Ijaw (sic) and is 'now imported, but apparently in the old days was found in some of the rivers, particularly those in the neighborhood of Benin and was polished by Bini artisans'.

References

Adams, C.J. (1823), *Remarks on the Country Extending from Cape Palmas to the Congo*, London.

Akobo, D.I. (1985), *Oral Traditions of Buguma: Iria Ceremony a Case Study*, Department of Library Studies, University of Ibadan.

Alagoa, E.J. (1970), 'Long-distance Trade and States in the Niger Delta', *Journal of African History*, vol. 11, no. 3, 319–29.

—— (1972), *A History of the Niger Delta*, Ibadan: University of Ibadan.

Daly, M.C. (1984), 'Kalabari Female Appearance and the Tradition of Iria', unpublished doctoral dissertation, University of Minnesota, Minneapolis.

—— (1987), 'Iria Bo Appearance at Kalabari Funerals', *African Arts*, vol. 21, no. 1, 58–61, 86.

——, Eicher, J.B., & Erekosima, T.V. (1986), 'Male and Female Artistry in Kalabari Dress', *African Arts*, vol. 19, no. 3, 8–51, 83.

Dike, K.O. (1956), *Trade and Politics in the Niger Delta 1830–1885: An Introduction to the Economics and Political History of Nigeria*, London: Oxford University Press.

Eicher, J.B. (1988, July 27), 'A Hierarchy of Cloth: A Kalabari Case Study', unpublished paper presented at the meeting of the International Federation of Home Economics, Minneapolis, MN.

—— (1993 23 Oct.), 'Dress, Gender Identity, and the Public Display of Skin as Expression of Kalabari Social Roles and Sexuality', unpublished paper presented at International Textiles and Apparel Association, White Sulphur Springs, WV.

—— (1995), 'Cosmopolitan and International Dress', in Roach-Higgins, M.E., Eicher, J.B. & Johnson, K.P. (eds), *Dress and Identity*, New York: Fairchild, 461–2.

—— (1996) 'Usi delle perle in una societa' africana: i Kalabari della Nigeria' ['The use of beads in an African society: The Kalabari of Nigeria']. *La Ricerca Folklorica*, no. 34, 35–42.

——, & Erekosima, T.V. (1993 23–25 April), 'Taste and 19th Century Patterns of Textile Use Among the Kalabari of Nigeria', unpublished paper presented at Dartmouth College Conference on 'Cloth, The World Economy and the Artisan: Textile Manufacturing and Marketing in South Asia and Africa, 1780–1950'.

——, & Erekosima, T.V. (1995), 'Why Do They Call it Kalabari? Cultural Authentication and the Demarcation of Ethnic Identity', in J.B. Eicher (ed.), *Dress and Ethnicity*, Oxford/ Washington, DC: Berg, 139–64.

——, & Sumberg, B. (1995), 'World Fashion, Ethnic and National Dress', in J.B. Eicher (ed.), *Dress and Ethnicity*, Oxford/Washington, DC: Berg, 295–306.

Erekosima, T.V. (1989), 'Analysis of a Learning Resource for Political Integration Applicable to Nigerian Secondary School Social Studies: The Case of Kalabari Men's Traditional Dress', unpublished doctoral dissertation, Catholic University of America, Washington, DC.

——, & Eicher, J.B. (1994), 'The Aesthetics of Men's Dress of the Kalabari of Nigeria', in M. DeLong & A.M. Fiore (eds), *International Textile and Apparel Association Special Publication on Aesthetics —7*, Monument, CO: ITAA.

Evenson, S.L. (1994), 'A History of Indian Madras Manufacture and Trade: Shifting Patterns of Exchange', unpublished doctoral dissertation, University of Minnesota, Minneapolis.

Francis, P., Jr. (1994), *Beads of the World: A Collector's Guide with Price Reference*, Atglen, PA: Schiffer Publishing, Ltd.

Fubara-Manuel, A. (n.d.), 'A History of Kalabari Part I: (Kalabari in Obu-Amafa from about 1370–1400 AD)', unpublished manuscript, Port Harcourt, Nigeria.

—— (1977), *The Period of King Amachree in Kalabari History*, Port Harcourt, Nigeria: Labomie Enterprises.

Gell, A. (1986), 'Newcomers to the World of Goods: Consumption among the Muria Gonds,' in Appadurai, A. (ed.), *The Social Life of Things: Commodities in Cultural Perspective*, Cambridge: Cambridge University, 110–38.

Horton, R. (1969), 'From Fishing Village to City State,' in M. Douglas and P. Kaberry, (eds), *Man in Africa*, London: Tavistock.

Iyalla, B.S. (1968), 'Womanhood in the Kalabari', *Nigeria Magazine*, vol. 98, 216–24.

Jones, G.I. (1963), *Trading States of the Oil Rivers: A Study of Political Development in Eastern Nigeria*, London: Oxford University Press for the International African Institute.

Liu, R.K. (1995), *Collectible Beads: A Universal Aesthetic*, Vista, CA: Ornament, Inc.

Lutz, H.A. & Eicher, J.B. (Oct. 1996), 'Gold Embroidered Velvets: From the Indian Embroiderer's Frame to the West African Dressed Body', unpublished paper presented at the 25th Annual Conference on South Asia, Madison, WI.

Michelman, S.O., & Erekosima, T.V. (1992), 'Kalabari Dress: Visual Analysis and Gender Implications', in R. Barnes & J.B. Eicher (eds), *Dress and Gender: Making and Meaning*, Oxford: Berg, 164–82.

Petgrave, M.D. (1992), 'Indian Madras in Kalabari Culture', unpublished Master's plan B thesis, University of Minnesota, Minneapolis.

Sumberg, B. & Eicher, J.B. (1995), 'India and West Africa: Transformation of Velvets', in J. Dhamija (ed.), *The Woven Silks of India*, Bombay, India: Marg, 141–54.

Talbot, P.A. (1926), *Peoples of Southern Nigeria: A Sketch of Their History, Ethnology and Languages with an Abstract of the 1921 Census*, vols I–IV, London: Oxford University Press.

5

Lantana Beads: Gender Issues in their Production and Use

Ann O'Hear

This chapter is designed to introduce the West African red stone beads called *lantana*, and to examine their production and uses with particular reference to gender-related issues.[1] In the nineteenth century and the first half of the twentieth, the production of these beads was a major industry in Ilorin, a city in northwestern Yorubaland, now part of Nigeria. Before this the beads had been produced in the city of Old Oyo, capital of the empire of the same name, to the west of Ilorin, and probably also elsewhere. When the Old Oyo empire collapsed in the early nineteenth century, the industry was transferred to the secessionist city of Ilorin, which proceeded to corner the export market in the beads. The pattern of trade in *lantana* beads is clear for the nineteenth and early twentieth centuries: there was an important trade from Ilorin to other parts of Yorubaland, and a particularly important trade to the kingdom of Benin and its neighbours. In earlier centuries, it is very likely that *lantana* beads were traded from Old Oyo to Benin.[2] It is certain, in any case, that these or very similar beads have been used in regalia for many centuries in Yorubaland, and that they have been imported and used by Benin, also in regalia, for centuries.

The present author's introduction to these beads was in the city of Ilorin. This is now the capital of Kwara State in Nigeria. It is largely Yoruba in population, with relatively small but powerful Fulani and Hausa minorities. The *lantana* bead makers, however, are said to have been all Yoruba, and their compounds are in the Yoruba-populated areas of the city. Ilorin rose to prominence in the early nineteenth century, first as the base of Afonja, a secessionist Old Oyo general. Then it was captured by Fulani Muslims, as part of the jihad which began in Hausaland in 1804, and became the centre of an emirate, and the southernmost outpost of the Sokoto/ Gwandu caliphate. It grew famous as an entrepot in the trade between the rest of the caliphate to the north, and the various Yoruba states to the south. However, it has also been important in production, with several major craft industries, producing for export from the city as well as for internal consumption. These include, in particular, horizontal narrow-loom weaving, carried on by Yoruba Ilorin men, which flourished in the nineteenth century, and is still doing well today; the manufacture of pottery by Yoruba women, which has actually come into its own as an 'export' product in the twentieth century; and the making of the red stone beads called *lantana*.

This last-mentioned was a large-scale, profitable industry in nineteenth-century Ilorin. It seems that Ilorin bead makers were able to profit from the fact that in the early nineteenth century Benin's trade with the Europeans was in serious decline, thus curtailing the supply of imported coral, and increasing the demand for *lantana*.[3] The mutual importance of the trade to both Ilorin and Benin was reflected in an annual presentation of beads by the Emir of Ilorin to his counterpart the Oba of Benin, who sent other products in return: this gift-exchange is still remembered today.[4] Some indication of the scale of the export trade, with Benin and other areas, may be gathered from the fact that in 1912 over 600 (male) bead makers were counted in a tax assessment exercise in Ilorin (Lethem 1912: Brief Report, para. 9).[5] In the late 1920s and early 1930s, however, there was a sudden and catastrophic decline in the Ilorin industry, and after that there was no real recovery. Some bead makers at least were still functioning as late as the 1950s, but to the best of my knowledge no one is making beads nowadays, although some people still remember the techniques and retain their old equipment.[6]

It has been suggested that this decline was set in motion by a shift of fashion among women caused by cheaper imported substitutes (imported copies of *lantana* were flooding the market in the late 1920s), but this explanation is incomplete. Many of the customers were men, chiefs or men of wealth, who bought the beads for regalia or prestige purposes, and certainly would not have been satisfied with cheap substitutes. What may well have happened is that, after the British takeover at the turn of the century, various factors (safer and easier transport for traders, a revitalized demand by rulers and other chiefs in Yorubaland for beads to serve as replacements for regalia lost during the incessant nineteenth-century wars) stimulated a production increase in Ilorin. But eventually the chiefs' demand would have been satisfied, and others, who converted to Islam, may have given up bead-wearing altogether. With beads still being produced in large quantities, their value would inevitably plummet (as indeed occurred), and former customers would turn to buying other prestige goods (O'Hear 1987: 510).[7]

The beads themselves are said, variously, to have been made of jasper, banded agates, chalcedony or carnelian (Frobenius 1913: vol. 1, 334; Daniel 1937: 7; Clarke 1938: 157; de Beauchêne 1969: 63; Fagg 1980: 10).[8] The stone from which they were made was quarried far to the north, in locations close to the River Niger, now in the Niger Republic. It was then brought down the Niger, and carried overland to Ilorin; presumably the same river route had been used earlier to bring the stone to Old Oyo. The finished beads are highly polished and reddish-brown in colour, though the shades of colour vary to some extent. They were fashioned in a wide variety of shapes and sizes; some idea of this variety can be seen in a diagram drawn by British educator and craft researcher J.D. Clarke, to accompany an article he published on the beads in 1938 (1938: 156). Some of the beads are long and cylindrical, some are barrel-shaped, others are small. Triangular pendants were made to hang from necklaces; and cone-shaped earplugs were also produced.

The manufacturing process was time-consuming and tedious, needing skill, strength and patience. First, the stone was chipped roughly into shape. Then it was pierced by rapidly tapping a small punch with a hammer, while the punch was twirled on the stone. It is said that many different punches were used, progressively finer ones as the work progressed (Clarke 1938: 156).[9] Then the bead was worked vigorously across a grinding-stone, and finally polished on a smooth board.[10]

An examination of various sources of information on this process suggests an interesting gender issue, which actually deserves far more detailed investigation than has yet been carried out. Nevertheless, the data available on *lantana* production are sufficient for some tentative conclusions to be drawn. Before these data are examined, it needs to be pointed out that craft production in general, in Yorubaland and in Nigeria (and indeed West Africa) as a whole, is strongly gender-based. In Ilorin, for example, pottery manufacturing, dyeing, spinning and the weaving of broad cloth on the upright loom have always (in the city's recorded history) been female occupations, while the weaving of narrow cloth on the horizontal loom has been done by men.[11] Virtually throughout Nigeria, women weave on the upright loom, and men on the horizontal. But it is not always true that a particular speciality is *invariably* the work of the same gender in Nigeria: dyeing in the north, for example, is a men's occupation (Shea 1975; Kriger 1993: 368). In exceptional cases, the same craft technology might be shared by both genders: in Benin City the upright loom has been used by the male court weavers as well as the female commercial weavers; and in the Bunu district, in far north-eastern Yorubaland, it was used by both males and females to produce prestige cloths (Ben-Amos 1978; Aronson 1992b: 38; idem 1992a: 53; Renne 1992: 64 and 102, note 2; Kriger 1993: 373, note 31). There is occasional evidence of gender shifts: in Ijebu, for example, while only women weave prestige cloths on the upright loom today, it is suggested that men also used to do so; but in the Ijo area narrow-loom weaving, although it was introduced by an Ijo man who had apprenticed himself to male Ewe weavers of eastern Ghana, has been taken over by women (Aronson 1992b: 38; idem 1992a: 53; Kriger 1993: 373, note 31).

The evidence on *lantana* production reveals some similar exceptions to the general rule. The evidence will be examined first with respect to Oyo, both the old city and the areas which made up its empire, and the new city which was founded, further south, in the nineteenth century, after the old empire had collapsed. An elderly informant in Ilorin, formerly a bead maker himself, tells the story that it was through the Alafin, or king, that stone bead making started in Old Oyo. The

Alafin would sit 'with a lady at his right, a lady at his left, and a lady at his back, smoothing beads on a stone . . . for feeling big, for proving he was a big man'.[12] And while this may simply be a reference to the work of the *ayaba*, or 'king's wives', under the charge of the Iya Kere, in keeping the royal beads polished and in good condition,[13] it may reflect the existence of female bead makers in the city. The present Alafin suggests that there *were* women stone bead makers in Old Oyo, who were, however, not Yoruba but Nupe, and who were dispersed after the fall of the old empire. None of them, according to his understanding, came to the new city.[14] Other informants connected with the Oyo palace are in agreement that there was one (male) slave craftsman in the new city, living in the compound of a major palace official, and producing a few stone beads for the then Alafin, until the bead maker's death during the British bombardment of 1895.[15] In the western Yoruba town of Iseyin, red stone beads were made in the past in two compounds, which may have been founded by Old Oyo refugees. In one of these the craft is said to have been carried on 'mostly by women'; in the other, a husband and wife team was mentioned, the man doing the drilling while the woman specialized in polishing and threading the beads.[16]

The reference to Nupe women bead makers is tantalizing. There was certainly an important stone beadworking industry in Bida (the capital of Nupe) in the nineteenth century (by that time at least concentrating on re-working old stone beads brought from the north),[17] but there is no available evidence to suggest that females were involved. S.F. Nadel, who investigated Nupe society in the 1930s, refers to the bead workers as males, and mentions women only as 'middleman' or 'capitalist' traders in the beads (1942: 283–4).

In Ilorin, however, there was some 'hidden' female participation in *lantana* bead making. While J.D. Clarke in the 1930s wrote of the practitioners as males, F. Daniel, at almost the same time, reported that they were of both sexes (Clarke 1938: 156; Daniel 1937: 8). Oral information from Ilorin confirms that women were involved, in the grinding and maybe polishing stages.[18] In the tax figures for 1922, along with over 800 males, 263 female bead makers were recorded (Priestman 1922: appendices 2 and 4).[19] The average income of male bead makers in that year was estimated at £24.00, that of the females at only 24s. This might suggest that the females were merely minor assistants, but is more likely to reflect their use, like apprentices, pawns and slaves, as a source of cheap labour, assigned to strenuous, repetitive and semi-skilled tasks, while male master-craftsmen did the initial rough shaping, and the piercing, generally oversaw the work, and garnered the profit and prestige (O'Hear 1994: 227, 229).

Thus, while the data are fragmentary with respect to gender and the production of *lantana* beads, they do reveal that both men and women participated, making this industry far less gender-specific than the norm; but the genders were still largely segregated into different stages of the process; and, in a high-profit and prestigious industry, males generally retained overall control. Lisa Aronson suggests that it was in weaving industries (Benin, Bunu and Ijebu) producing cloth for high-status and prestige individuals that men involved themselves in production otherwise carried on by women (1992b: 38; 1992a: 53): it is likely that some similar process was at work in the male control of *lantana* bead making in Ilorin.

Red stone beads have formed part of the royal and courtly regalia of numerous kingdoms over hundreds of years. They were certainly used, together with coral, in the regalia of the Alafin in Old Oyo. They were stored and polished in the palace, under the charge of the Iya Kere, the female keeper of the king's regalia.[20] They are still used in New Oyo, especially by the Alafin. It is said that he wears them in large numbers, while some members of the Oyo Mesi, or Council of State, wear only a single necklace, and minor chiefs wear only bracelets. The beads are still kept polished by the *ayaba*, or 'king's wives', using camwood powder; these women also wear necklaces of *lantana*-type beads, procured for them by the Alafin.[21]

Such beads have also been used in the regalia of other Yoruba kingdoms, especially in eastern Yorubaland. They may even have been utilized in ancient times in the regalia of the Oni of Ife, if William Fagg's suggestion is correct, namely, that the red paint on the beads portrayed on bronze figures from the 'classical period' represents red stone (1980: 10; 1963: plate 9, caption).[22] They have also been used in crowns. Fagg describes an old crown, called *ade Odudua*, in the possession of the Owa of Idanre, which 'appears to date at least from the eighteenth century', and 'consists largely of strings of red beads which are mostly stone' (1980: 10, 12, and fig. 6). *Lantana* may also have been used in the past in a crown of the ruler of Okuku (Beier 1982: 60).

Elsewhere in eastern Yorubaland, a royal burial of the late nineteenth century in Ilesha was found to contain the body of an *oba* (king) wearing necklaces of red stone beads (Pokornowski 1979: 110, citing Willett 1960: 10). *Lantana* necklaces are often worn by chiefs in the Ekiti area, including, in one documented case at least, a female regent.[23] They are also worn by Igbomina chiefs (Drewal and Pemberton 1989: 36, plate 37, photograph by Pemberton).

A photograph in the catalogue, *Yoruba: Nine Centuries of African Art and Thought*, serves to introduce a particularly spectacular use of the beads in the eastern Yoruba kingdom of Owo. Here, the Olowo (ruler) is seen wearing a blouse and strings of beads: while the blouse is very likely coral, the strings of beads are *lantana* (Drewal and Pemberton 1989: 17, plate 4, photograph by Drewal). The Owo art history specialist, Robin Poynor, confirms the use of red jasper beads in Owo regalia, and his research suggests very strongly that in the nineteenth century they were obtained from Ilorin. In Owo, coral or jasper beads were given by the king to chiefs he had installed, as 'beads of recognition'. This is very similar to Benin custom, but the correspondence goes much further. As Poynor points out, although Owo claims that its ultimate origin is from Ife (by tradition, the 'original' or spiritual home of the Yoruba), there were times when Benin exerted a great deal of influence on it: as a result, the 'ritual, paraphernalia and costume' of the Owo court are clearly 'of Benin derivation'. The great period of 'Benin-ization' was in the eighteenth century, and while the holders of older titles simply wear a single necklace of coral or jasper (the paucity of beads is said to reflect their loss of influence), the king himself and the newer, more powerful chiefs with Benin-derived titles wear the much more 'ostentatious' *agokun* costume, which closely resembles Benin models, and consists of 'accumulations of coral and jasper beads' (Poynor 1978: 24; idem 1989: 133, 135–8; also personal communication, 23 September 1991).[24] Thus, although *lantana* beads are recognizably 'Yoruba' in origin and identity, some parts of Yorubaland which are particularly avid users of them, like Owo and Ekiti, have also been very much influenced by Benin. In Owo, specifically, one can see a basic 'Yoruba' use of the beads in chiefly necklaces; in the more elaborate costumes this is overlaid by the influence of Benin.

In Benin itself, red beads are of paramount importance in the regalia of the *oba* and his court. They are worn not only by males, but also by the Queen Mother and the king's wives.[25] Benin is famous for its use of coral, but red stone beads also have a long history there. According to the Benin historian Jacob Egharevba, they were introduced to the city in the fifteenth century (1949: 60).[26] In fact, many of the beads that are called, generically, 'coral' in Benin are actually *lantana* stone,[27] as a number of European travellers and chroniclers were in fact aware. In the early years of this century, Frobenius made a point of finding out about them:

> the chroniclers . . . tell of a very special festival of the King of Benin, which they called the 'Festival of Corals', on which he lent out chains of red beads which the old historians took to be 'corals'. I got some of these, which are still considered in Benin to be of great value, and was told that they were a kind of red jasper . . . They are mostly wonderfully cut tubes, with an absolutely magnificent polish . . . in Nupeland . . . I was told that these stones, called Susi or Lantana, were mined in the North and cut in Ilorin. So I sent Martius to the Niger and Ilorin to investigate further. He got the statement confirmed (1913: vol. 1, 334–5).

The seventeenth-century account by Dapper also refers to 'jasper' on display at the coral festival. This author also mentions the 'fiadors or state councillors', who were the officials charged with the European trade at the port of Ughoton, and who, on first meeting the European traders, were dressed 'in court dress, with jasper round their necks'. In what is presumably a reference to the junior palace association members in Benin, he relates that '[t]here are men at the King's court, twenty and twenty-four years old, who . . . go about naked, only wearing a chain of corals or jasper round their necks'.[28]

Lantana beads have been used in a variety of ways in Benin. Smaller ones, for example, are worn by some chiefs, threaded on a wire, which gives a stiff round shape to the necklace. Pendants have also been included on necklaces. Large beads have been used in necklaces, and also for special ornaments; this last may well have included the 'carnelian cylindrical beads on stout wire' which according to William Fagg were used on the 'winged' type of *oba*'s cap, forming 'long arms . . . which pass from the ears in front of the cheeks and nearly meet in front of the nose'.[29]

The beads are also found, as would be expected, in the regalia of neighbouring polities which were influenced by Benin. In 1912 it was said in Ilorin that buyers for *lantana* beads would come from as far away as Warri (Lethem 1912: Progress Report, para. 32). They are used in petty states in the western Igbo area, apparently interchangeably with coral.[30]

Lantana-type beads are used in Yorubaland in connection with religious cults. In (New) Oyo, they are worn by priests (*mogba*) and devotees of Sango associated with the royal shrine at Koso. There is clearly a strong royal connection here, as Sango worship has been closely associated with the Alafins and their interests, and a present-day female devotee, born into the Mogba family, explains that devotees wear the beads as symbols of Sango himself, who, they believe, wore them when he was the Alafin.[31] The followers of Oya, wife of Sango, are also 'distinguished by tubular maroon beads worn in strings around the neck'.[32]

As has been demonstrated, the beads are widely used by rulers and titleholders in Yorubaland. This is not the case in Ilorin, however, although it is a largely Yoruba city. But it is also very largely a Muslim city, and in fact the *non*-wearing of beads by Ilorin men, especially the chiefs, seems to be used as a symbol of their religious affiliation. Given the non-Islamic cult connections of *lantana* and other beads, this is only natural. But several of the Yoruba titleholders in the city used to have stone bead makers in their compounds or associated with their families, and it is said that the heirs of two of these titleholders (one of whom is the Balogun Alanamu, and the other is the Magaji Are, direct descendant of Afonja, the pre-Fulani ruler) still wear beads, as a symbol of their position. In these cases, it looks as if the beads are used as a symbol of the *Yoruba* identity of these chiefs and their people, as against the northern identity of the Hausa, Fulani and other northern-origin inhabitants of Ilorin.[33]

In this city, however, *lantana* beads have mostly been used by women rather than men. Old women still sometimes wear them, and they are also worn by brides. Newly-married women in Ilorin wear a choker containing a number of *lantana* or other large beads of similar colour and shape, and it does not seem that this custom is entirely confined to those of Yoruba descent. The bridal choker may also be combined with necklaces, again including *lantana* beads. This seems much like the custom reported (for Yorubaland in general?) by Samuel Johnson, in which a new bride 'is covered with trinkets (consisting chiefly of corals and other costly beads, [and] gold necklaces where they are obtainable, etc.)' (1921: 115). *Lantana* beads are also said to be worn by women during their marriage ceremonies in the western Yoruba town of Iseyin.[34] Nevertheless, it may be suggested that the survival of women's beadwearing in Ilorin is as much or more a symbol of their *female* than their Yoruba identity: an indication that less was expected of them, as Muslims, in the past than was expected of the men. As Paul Lovejoy has pointed out, in the caliphate of which Ilorin was a part, 'Islam was essentially a man's religion', and 'most women were only nominally Muslim, or they were beyond the pale entirely' (1990: 173). In this connection, it may be noted that some other types of beads available nowadays in Ilorin are said to 'come from Mecca',[35] and while this is very likely to be a true statement, it may well also represent a present-day attempt to legitimize the continued use of beads by Ilorin women, who are nowadays more actively Muslim, and who have in many cases performed the pilgrimage to Mecca.

To summarize the gender issues involved in the use of *lantana* beads, it can be said that they are widely worn by male titleholders as part of their regalia, both in Yorubaland and elsewhere, but that this in no way precludes their use by women titleholders as well. In Ilorin, by contrast, where the use of beads as regalia has largely disappeared, the use and non-use of beads by women and men is a symbol of their discrete gender identities.

Notes

1. Much of the information given in this paper on the history of *lantana* beads is to be found in O'Hear 1983: chapter 2; 1986: 36–9; 1987: 509–11; and 1993. I would like to thank Suleiman Ajao, Barbara Blackmun, Mark Duffill, Peter Morton-Williams, Joseph Nevadomsky, Ade Obayemi, Robin Poynor, J. Richardson, Frank Willett and others for information and advice; and R.O. Lasisi, Boniface and Felicia Okonkwo, Kayode Abubakar Ibrahim, A.I. Alesinloye and H.J. O'Hear for conducting interviews on my behalf.

2. Though this is not yet absolutely proven. For arguments strongly suggesting an Old Oyo–Benin trade, see O'Hear 1993: note 21.

3. For the decline in Benin's European trade in the early nineteenth century, see Ryder 1969: 11–12. The Benin historian Jacob Egharevba's reference to a 'new source of supply of stone beads' for Benin being found in the reign of Oba Osemwende is surely a reflection of the opening of trade with Ilorin, and the fact that this event has been remembered in Benin tradition is a reflection of its importance (1949: 60). I am indebted to Barbara Blackmun for pointing out to me this reference and its significance.

4. This gift exchange was a subject of discussion between Oba Erediauwa and Emir Sulu Gambari in 1982, during the former's visit to Ilorin on his post-installation tour. Interview with His Highness Alhaji Sulu Gambari, Emir of Ilorin, 8 December 1982.

5. In a further tax report ten years later, a figure of 851 was given. It is likely that this higher figure reflects a more intensive (and therefore more accurate) tax count, rather than any major increase in bead makers' numbers between 1912 and 1922, since differences of the same order are also found on comparing the 1912 and 1922 figures for other occupations (Priestman 1922: appx 4).

6. On the reasons for the decline, see especially O'Hear 1987: 510. I am grateful to Frank Willett (personal communication, 9 April 1993) and Peter Morton-Williams (personal communication, 9 May 1993) for details of bead making in Ilorin in the 1950s.

7. I am indebted to Ade Obayemi for the suggestion that a production increase was stimulated by a demand for replacement regalia.

8. Also information from J. Richardson, formerly of Kingston Minerals, Ilorin, 1979; and information from mineralogists at Union Carbide Metals, Niagara Falls, USA, August 1981. I am grateful to Mark Duffill for drawing my attention to the report by G. de Beauchêne.

9. When Frank Willett observed the bead makers in 1957, he saw a large number of punches but they all appeared to be the same size (personal communication, 9 April 1993).

10. The process has been described in Clarke 1938: 156–7, and Daniel 1937: 7–8. I am also indebted to Peter Morton-Williams for describing the process, and for copies of his photographs (personal communication, 20 October 1993).

11. Though there is some suggestion that a few women are nowadays practising this craft in the privacy of their homes (information from Suleiman Ajao).

12. Interview with Baba Elesin, Ile Agba, Ilorin, 7 May 1985.

13. For this, see below.

14. Interview by R.O. Lasisi with Oba Lamidi Adeyemi III, Alafin of Oyo, 11 April 1991.

15. Interviews by R.O. Lasisi with Tijani Alamu, head of palace servants, Alafin's Palace, 12 April 1991; Karimu Akangbe, Osi Efa, 13 April 1991; and Aduuola Ejide, Iya Kere, Kere Quarters, Alafin's Palace, 26 May 1991.

16. Interviews by R.O. Lasisi with Sabitiyu Abake, Koso, Iseyin, 20 June 1991; and Ayisatu Alake, Atori, Iseyin, 22 June 1991 (reporting on her natal compound of Isanlu, Iseyin).

17. Certainly this was their major occupation by the time Frobenius visited Bida in the early years of the twentieth century, although he noted that pieces of *lantana* stone were found there (1913: vol. 2, 444–5). Later, S.F. Nadel (1942: 283) also reported that the work of the Bida bead workers consisted in 'refining' beads brought from the north.

18. Interview with Alhaji Abdulkarim and others, Ile Ashileke, Ilorin, 29 May 1980; information from Bayo Abubakar Yahaya, Ile Onileke, Ilorin, 9 June 1982; information from Kayode Abubakar Ibrahim, Ile Magaji Are, 6 September 1982.

19. Since the 263 females were listed together with the males, and 'girdlemakers' (women making an altogether different type of bead, from palm kernel or palm nut shells) were listed separately, it is clear that the 263 females were indeed involved in the stone bead industry; this is further corroborated by the fact that no female bead makers were listed in areas of the city where there were no males. Within the bead-making areas, however, there is no correlation between the numbers of females and males listed, but this is

likely to reflect simply the difficulty of assigning primary occupations to women who might each engage in a number of activities on a part-time basis. On the numbers of males given in this report, see note 5 above.

20. Lasisi interview with the Alafin of Oyo, 11 April 1991. For the Iya Kere as custodian of the Alafin's regalia, see Johnson 1921: 64. For the Alafin's use of coral, see e.g. Clapperton 1829: 381.

21. Lasisi interviews with the Alafin and the Iya Kere; and with Salami Adio, the Otun Efa, said to be the 'second senior palace official in charge of wearing apparel', 26 April 1991.

22. See also Eyo and Willett 1982: 98, colour plate 45.

23. Slides illustrating Omari-Obayemi, 1992. The importance of *lantana* in the Ekiti area is underscored by the fact that a small trade in used beads from Ilorin was still being carried on with that area until very recent years at least. Interview with Baba Elesin, 13 September 1988.

24. Note that the photograph in Drewal and Pemberton 1989: 36, plate 37, is not of the complete *agokun* costume.

25. Duchâteau 1994: 31 (quoting Ben-Amos 1980: 25, caption to plate 23), and 53 (on heads of Queen Mothers). See also de Negri 1962: 44, photograph captioned 'Benin women wearing coral-bead necklaces with traditional hairstyles featuring coral-bead decorations'. One of the women in this photograph is clearly wearing *lantana* necklaces.

26. Red stone beads are sometimes referred to as the 'original' or 'authentic' coral, and 'older than the other coral' (personal communication from Joseph Nevadomsky, 10 November 1990). According to R.E. Bradbury, they were called *ivie-egbo* ('forest *ivie*'), in contradistinction to coral (*ivie-ebo*), and were said to have been known in Benin longer than any other bead; Benin tradition, however, as in Egharevba's account, also has it that there is one other type of bead considered to be the oldest of all. R.E. Bradbury, information cited in Fage 1962: 346, 347; Egharevba 1949: 60; personal communication from Barbara Blackmun, 22 June 1991.

27. Personal communications from Barbara Blackmun and Joseph Nevadomsky. For an illustration of the variety of red beads used in Benin, see Nevadomsky 1986: 43, plate 3.

28. Translation of Dapper quoted in Roth 1968: 24, 74, 134, 135. On Dapper's work, and this translation, see ibid.: 2, and note 1.

29. For the 'winged' cap, see Fagg 1964: 37, and plate 15; also Eyo and Willett 1982: 44, figure 35; for pendants on necklaces see Duchâteau 1994: 110, plate 118; the rest of the information in this paragraph was provided by personal communications from Barbara Blackmun and Joseph Nevadomsky.

30. Information on the western Igbo area was provided by Boniface and Felicia Okonkwo, August 1993.

31. Interview by R.O. Lasisi with Sangowoyin Igboo, Ile Kuluku, Ashipa Oyo (natal compound Ile Mogba, the compound of the Sango priests of the royal shrine at Koso), 26 May 1991. Shittu Akande, the Mogba or 'head of Sango worshippers in Oyo', also confirms that the beads are worn (interview by R.O. Lasisi, Ile Mogba, 25 May 1991). For the association of the Mogba priests and the Sango cult in general with the Alafin's

interests, see Law 1977: 104. There may well be a link here with *lantana* bead making in Ilorin, since the members of Ile Ashileke, one of the most important bead-making compounds in that city, claim an Old Oyo origin and a relationship with 'Ile Mongba' in New Oyo, and say that they were 'worshipping Sango' before they came to Ilorin. Interview in Ile Ashileke, 1 June 1980.

32. Pokornowski 1979: 107, citing Bascom. Peter Morton-Williams confirms the connection of *lantana* beads with the cult of Oya.

33. Information from K.A. Ibrahim, 13 and 18 September 1982, 28 April 1983; interview by A.I. Alesinloye (Ile Baba Isale, Ilorin) and H.J. O'Hear with the Sarkin Gobiri (a title-holder of Hausa origin), Ilorin, 23 April 1983.

34. Interview by R.O. Lasisi with Karimu Ishola, Basorun of Iseyin, 7 June 1991.

35. Interview with Baba Elesin, 18 February 1985; interview in Ile Ashileke, 1 June 1980. An informant from Igboho also reports that beads are now brought back by people who have been on pilgrimage to Mecca. Interview by R.O. Lasisi with Shittu Alamu, Bale of Madeke Compound, Igboho, 12 July 1991.

References

Aronson, L. (1992a), 'Ijebu Yoruba *Aso Olona*: A Contextual and Historical Overview', *African Arts*, vol. 25, no. 3, 52–63, 101–2.

—— (1992b), 'The Language of West African Textiles', *African Arts*, vol. 25, no. 3, 35–40, 100.

de Beauchêne, G. (1969), 'Report to Third Conference of West African Archaeologists', in D. Calvocoressi (ed.), *Report on Third Conference of West African Archaeologists*, Accra.

Beier, U. (1982), *Yoruba Beaded Crowns*, London: Ethnographica.

Ben-Amos, P. (1978), 'Owina n'ido: Royal Weavers of Benin', *African Arts*, vol. 11, no. 4, 49–53.

—— (1980), *The Art of Benin*, London.

Clapperton, H. (1829), *Journal of a Second Expedition into the Interior of Africa*, Philadelphia.

Clarke, J. D. (1938), 'Ilorin Stone Bead Making', *Nigeria*, no. 14, 156–7.

Daniel, F. (1937), 'Bead Workers of Ilorin, Nigeria', *Man*, January 1937, items 2, 28.

Drewal, H., Pemberton, J., with Abiodun, R. (1989), *Yoruba: Nine Centuries of African Art and Thought*, New York: Center for African Art.

Duchâteau, A. (1994), *Benin: Royal Art of Africa from the Museum für Völkerkunde, Vienna*, Vienna: Prestel-Verlag.

Egharevba, J. U. (1949), *Benin Law and Custom*, 3rd edn, Benin City: J. U. Egharevba.

Eyo, E. & Willett, F. (1982), *Treasures of Ancient Nigeria*, London: Collins.

Fage, J. D. (1962), 'Some Remarks on Beads and Trade in Lower Guinea in the Sixteenth and Seventeenth Centuries', *Journal of African History*, vol. 3, no. 2, 343–7.

Fagg, W. (1963), *Nigerian Images*, New York: Praeger.

—— (1980), *Yoruba Beadwork*, New York: Rizzoli.

Frobenius, L. (1913), *The Voice of Africa*, trans. Rudolf Blind, New York: Blom.

Johnson, S. (1921), *History of the Yorubas*, Lagos: CMS Bookshops.

Kriger, C. (1993), 'Textile Production and Gender in the Sokoto Caliphate', *Journal of African History*, vol. 34, no. 3, 159–89.

Law, R. (1977), *The Oyo Empire c.1600–c.1836*, Oxford: Clarendon Press.

Lethem, G.J., Assistant Resident (1912), Nigerian National Archives Kaduna, Ilorinprof 4 900/1912, Ilorin Town Reassessment Report.

Lovejoy, P. E. (1990), 'Concubinage in the Sokoto Caliphate (1804–1903)', *Slavery and Abolition*, vol. 11, no. 2.

Nadel, S. F. (1942), *A Black Byzantium*, London: Oxford University Press.

de Negri, E. (1962), 'Nigerian Jewellery', *Nigeria Magazine*, vol. 30, no. 74: 43–54.

Nevadomsky, J. (1986), 'The Benin Bronze Horseman as the Ata of Idah', *African Arts*, vol. 19, no. 4, 40–7, 85.

O'Hear, A. (1983), 'The Economic History of Ilorin in the 19th and 20th Centuries: The Rise and Decline of a Middleman Society', unpublished PhD thesis, University of Birmingham.

—— (1986), 'Ilorin Lantana Beads', *African Arts*, vol. 19, no. 4, 36–9, 87–8.

—— (1987), 'Craft Industries in Ilorin: Dependency or Independence?' *African Affairs*, vol. 86, no. 345, 505–21.

—— (1993), 'Lantana Beads: Trade and Regalia in Yorubaland and Benin', paper presented at African Studies Association (USA) Annual Meeting.

—— (1994), 'Pawning in the Emirate of Ilorin', in T. Falola and P. E. Lovejoy (eds), *Pawnship in Africa*, Boulder, Colorado: Westview.

Omari-Obayemi, M. S. (1992), 'Obinrin-Kunrin (Female Men): Ritual and Artistic Portraits of Yoruba Women of Power', paper presented at Arts Council of the African Studies Association Triennial Symposium.

Pokornowski, I. (1979), 'Beads and Personal Adornment', in J. M. Cordwell and R. A. Schwarz (eds), *The Fabrics of Culture*, The Hague: Mouton.

Poynor, R. (1978), 'The Ancestral Arts of Owo, Nigeria', unpublished PhD thesis, Indiana University.

—— (1989), 'If the Chiefs Are Like This, What Must the King Be Like? Chieftaincy Garb as Indicators of Position in the Owo Court', in B. Engelbrecht and B. Gardi (eds), *Man Does Not Go Naked*, Basel: AC Verlag.

Priestman, H. E. (1922), Nigerian National Archives Kaduna, Ilorinprof 4/13 D 149/1922, Assessment Report Ilorin Town.

Renne, E. P. (1992), '*Aso Ipo*, Red Cloth from Bunu', *African Arts*, vol. 25, no. 3, 64–9, 102.

Roth, H. Ling (1968), *Great Benin: Its Customs, Art and Horrors*, new edn, London: Routledge and Kegan Paul.

Ryder, A. F. C. (1969), *Benin and the Europeans 1485–1897*, Harlow: Longmans.

Shea, P. (1975), 'The Development of an Export-oriented Dyed Cloth Industry in Kano Emirate in the 19th Century', unpublished PhD thesis, University of Wisconsin.

Willett, F. (1960), 'Recent Archaeological Discoveries at Ilesha', *Odu*, no. 8, 5–20.

6

A Short History of Rosaries in the Andes

Penny Dransart

A rosary is both a form of prayer and, in a material manifestation, a string of beads used by Christians in meditation as part of a programme of prayer. It was introduced to the Andes in the sixteenth century as an item of Christian faith,[1] when it served in the confrontation between native Andean and invading European peoples. The rosary played an important role in the accommodation of the new religion. In fact, during the early days of the colonial period in the Andes, the Christian rosary was likened to the *quipu*, a series of knotted cords used by the Inkas and other Andean peoples for keeping administrative records. It was therefore received into a cultural context for which there were existing Andean categories.

The form of rosary most widely known today is a circlet consisting of a string with five sets of ten beads, each set being separated by a larger or differently coloured bead. A pendant hangs from this circlet, containing one large bead, three small ones and a further large bead. The sets of ten beads are used for repeating the prayer *Ave Maria* (Hail Mary) ten times, each set preceded by *Pater Noster* (Our Father) on the single large beads and the *Gloria* (Glory be) afterwards, on the string or chain. This sequence is known as a decade, five of which constitute a chaplet, or lesser rosary. The number of beads present corresponds with a chaplet, but the beads may be counted more than once, in groups of one hundred or one hundred and fifty (Gorce 1937: 2093). Hence a full rosary involves the repetition of fifteen decades of Ave Marias. This form of prayer became standardized in Europe in the fifteenth and sixteenth centuries. However, rosaries had already been associated with devotions which had acquired Marian connotations since the eleventh century (Gorce 1937: 2092; Wakefield 1983: 339).

In the colonial period, the rosary was used by women and men alike. However, late in the twentieth century, among bilingual Aymara–Spanish speakers of Isluga, northern Chile, the rosary has undergone considerable modification. It is now associated with women, rather than men. Its appearance has also been modified. Isluga rosaries consist of brightly coloured glass beads interspersed with charms of silver, or silver coins (Figure 6.1). If it were not for the silver crucifix, it might not be recognized as a rosary. The identification is made by the women themselves.

Figure 6.1 Aymara rosary, collected in Isluga, 1989.

However, Aymara women speak of the amuletic protection offered by the rosary, rather than referring to it as an aid in their devotions. Until recently, it was an important item of dress worn at religious festivals, which tend to have a highly charged and ambiguous character. It was one of a number of items that Aymara women consider to possess amuletic attributes. In particular, woven belts wrapped round the waist form a counterpart to the rosary, which encircles the neck.

The form of the contemporary rosary in Isluga is a reinterpretation of that introduced in the sixteenth century. Indeed the Aymara rosary, as worn until recently, may be regarded as a parallel version of the orthodox Christian form.

In the course of this chapter, I propose to explore the role of rosaries in religious observance in Isluga. I will then consider, at a more general level, the historical background in the seventeenth century (a period for which there is historical material available), and the relationship between rosaries and *quipus*. I wish to examine how women's and men's religious experience focusing on the rosary has changed through time. Before proceeding to discuss how a rosary gives its wearer the confidence to participate in the active religious observance of the community in Isluga, I will briefly introduce Isluga and some of the more important Christian festivals observed by the community.

Isluga – The Place

Isluga is situated to the east of Iquique, adjacent to the Chilean–Bolivian frontier. It is bounded by the Salar de Surire to the north, and the Salar de Coipasa (most of which is in Bolivian territory) to the south. To the west, it stretches as far as a chain of high volcanic peaks beyond which lie the valleys of the precordillera and the Atacama Desert proper. In contrast with the desert vegetation characteristic of lower altitudes, these high altitude lands are covered by more extensive pastures that are fed by melted waters from the snow-capped volcanic peaks, and seasonal rainfall. Isluga is one of several Aymara communities in the region occupying territories where the vegetation is regarded as marginal grazing lands by outsiders. However, the Aymara have long worked in partnership with their environment to make it productive and the basis of a predominantly pastoralist economy.

Isluga, and the Tarapacá Region to which it belongs, were formerly part of Peruvian national territory. The Chilean military incursion into Tarapacá took place in 1879, to gain access to lands rich in nitrates and other mineral resources. A plebiscite was held in 1929, following which Tarapacá remained under Chilean control. This historical event is represented in the rosary in Figure 6.1 in the form of a Peruvian coin. The other coin to have survived in this rosary is Chilean.

In 1974, internal boundary changes reshaped the departments, known as *comunas* in Chile. The main parts of the lands of two ethnic communities, Isluga and

Cariquima, were joined together in a district called Los Cóndores, while remnants of these two territories were split and incorporated into three neighbouring districts. Instead of making the central, ceremonial town known to the Aymara as Islug marka (Isluga town) into the administrative headquarters, the Chilean state established its presence in a tiny hamlet, Colchane. Previously, Colchane consisted of a small cluster of houses belonging to the members of one family (Martínez 1975: 404; Provoste 1978: 11). It now has a police station, a boarding school, a health centre and a large church. However, the Roman Catholic Church does not maintain a constant presence in the highlands, and its operational centre is outwith Isluga in the cathedral of Iquique.

The vestiges of a more traditional Andean social organization have survived in Isluga. This takes the form of two geographically based moieties known as *parcialidades* in Spanish and *saya* in Aymara. Manq"asaya is literally the 'inner' moiety, usually referred to in conversation as 'below'. It incorporates the villages located between the central town of Islug marka and the Bolivian border. Araxsaya is the upper moiety, and it includes villages located north or 'above' the central town of Islug marka. It was in the upper moiety that I was based during my period of fieldwork (1986, 1987–1988, 1989 and 1995).[2] The upper moiety was where women continued to wear their traditional form of dress longest, presumably because the area was more remote from Colchane, the centre of Chilean administration. When I began my fieldwork in March 1986, a considerable number of women wore an ancient style of dress – the *urk"u* – on a daily basis. By 1989, it was often used only for festive occasions, as has been the practice in Manq"asaya, the lower moiety. During the mid 1980s, the rosary was also falling into disuse in Araxsaya. Nevertheless, strings of glass or predominantly red ceramic bead necklaces constituted a standard item of dress. Necklaces have continued to be worn with the *urk"u*, although they now usually consist of plastic beads.

Islug Marka

The herding lifestyle of Isluga means that the population is highly mobile, and many of the festivals observed throughout the year are held in the various villages and hamlets of Isluga. There are several major events of community-wide importance that have traditionally been held in the central town of Islug marka. These are the Day of the Dead, at the beginning of November; the celebration of Saint Thomas, on 21 December (formerly this was preceded by nearly a month of festivals); and the celebration of Carnival, which begins on the Saturday immediately before the first day of Lent. An examination of the character of these festivities is important for understanding the context in which Aymara women have worn rosaries.

In Isluga, Saint Thomas is the patron, and the people refer to themselves as the 'children of Saint Thomas'. Yet, inside the old, colonial style church in Islug marka it was the Virgin of the Immaculate Conception (Concepción) who occupied the uppermost and most elaborate niche behind the altar, at the west end of the church (Martínez 1989: figure V).[3] In Isluga, the churches have the entrance at the east end, which means that the saints face outward to the rising sun. Concepción was carried in procession not only on her own festival, 8 December, but she also accompanied Saint Thomas on 21 December. The Virgin is a complex figure in Andean cosmologies. In this region, Concepción is associated with the moon, and is venerated as *Tayksa María Awajistu*, or 'Our Mother Mary who is herding us' (Martínez 1989: 132). Other aspects of the Virgin are associated with the church in Islug marka. The Virgins of the Candelaria and the Rosary (Rosario) are housed in separate niches, in the lower level of saints, in the west wall of the church (Martínez 1989: 129).

It is interesting to note that Rosario, the aspect of the Virgin Mary who carries a rosary in her hand, is one of the saints that Gabriel Martínez identified as no longer having an active cult when he did his fieldwork in Isluga during the 1970s (1989: 135). With the theft of Concepción from the church, Rosario has been brought into use to accompany Santo Tomás in the procession round the square on his feast day, in place of Concepción. In some parts of the Andes, Rosario is associated with seeds, and the sowing of seeds (Arnold, personal communication). Apparently people do not make this connection in Isluga, where seed-time is associated with the Virgin of the Assumption. Since the herding of animals is such a dominant economic activity in Isluga, the association between the Virgin of the Rosary and her aspect as shepherd or herder may be relevant here. The historical aspects of the iconography, as depicted in colonial art are briefly considered below.

The saints of the Catholic pantheon are seen as powerful figures. They are believed by many to be ready to castigate those people who do not make appropriate religious observance to them. For example, Saint Barbara (Barabara), another personage whose effigy was housed in the church, is very much associated with thunderbolts. Her rays are said to fall with increased vigour if her day (4 December) coincides with a Tuesday or Friday, which are not propitious days of the week.[4] These saints are often portrayed as both powerful and vengeful if their observance is neglected.

This point was clearly expressed to me after the festival of Candelaria (the feast of the Purification of the Virgin) was observed in a neighbouring village to the one in which I resided. An old lady had been unable to attend, and she felt very uneasy that her own family had not honoured the occasion. She said that Candelaria was 'powerful', recalling that in the past one of the villagers had failed to recognize the festival, as a result of which one of his mules was killed in 'punishment'. Her feelings of unease were compounded by her dream of plenty during the previous night. She went on to say that in the past, when the full month of festivals was held in Islug marka in December, the harvests of quinua and potatoes (virtually the only crops which can be grown at such high altitudes, in limited areas within Isluga) were 'beautiful'. Now, she said the nights were clear, and the quinua frosted and small. Her deeply felt reactions to local events fully demonstrate that the cult of the saints is profoundly interrelated with the horticultural cycle in Isluga. Her response also demonstrated that in the Andes, the Virgins do not possess the passive character which is such a marked feature of the Virgin Mary as perceived in Europe, where she is noted for her chastity, humility and gentleness (Warner 1990: xx and xxiv).

In addition to the community-wide festivals held in Islug marka, there are smaller-scale celebrations organized in outlying villages. The most important of these is a family-based event known as the *wayñu* in Isluga, held in honour of the llamas, alpacas and sheep (Dransart: 1997). This is an elaborate ritual act undertaken by families to enhance the reproductive powers of their animals. It also involves the acknowledgement of the Wirjin Tayka, who is the divinity of earth and time (addressed more generally as the Pachamama in the Andes), and of the spirits of the hills. The *wayñu* does not possess the predominantly Christian character of the major events observed in Islug marka. Outwardly it seems largely non-Christian, and deeply rooted in Andean traditions. Yet in making ritual libations, the people themselves are conscious of the identity of the beings they are addressing during the ceremonies. The blood of a sacrificial llama, and substances such as alcohol, maize flour, sugar and coca leaves are offered to the Wirjin Tayka and spirits of the hills. In contrast, smoke from fragrant embers is wafted to the Christian Virgin. It should also be noted that the name of the Isluga earth mother is, in fact, Aymara for 'Virgin Mother'. The relationship between the Andean Wirjin Tayka and the Christian Virgin provides another manifestation of parallelism in religious observance among the Aymara.

During all the different festive events, people remember the saints, the Wirjin Tayka and spirits of the hills. Traditional acts of remembrance involve the supplicant in feeding and nourishing these beings, which are in turn held to nourish fortunate persons with large herds of llamas and good crops of quinua and potatoes. Through ritual drunkenness during fiestas people make libations and drink alcohol in order to remember the specific entities that are being honoured on particular occasions during the year. Olivia Harris has said of drinking among the Aymara, 'drunkenness is virtually an obligatory state in order to worship the divine beings of the Andean cosmos' (1989: 233). It is significant in this respect that the rosary in Figure 6.1 is incomplete. The woman who sold it to me in 1989 explained that she was drunk, the string broke and she lost some of the beads and charms.

Dress and Gender Codes

Isluga women wear a form of dress which is descended from the main garment worn by Inka and other highland women in prehispanic times (Gisbert *et al* 1987: 67; Dransart 1992: 146). A consideration of both women's and men's dress in more detail will help clarify differences in the presentation of oneself (whether female or male) when addressing divine or supernatural personages. Do differences expressed in dress codes affect the manner in which women and men supplicate divinities? By establishing such differences, it will be possible to elucidate why the Aymara rosary has been associated only with women in recent times.

The main female garment, the *urk"u*, is normally dark brown or black, enlivened by a narrow band of bright hues at the hem. It is held in place by several belts wrapped tightly round the waist; these are also of strong colour. At the shoulders, the dress is fastened by pins. On festive occasions, a shawl is worn of light beige or grey, with narrow bands of bright colours. All these items of clothing (dress, belts and shawl) are handwoven, usually, in the case of adult women, the products of the wearer's own labour.

Whereas women wear western style garments of industrial manufacture underneath the *urk"u* (especially acrylic jumpers and cardigans), men tend to wear western style clothing (shirt, pullover, jacket and trousers) in a more outward manner. They, like women, wear traditional handwoven belts around the waist, but, unlike women, the belts are obscured from view under the outer clothing. For both women and men, Aymara belts are considered to have a protective function, to preserve the wearer from illness. The perceived effectiveness of such belts has to do with the strong colours, which are believed to deflect danger or to prevent illness from 'seizing' the wearer. Older women, especially, express a horror against too much strong colour, such is its perceived power (Dransart 1988: 46–8). Therefore 'traditional' Aymara garments consist of large expanses of natural, undyed colour (the browns, black and grey of camelid fleece), offset by small amounts of dyed hues.

Men are less likely to wear 'traditional' Aymara style clothing than women. Martínez reports that Isluga men went through a process of 'modernization' in dress, a process that was resisted by the women to a much greater extent (Martínez 1975: 421).[5] Given that Isluga women tend to display their Aymara identity in an outward fashion, while men tend to hide items which mark Aymara identity beneath western style garments, it is tempting to make a comparison with the Cuna of Panama. The dress of Cuna women is in marked contrast to that of their menfolk who, for at least a century, have adopted western style clothing. Cuna women are elaborately and lavishly dressed in clothing of their own making, including intricately embroidered *molas*. Since they are attired in *molas* and nose-rings, in Michael Taussig's appraisal of the situation, they are responsible for signalling to the outside world their 'radical Alterity' (Taussig 1993: 185).

However, the comparison between the Cuna of Panama and the Aymara of Isluga is ultimately superficial. In Taussig's analysis, the lavishness of women's self-imaging is controlled by Cuna men; it serves to protect women from non-Cuna men. The gaze of westerners is deflected by the gorgeous garments – yet at the same time, in Taussig's interpretation of the situation, women's industry has meant that Cuna women 'sew themselves into an iron cage' (Taussig 1993: 184). It is true that Isluga women express their alterity to non-Aymara Chileans in terms of dress codes, while men apparently attempt to de-emphasize the contrast by donning western dress. However, the situation becomes considerably more complex when we consider relations between Isluga people and the divinities and supernatural beings which they honour through the course of the annual herding and horticultural cycle. There are times, especially during festivals, when Isluga men don 'traditional' Aymara garments, including a poncho and carrying shawl. These garments are woven by women, usually the wife of the wearer. Unlike the Cuna, there are occasions when Isluga men's self-imaging is controlled by the women,[6] since the garments they weave for their menfolk are worn outwardly, above western style trousers and pullovers.

Spiritual Encounters

It follows, then, that both men and women benefit from the protective function of the garments with which they are clothed. Clothing protects against physical dangers, against the cold and against abrasion. Western style garments would be adequate for such purposes, but Aymara dress is chosen instead and considered to be effective in protecting against dangers arising from metaphysical sources. In particular, dangers arise when humans encounter supernatural phenomena. Such beings may be sought out and addressed by humans, as in the *wayñu* ceremonies, but they may also be encountered unexpectedly in the course of daily routine. Dress also may include other accessories, most notably for women, silver or chrome pins, hair slides, bead necklaces and, of course, Aymara rosaries. All these items may be referred to as possessing amuletic properties. It remains to be seen why women feel a greater need for them than men.

There are, in Isluga territory, certain spots in the landscape which are accorded special status. On the one hand, they are connected with the inner world and good fortune, but on the other hand, they are considered to be potentially dangerous to human beings and animals. The most dangerous places are accorded the epithet fierce (*bravo* in Spanish; Martínez 1976: 292–5). In an interview with a man from one of the villages of Manq"asaya, Martínez asked if his respondent was frightened to go, as part of the *wayñu* ceremony, to a notoriously fierce location in moist pastures where his family herded llamas. Although he went alone, in the darkness of night, his fear was dissipated as he had been drinking. 'With a little drink, one has more head', he admitted to Martínez (1976: 286). This enabled him to shout out to the spirit of the place. Yet he also recognized the dangers of the place; local people would never sleep there, or even lie down when herding animals (ibid.: 292). He identified that particular spot as being masculine, a 'devil' which was particularly threatening to women of all ages. Since girls had fallen ill there (ibid.: 293), women were encouraged to avoid it.

Yet young girls and women take a full and active part in the herding of animals, and they often venture into lonely spots in search of animals. While doing fieldwork in Isluga, I was constantly being advised of the dangers of walking in the hills, and was warned of stories concerning spirits of the hills taking human form and approaching lone women, who died after taking ill if a llama was not sacrificed in time. Besides, there were other, albeit lesser, dangers nearer home. Some of the corrals and horticultural plots near the village contained large stones referred to as 'grandparents'. These were connected with the ancestors of the place, and the stones were understood to have the ability to cause one's teeth to hurt, or a woman's stomach to swell when approached. For all these reasons, women fortify themselves against unanticipated dangers in their dress, adding belts, pins and necklaces accordingly. In contrast, men take fewer precautions, in the form of belts wound tightly round the waist.

All these items acquire specific importance at religious festivals, which as I have mentioned above, have a highly charged and ambiguous character. In their function as amulets, rosaries and other items of dress enable the wearer to participate in activities involved in the religious observance of the community, just as the taking of alcohol gives mere mortals the courage to confront the most fearsome of spiritual beings. Men are more likely to resort to the taking of alcohol in order to address the spirits of the hills. Women tend to restrict their consumption of alcohol, although they are responsible for the making of *chicha*, from fermented maize or quinua seeds. Only during the *wayñu* ceremonies do women exhort each other to drink alcohol: 'You have to drink until you fall down', one woman instructed me. The wearing of an Aymara rosary by women should be understood in this context of ritual drinking and making libations.

Historical Considerations

In Europe, the rosary, as a string of beads, achieved its 'definitive' form with the attachment of a crucifix only in the sixteenth century (Gorce 1937: 2908). As a form of prayer, it had antecedents in the meditation and devotions associated with St Bernard of Clairvaux (d. 1153) and the Cistercian order, of which he was a member. St Bernard is accredited with promoting the twelfth-century chaplet of fifty recited, or sung *rosae spirituales,* mystic roses, with which to hail Our Lady (Gorce 1937: 2904). By the fourteenth century, the meditations had become associated with five, seven, fifteen or twenty 'joys' *(gaudiae)*, a series of mysteries concerning the life of Jesus and Mary.[7]

Members of the Dominican order also encouraged people to use the rosary. A long Dominican poem dating to the first half of the fourteenth century, the *Rosarius,* addressed the Virgin as the new rose ('Tu es la rose nouvelle') (Gorce 1937: 2904). At the end of the fifteenth century, a Dominican priest, Alanus de Rupe (d. 1475), author of *De Utilitate Psalterii Mariae,* was a staunch advocate of the use of the rosary (ibid.: 2908; Warner 1990: 306). He recommended the rosary as the means for obtaining mercy and protection from the Virgin.

By this stage, the rosary had become extremely widespread in Europe as a means for devout Christians to meditate on the life of Jesus and Mary in the repetition of prayers which were embedded in the medieval symbolism of the rose. Officially, the rosary was granted the approval of the Holy See by Pope Alexander VI in 1495 (Warner 1990: 306). When Europeans invaded the Andes in 1532, friars and priests began to evangelize in the former Inka empire in order to convert people to Christianity. A Dominican friar, Vicente de Valverde accompanied Francisco Pizarro in the invasion of the Inka empire.[8] Other orders to work actively in the Andes included the Franciscans, the Augustinians, the Mercedarians, and the Jesuits. One of the tools they took with them was the rosary.

Other items used by the Spanish as aids for promoting Christianity were paintings and effigies of saints. This gave rise to native American appellations, which were linked to the places where a particular image was enthroned. Among the Andean Virgins, one of the best known is that of Pomata, enthroned by Dominican priests in Pomata, near Copacabana on the shores of Lake Titicaca (Gisbert 1980: 82–3). This image was a version of the Virgin of the Rosary (Rosario), whose patronage was extended to native Andean peoples and blacks. In the words of Teresa Gisbert, 'Pomata is without doubt, the American Virgin par excellence with her headdress of Indian feathers and protection of natives and slaves' (1980: 83).

One of the most prominent attributes of Rosario is, of course, the rosary, but this feature is also shared in the iconography of a related version, the Virgin of the Shepherds (Damian 1995: figure 22). In this respect, a painting dated 1703, entitled *La Divina Pastora* (The Divine Shepherdess) in the Museo Nacional del Arte, La Paz, Bolivia, is of interest. In this picture the Virgin is surrounded by sheep which have roses in their mouths and rosaries of black beads hanging over their backs. Alternatively, some of the sheep have the characteristic knotted belt cords which form part of a Franciscan monk's habit draped over their backs. In the background, a lamb wearing a black rosary with a pendant crucifix has a speech scroll emanating from his mouth, bearing the words 'Ave María'. He is threatened by a fox, which is struck by lightning sent by an archangel in the sky. It is perhaps this association between rosaries and herded animals as flowers which became traditional in Isluga, rather than the associations between the Virgin of the Rosary and seeds, which comes to the fore in other, more agricultural parts of the Andes.[9]

Rosaries were used by people in all walks of life, whatever their race, sex, class or status, in the Andes during the early and mid colonial period. Evidence for this widespread usage is provided in the work of a native Andean author of the late sixteenth and early seventeenth centuries, Felipe Guaman Poma de Ayala. In a document entitled *Nueva corónica y buen gobierno* (*ca* 1615), addressed to King Philip III of Spain, Guaman Poma included a series of informative line drawings which complement his text. The people depicted with rosaries include members of the Inka nobility, Queen Curi Ocllo (f. 757); local functionaries (f. 753 and f. 755); a married Quechua couple at prayer (f. 821, figure 2); an old lady, too poor to pay her taxes (f. 886); a couple of black slaves 'from Guinea', who are praying in front of an effigy of the Virgin (f. 703); the extirpator of idolatry, Cristóbal de Albornoz (f. 675) and the author himself (f.18).[10]

In a study of the work of Guaman Poma, Rolena Adorno (1989) argues that the rosary served as a metalinguistic sign. According to Adorno, it denotes the most powerful of cultural values imported from Europe and used in an Andean sphere. In Guaman Poma's series of portraits of ethnic Andean functionaries, Adorno suggests that the depiction of the rosary is a means of saying that within an Andean domain, European spiritual values were accepted, but not a European domination which rejected indigenous political and social hierarchies (1989: 189). For Adorno, the use of the rosary is not a sign of acculturation, instead it affirms that Andean and European cultural space constituted separate and different entities (1989: 204). The rosary is a sign which was understood in both spheres, but in Adorno's analysis it helps de-emphasize the exotic quality displayed in the dress of Andean peoples to a European readership. She considers one of the main themes of Guaman Poma's work to be an expression of the relationship between Andean peoples and symbolic Christian values (1989: 205). This perspective is perhaps relevant to further our understanding of the historical antecedents, and how the Aymara women of Isluga have adopted the rosary and converted it into a cultural form of their own. However, in Isluga the rosary has been transformed into a particularly Aymara cultural form which is no longer readily understood by outsiders.

Rosary Beads and Knotted Cords

It should also be recognized that the rosary was accepted in the Andes as an intrinsic part of Christianity, a religion which had, at times, what the Christian priests and missionaries thought to be uncanny similarities to aspects of American religions

(Cervantes 1991: 22–3). The rosary had its counterpart in the *quipu*, in which the beads of the rosary, used to count prayers, were likened to the knotted cords used in Andean accounting systems.[11]

The Spanish Jesuit José de Acosta (1540–1600) attributed such similarities to the work of deception undertaken by the devil (1954: 140–1). He equated pagan religious observance among the peoples of the Americas with idolatry. However, he was an acute observer of customs in the Andes and in 1590 he wrote:

> *Quipos* are aids to the memory or registers made of strands, in which various knots and various colours mean different things. It is incredible what they achieved in this manner . . . just as we have twenty four letters arranged in different ways that we take out an infinity of words, so these knots and colours have innumerable meanings (Acosta 1954: 189).

He went on to relate how he saw an Andean woman make a general confession of her life, using a *quipu* to aid her memory. He commented:

> . . . and I even asked about some little threads which seemed slightly different, and they were certain circumstances which required the sin to be confessed entirely (Acosta 1954: 190).

This careful record keeping of the most detailed actions undertaken by individual persons would seem to have prehispanic precedents. In the days of the Inka empire, specially trained keepers of *quipus* kept detailed accounts of the animals and produce owned by the deities honoured by the Inka state. However, records were also kept of the offerings that the Inka emperors made to every *wak'a* (shrine, holy place or thing) in all parts of the empire, in case some neglected *wak'a* should wreak its anger on the monarch (MacCormack 1991: 201).

A related notion concerning the accounting of religious observance was expressed by Guaman Poma when he appealed to the Christian charity of his readers, saying 'Pay me now your prayers' (1980: 702[716]). In fact, the Spanish word for a bead is *cuenta*, which may also refer to an account. Elsewhere, Guaman Poma refers to a rosary carried by a mendicant priest as 'another *quipu* for alms' (1980: 638[652]). The common theme here is that not only must one's sins be accounted for, but that also prayer or good deeds throughout one's lifetime may be counted as part of the final reckoning.

Concluding Comments

Among the contemporary Aymara of Isluga, the rosary is no longer employed in elaborate accounting systems as practised in Inka and colonial times. Nor, as mentioned above and as depicted by Guaman Poma (1980: 761 [775] and 811[825]), do men wear it nowadays round the neck (Figure 6.3). However, the women of Isluga have worn it until recently, and they associate it with protective powers. In this respect it may be seen to be part of a tradition which may be traced back to the fifteenth century work of Alanus de Rupe, with its emphasis on the protection offered through the use of the rosary.

The transformation of the rosary into an amulet has not only been affected by the Aymara, as there is evidence for such a usage by urban-dwelling taxi drivers who wind cheap plastic rosaries round their rear-view mirrors in Latin American cities. Where Aymara rosaries differ from their orthodox Christian counterparts is in the proliferation of shiny, coloured glass beads and silver charms. These substances are considered to possess apotropaic qualities. Items which are shiny and charged with colour are regarded with ambivalence in Isluga (Martínez 1976: 284; Dransart 1988: 47–8).

The Aymara rosary may therefore be regarded as a parallel form. It is a material manifestation of a related phenomenon reported by Arnold, Yapita and Jiménez Aruquipa, whose analysis of ritual language among the Aymara, northern Potosí, Bolivia, indicates that the doctrine of the Trinity has been reinterpreted (1992: 136–41). Equally, the saints in the Andes, powerful, beneficent and sometimes vengeful, constitute a heterodox reinterpretation of their European counterparts. The cult of the saints was briefly discussed above with reference to the ritual centre of Islug marka. An understanding of the celebrations of saints' festivals is important as such events provided the occasions when Aymara women wore their rosaries while making ritual libations.

Ritual drunkenness is an important aspect of such celebrations, and this aspect of traditional religious observance especially is being challenged by active missionizing on the part of Evangelical Protestants among the Aymara communities of Chile and Bolivia. The paradoxes of maintaining a commitment to ritual drinking have been highlighted by Harris (1989: 233), and tensions arising from different attitudes towards alcohol among Protestants and Catholics form part of an ongoing debate in Isluga (Dransart 1997: 98). Although alcohol is still important when ritual libations are performed in Isluga, women no longer wear rosaries during such ceremonies.

Ultimately, the woven belt has proved to be more enduring as a protective device in Isluga. The rosary, although Aymaraized and converted into a form which was always associated with the *urk"u* and never with western style dress, still retains an association with Catholicism. Its use bears witness to an outward display of Aymara allegiance to the saints, the Wirjin Tayka and the spirits of the hills. Given the rise in support for the Evangelical Pentecostal Church in the area, it is increasingly difficult for individuals to make such outward expressions of identification. In contrast, even devout Protestant women still weave belts for

Figure 6.2 Drawing by Felipe Guaman Poma: 'Principal, good Christian, principal, lord and lady of a province' (1936 f. 761).

Figure 6.3 Drawing by Felipe Guaman Poma: 'Married Indian Christians' (1936 f. 821).

members of their family, wrapping them round the underwear, underneath their outer garments, to ensure the good health of their children.

Notes

1. Rosaries or prayers beads are characteristic of different religions, including Hinduism, Buddhism and Islam, as well as Christianity. Although rosaries are often thought to be associated with Roman Catholicism, they are also used by some non-Roman Catholic Christians.
2. I would like to thank the people of Isluga for making it possible to work with them. I also wish to acknowledge financial support from the Emslie Horniman Anthropological Fund, the Pirie-Reid Scholarship fund and the British Council.
3. In recent years there has been increased support for the Evangelical Pentecostal Church in Isluga. Many people blamed members of this church for a situation which led to the theft of some of the saints (including Concepción, Candelaria, Santa Barbara and Santísimo) for sale on the international art market. One of the pastors from a neighbouring community was alleged to be responsible.
4. It should be noted that in the Roman Catholic calendar, Tuesday and Friday of every week (and Sundays in Lent) are the days on which the five Sorrowful Mysteries are remembered in the programme of prayer which constitutes the rosary. See note 7.
5. Isluga women do not adopt the fashions followed in the Chilean cities. When they wear western style garments, they prefer wide flaring skirts, often checked, and bright but monochrome cardigans and jumpers. Hence clothing still constitutes an expression of ethnic identity.
6. The point has been made most cogently that in weaving ponchos for their menfolk and shawls for themselves, it is the women of Qaqachaka, Bolivia, who actively define the limits and obligations of each sex as social constructions (Arnold 1994: 112).
7. These are now separated into cycles of Joyful, Sorrowful and Glorious Mysteries. See note 4 above.
8. It was his bible or breviary which the Inka emperor Atahuallpa cast to the ground in a famous incident which led the Spanish soldiers to take the emperor hostage.
9. It is interesting to note that Isluga herders refer to their llamas and alpacas as their 'flowers' during the *wayñu* ceremony (Dransart 1997: 93). Elsewhere in the Andes, similar festivals to the animals are sometimes known as the *floreo*, or the flowering of the animals. The imagery of the Virgin as the Divine Shepherdess was inspired by a vision experienced by a Capuchin friar early in the eighteenth century.
10. The folio numbers listed follow Guaman Poma's own pagination, as reproduced in the facsimile edition of his work in 1936. The corrected folio numbers in the edition of J.V. Murra and R. Adorno (1980) are as follows: f. 757 [corrected number f. 771]; f. 753 [767]; f. 755 [769]; f. 821 [835]; f. 886 [900]; f. 703 [717]; f. 675 [689] and f. 18

[18]. Hereafter, references to Guaman Poma's work will give references to the original folio number, followed by the corrected number in square brackets.

11. For further information on *quipus*, see Ascher and Ascher (1981).

References

Acosta, J. de (1954 [1590]), 'Historia natural y moral de las Indias', in *Obras, in Biblioteca de Autores Españoles*, vol. 73, 1–247, Madrid: Ediciones Atlas.

Adorno, R. (1989), *Cronista y Príncipe. La Obra de Don Felipe Guaman Poma de Ayala*, Lima: Pontificia Universidad Católica del Perú Fondo Editorial.

Arnold, D.Y. (1994), 'Hacer al hombre a imagen de ella: aspectos de género en los textiles de Qaqachaka', *Revista Chungará*, vol. 26, no. 1, 79–115.

——, Jímenez Aruquipa, D. & Yapita, J. de D. (1992), 'Simillt'aña: Pensamientos compartidos acerca de algunas canciones a los productos de un ayllu andino', in D. Arnold (ed.), *Hacia un Orden Andino de las Cosas*, La Paz: Hisbol and ILCA, 109–73.

Ascher, M. & Ascher, R. (1981), 'El quipu como lenguaje visible', in H. Lechtman & A.M. Soldi (eds), *La Tecnología en el Mundo Andino Runakunap Kawsayninkupaq Rurasqankunaqa*, Mexico: Universidad Nacional Autónoma de México, 407–32.

Cervantes, F. (1991), *The Idea of the Devil and the Problem of the Indian: The Case of Mexico in the Sixteenth Century*, London: Research Papers no. 24, University of London, Institute of Latin American Studies.

Damian, C. (1995), *The Virgin of the Andes: Art and Ritual in Colonial Cuzco*, Miami Beach: Grassfield.

Dransart, P. (1988), 'Continuidad y cambio en la producción textil tradicional aymara', *Hombre y Desierto: una Perspectiva Cultural*, vol. 2, 41–57. Antofagasta, Chile.

—— (1992), 'Pachamama: the Inka Earth Mother of the Long Sweeping Garment', in R. Barnes & J. Eicher (eds), *Dress and Gender: Making and Meaning in Cultural Contexts*, New York and Oxford: Berg, 145–63.

—— (1997), 'Cultural Transpositions: Writing about Rites in the Llama Corral', in R. Howard-Malverde (ed.), *Creating Context in Andean Cultures*, New York and Oxford: Oxford University Press.

Gisbert, T. (1980), *Iconografía y Mitos Indígenas en el Arte*, La Paz: Gisbert y Cía S.A.

——, Arze, S. & Cajías, M. (1987), *Arte Textil y Mundo Andino*, La Paz: Gisbert y Cía.

Gorce, M.-M. (1937), 'Rosaire', in A. Vacant, E. Mangenot and E. Amann (eds), *Dictionnaire de Théologie Catholique*, Paris: Librairie Letouzy et Ané, vol. 13, 2902–11.

Guaman Poma de Ayala, F. (1936 [1615]), *Nueva Corónica y Buen Gobierno (Codex Péruvien Illustré)*, Paris: Travaux et Mémoires de L'Institut d'Ethnologie, vol. 23.

—— (1980 [1615]), *Nueva Corónica y Buen Gobierno*, J.V. Murra and R. Adorno (eds), Mexico City: Siglo Veintiuno.

Harris, O. (1989), 'The Earth and State: The Sources and Meanings of Money in Northern Potosí, Bolivia', in J. Parry & M. Bloch (eds), *Money and the Morality of Exchange*, 232–68.

MacCormack, S (1991), *Religion in the Andes: Vision and Imagination in Early Colonial Peru*, Princeton, New Jersey: University of Princeton Press.

Martínez, G. (1975), 'Características de orden antropológico y socio-económico de la Comunidad de Isluga (I Región)', *Norte Grande*, vol. 1, nos 3–4, 403–26.

—— (1976), 'El sistema de los uywiris en Isluga', *Anales de la Universidad del Norte (Chile)*, vol. 10, 255–331.

—— (1989), 'Estructuras binarias y ternarias en Pueblo Isluga', in G. Martínez, *Espacio y Pensamiento. I Andes Meridionales*, La Paz: Hisbol, 109–48.

Provoste, F.P. (1978), Consideraciones para promover organizaciones colectivas en Isluga, Iquique: Universidad del Norte, Dirección Académica Sede Iquique, Centro Isluga de Investigaciones Andinas. Mimeographed.

Taussig, M. (1993), *Mimesis and Alterity: A Particular History of the Senses*, New York: Routledge.

Wakefield, G.S. (1983), *A Dictionary of Christian Spirituality*, London: SCM Press.

Warner, M. (1990), *Alone of all her Sex*, London: Picador.

7

Why Do They Like Red? Beads, Ethnicity and Gender in Ecuador

Lynn A. Meisch

Introduction

One of the pleasures of attending the weekly markets in highland Ecuador is admiring (or buying) the strands of antique and contemporary beads that are heaped on tables, hung from market stalls or piled on cloths on the ground. The beads are avidly and carefully examined and sometimes bought by indigenous women because beads constitute an essential part of female dress (Figure 7.1). By dress or costume I mean a person's hairstyle, headgear, clothing, jewellery and other bodily adornment (following Barnes & Eicher 1992; Eicher 1995; Meisch & Rowe, in press [1997]). Pre-Hispanically, however, both males and females in the three major geographic regions of Colombia, Ecuador and Peru (the Pacific coast, Amazon basin and Andean highlands) wore beads in a variety of ways: as earrings, necklaces, pendants, wristwraps, upper arm wraps, anklets, upper calf wraps (worn just below the knee) and as ornaments sewn onto clothing, depending on local custom (for Pre-Hispanic Ecuador see Meggers 1966: plates 22–9; Crespo Toral & Holm 1977: photographs on pp. 1, 102, 118, 119, 121, 126–9, 133, 134, 154, 205, 214, 222, 227, 232, 249; Valdéz 1992: Figures 1, 4, 11, 13, 14, 15, 16, 18. For examples of the stunning beads worn by high-ranking male Moche of Pre-Hispanic Peru see Alva & Donnan 1994). This chapter examines the importance of beads as a gender, ethnic and sometimes religious marker in contemporary Ecuador, and analyses the reasons why patterns of bead use have changed over the centuries.

Today males of such indigenous groups as the Cofán in the northern Ecuadorian Amazon (S. Oriente)[1] wear glass and natural seed bead necklaces and sometimes glass bead headbands and bracelets, but basically beads are considered a feature of indigenous female dress in the Oriente and especially in the highlands of Ecuador (Figure 7.1), and are worn in the form of necklaces, bracelets, earrings, and rosaries.[2] If non-indigenous women wear beads they wear a single-strand necklace, perhaps of pearls, or faux pearls; masses of beads in a necklace signify indigenous ethnicity. Neither males nor females wear beads in the highlands of Peru, Bolivia, Chile,

Figure 7.1   Young women in San Bernardo, Chimborazo province. The one on the left is wearing a gilded glass necklace more typical of Otavalo. (Photo: Lynn A. Meisch.)

Argentina, or Colombia (except the Kágaba, and Páez), and this is puzzling given that the region shares many pan-Andean textile and costume traditions. The population of contemporary Ecuador, a country the size of Oregon, is 11,566,000 persons. About 40 per cent are indígenas, meaning descendants of the aboriginal population of the region, 5 per cent African-Ecuadorian and 55 per cent whites-mestizo. These categories are socially constructed, fluid, and based for the most part on cultural characteristics (language, dress, residence, self-identification), rather than on phenotype. Both the Quichua and Spanish languages are foreign impositions, the result of the Inka and Spanish conquests of Ecuador in the fifteenth and early sixteenth centuries; today these languages have replaced aboriginal languages and are used to describe dress and ethnicity.

In the Amazon lowlands, language and territory are the salient ethnic markers, while in the highlands dress is the most important ethnic diacritica. Both the use of beads in Ecuador and the preference for certain colours have deep historical roots. In every highland indigenous ethnic group females wear beads. The size, colour, and how the beads are worn vary according to local custom, although red and coral-coloured beads are most common. Other features of indigenous female dress include a rectangular wrap skirt or full, gathered skirt, rectangular shoulder wrap which is sometimes pinned shut with a stick pin, a belt which is usually handwoven, an embroidered blouse in some communities, and a headcloth or handmade or factory-made felt hat.

Beads are also one of the ways in which gender is marked in infants. Baby girls have their ears pieced almost immediately after birth. A loop of string, sometimes with beads, is inserted in the hole. Baby girls often wear bead necklaces, and in those communities where wristwraps are common they sometimes wear tiny versions of the same. The only beaded item worn by both sexes is a small, red, seed bead bracelet, usually with a charm attached. These bracelets are sold in markets throughout the central sierra to protect babies against the evil eye.

Spondylus

Why are beads so important and why do contemporary indigenous women like red or coral? Part of the answer lies in the Pacific ocean off the Santa Elena peninsula of Ecuador. These waters and the Pacific ocean as far north as Baja California contain two species of Spiny Oyster or Spondylus, a bivalve mollusk. Spondylus princeps is a solitary species, living on the ocean floor between 40 and 65 feet deep. Princeps has beautiful coral or red outer shell with projecting spines, hence the name Spiny Oyster, and a lining of red or coral on the inside rims. Spondylus calcifer is a more gregarious species growing at shallower depths, and has purple colouration. Although Spondylus princeps is more coral or red coloured and calcifer is more purple coloured, there is enough overlap in colour to make it difficult to tell the two species apart when they have been cut into beads.

Spondylus beads, called *mullu (muyu)* or *chaquira* in Quichua, were highly prized and traded throughout the Andes beginning in the Formative epoch (Murra 1975; Marcos & Norton 1981; Norton 1986). Spondylus beads and shells were not only worn, but used as offerings, most likely because of their association with the ocean, water and fertility. So many Spondylus, Strombus, and Malea shells were excavated from the subfloor of the main plaza at La Tolita on the north coast of Ecuador, a sacred space dating to 400–200 BC, that the plaza is still called 'the shell place' (Valdéz 1992: 237). In pre-Hispanic times a Spondylus diving and bead-making industry was centred on Isla Puná, off the coast of Ecuador near Guayaquil. Bruhns (1989) excavated a beautiful Spondylus and turquoise necklace at Pirincay dating from approximately 1200–1000 BC in the Formative Period (Figure 7.2). The Formative site of Pirincay was situated on the Rio Paute in southern Ecuador to control traffic between the jungle and the sierra. Bruhns' find is the earliest known complete necklace found in Ecuador. The Spondylus came from the Ecuadorian coast and the turquoise probably came from the lower Jubones valley to the southwest of Cuenca or from deposits in northern Peru. We do not know, however, whether this necklace was worn by males, females or both.

Bruhns' excavations revealed workshops for the manufacture of rock crystal beads, which were traded to the coast, perhaps in exchange for Spondylus. Bruhns also excavated beads made of the following local materials, dating from the Later Formative, c.1400 BC: slate, shale, volcanic tuff, bone, jadite, white quartz and clay (one bead). She also found beads made from such materials of non-local origin (besides the Spondylus and turquoise mentioned earlier) as Strombus, mother of pearl, and red and green chalcedony (1989: passim). Meggers, Evans and Estrada also excavated Formative Period beads from the Valdívia and Machalilla phases. They identify eleven perforated disks between 1.1 to 2.8 cm in diameter, with thickness of 1.5 to 3.0 cm., as 'probably beads'. Eight were cut from the flat portions of large, unidentified shells, two from the pearl oyster (Pinctada mazatlanica Hanley), one from Spondylus, and three from the spiral end of the Olive shell (Oliva peruviana Lamarck) (1965: 38).

Leon Doyon recently excavated more than five kg of Spondylus calcifer and princeps beads from the tombs of the late Regional Development Period site of La Florida, Pichincha province, just outside of Quito (c. AD 500). Some of the beads were strung on cotton strings (Doyon-Bernard n.d. [1992]: 27), although the author did not give additional information on how the beads might have been worn (as necklaces, bracelets, armbands, anklets, headbands, decoration on cloth, and so on).

Tiny, cylindrical or barrel-shaped gold beads 7 mm long from La Tolita on the north coast (Orchard 1975: 61, Figure 59) also dating to the Regional Development

Figure 7.2 Spondylus and turquoise necklace dating to approximately 1200 to 1000 BC and excavated by Karen O. Bruhns at Pirincay in southern *sierra*. (Photo: Karen O. Bruhns.)

Period (500 BC to AD 500) are identical to brass beads that are still made in Cotacachi, near Otavalo in the highland province of Imbabura. Similar small gold beads, called *chaquira de oro* by the Spanish, are known archaeologically on the coast from Puná Island to the Colombian border and were associated with noble burial and tribute to the elite (Salomon 1986: 91). The La Tolita beads are distinguished by a tiny collar or rim at each end, and it may be that in colonial times jewellers began to replicate pre-Hispanic gold beads using baser metals. The Cotacachi barrel-shaped brass beads that have a small collar at each end are called '*cuentas Quiteñas*' (S. Quito beads) by antique vendors in the Otavalo market and are said to be the older style, while the small cylindrical beads with diagonal lines are called '*cuentas de Cotacachi*'. Today these beads are made only in Cotacachi, but they are found on necklaces and wristwraps throughout the sierra.

García & Pérez (1986) excavated 7,540 beads in Atacames on the north coast of Ecuador, dating to the Regional Integration Period (AD 500–1000). These beads were made of many materials: Spondylus, clay, stone, bone and metal. The clay beads were coloured red, brown and black, obtained from ochre; and white, obtained from ground up shells. Other local materials used for beads found in archaeological excavations include black coral, serpentine, quartz, gold, platinum, jasper and sodalite (a transparent or translucent mineral) (Kessler 1986: 50). Some people have argued that the tiny ceramic spindle whorls excavated in quantities on the Ecuadorian coast were worn as beads, but these are the right size and weight for spinning cotton, and are so similar to ceramic spindle whorls found on spindles with yarn on the central and north coasts of Peru that I think they were in fact used as spindle whorls. Liu (1978) and Wilbert (1974) also identify the Ecuadorian clay artefacts as spindle whorls rather than beads.

Realistic pre-Hispanic Ecuadorian ceramic figurines suggest that beads were worn by men and women on the coast and in the sierra (Crespo Toral & Holm 1977; Meggers 1966; Valdéz 1992) from Formative times through the Spanish conquest and beyond. Historical evidence confirms that beads were worn by both genders in the Amazon basin pre-Hispanically, and in the colonial era (Salomon 1986: 90–6). Both women and men wore beads in almost every conceivable style, as mentioned above. We also know from archaeological evidence that women occasionally wore earrings made from loops of beads (Karen Bruhns, personal communication), as they do today in the central sierra.

Salomon (1986: 91–6) has documented the pre-Hispanic importance of beads as trade items within Ecuador and between Ecuador and regions to the north and south. He notes that colonial sources are unanimous in insisting that certain red or white beads, called *carato* (etymology unknown), which were traded throughout Amazonia and the northern Ecuadorian sierra, were made of bone (Ibid.: 91–2). Spondylus, gold and silver beads were also involved in this trade. Northern Ecuadorian indigenous merchants travelled throughout the northern Andes and 'specialized in the importation of extra-sierran goods, from the lowlands and transverse river canyons, usually of high prestige and high unit value'. The mindalaes paid tribute to their own lords in gold, textiles and beads (Ibid.: 105). When Pedro de Cieza de León rode through Ecuador in AD 1545, shortly after the Spanish conquest, he commented on the beads worn by the indígenas of Puerto Viejo on the Ecuadorian coast:

> The women of these Indians . . . wear gold jewelry, and some very small beads called red *(colorada) Chaquira*, which were a valued item of trade . . . In other provinces I have seen that these *chaquira* were so valued that they paid a large quantity of gold for them. In the province of Quimbaya [modern Colombia], where the city of Cartago is located, certain chiefs and officials paid more than 1,500 pesos for less than a *libra* (pound) [of *chaquira*] (Cieza de León 1984: 154, my translation).

European Trade Beads

Columbus, Cortés and Pizarro brought beads to the New World as trade items (Dubin 1987: 254), including such Venetian glass beads as red *cornaline d'Aleppo*, called white hearts among bead collectors, *veintimilla* in Ecuador and *coral de los indios* (S. Indian coral) in southern Colombia. *Cornaline d'Aleppo* means carnelian from Aleppo, Syria, and these beads were probably made in imitation of real carnelian. The ones found in Ecuador are distinguished by an outer layer of red or coral-coloured glass over a white glass core, and range in size from tiny seed beads under 2 mm long to larger ones 1 cm (measured parallel to the hole). These beads have been excavated at Fountain of Youth Park in Florida dating to as early as AD 1580, but are most common at European-influenced sites in the Americas from the late seventeenth through the eighteenth centuries (Deagan 1987: 168, 172). The *veintimilla*, then, probably arrived in Ecuador much earlier than I have thought, as I previously associated them with the 1876–83 presidency of General Ignacio de Veintimilla (Meisch 1987: 135). White hearts are still manufactured (in Czechoslovakia), which makes it difficult, if not impossible, to date these beads when they are found on necklaces and bracelets.

In AD 1598, an Ecuadorian indígena don Diego Collín died leaving a last will and testament. He was the indigenous lord of Machachi, a town located in the sierra just south of Quito. Don Diego willed to his heirs 'eight collars of *chaquira* . . . so that they may honor and celebrate the feasts of the calendar with them, as is the custom among the native lords' (Caillavet, cited in Salomon 1986: 124). A bracelet and diadem of *chaquira* were also included in the will along with beads called catuc (etymology unknown), from the Oriente. While the word collars (S. *collares*) generally means necklaces, we do not know which gender wore these or how they or the other pieces were used in the ceremonies don Diego mentioned. The *chaquira* were important in the celebration of traditional fiestas because they had symbolic as well as aesthetic and monetary value.

Another colonial will offers evidence of the continuing importance of beads to indigenous Ecuadorians. Doña Lucia Coxilagunago was a Caranqui-Cayambe indigenous woman from a noble family who died in AD 1606. She was the wife of the indigenous governor general of the repartimiento of Otavalo and therefore of high status by virtue of her husband's position as well as her own. Doña Lucia willed various costume items to her three daughters, including eight different *sartas*, or strings of beads, mainly silver beads (S. & Q. *una sarta de chaquira de plata*), mixed with other beads she called coral and pearls. This coral came in red, blue and purple. She also lists a string of white and blue beads (Caillavet 1982: 51–2).

Portraits of Europeans from the fifteenth and early sixteenth centuries show women with various kinds of jewellery including bead necklaces. The use of jewellery, especially necklaces, bracelets, chokers and earrings, had female assoc-iations according to European norms and were considered inappropriate for males. The Spanish were perplexed by Andean practices that violated their gender norms (Silverblatt 1987). For example, they commented on the enlarged earlobes and earplugs worn by Inka male nobility, and called the men '*orejones*' (S. big ears). Cieza de León, mentioned above, was offended in the 1540s by the practices he observed among the Cañaris of southern Ecuador: 'It is the women who till and plant the fields and harvest the crops, while their husbands for the most part stay indoors spinning and weaving and preparing their arms and clothing and caring for their faces, and other feminine occupations' (1959: 71–2).

In short, I see the Spanish conquest as a turning point in bead use as highland indígenas, who were more exposed to the presence of Europeans of both genders than were rainforest dwellers, adopted European attitudes toward the appropriate gendered use of jewellery. While I have no evidence that the Spanish outlawed the male use of beads, we know that at various times in the colonial era, especially after the great uprisings of 1780–82 that the Spanish prohibited the use of certain indigenous garments including the Inca headdress, tunic, breechcloth and cloak (Adelson and Tracht 1983: 56–7). We also know from Guaman Poma's drawings from the early seventeenth century that indigenous males were much quicker to adopt European-style dress than were indigenous females (1980 [1583–1615]).

To return to doña Lucia, it is difficult to determine all the possible materials and origins of her beads. The red and purple 'coral', for example, could have been Spondylus. Doña Lucia's red beads also could have been imported Mediterranean coral, *cornaline d'Aleppo* or clay, although the latter is the least likely material given her high status. There is yet another possibility. Salomon (1986: 91–2) notes that colonial sources are unanimous in insisting that certain red or white beads called *carato*, mentioned above, which were traded throughout Amazonia and the northern Ecuadorian sierra, were made of bone. The *carato* were highly valued and that they should be of bone is puzzling since it would seem they would be easy to counterfeit, unless they were so distinct that this was impossible.

Doña Lucia's blue beads may have been lapis lazuli, imported from Chile or the beautiful blue or turquoise Nueva Cádiz beads, which arrived in Peru and Ecuador (Liu & Harris 1982: 1) immediately after the conquest.

> Of particular interest is the Nueva Cádiz bead, named for an archaeological site on an island off the coast of Venezuela, occupied by the Spanish from 1498 to 1545 . . . Their distribution was primarily limited to the Spanish New World, particularly Peru, between the late 1400s and 1560 . . . Nueva Cádiz beads disappeared after 1560, perhaps as a result of the Spaniards' newly achieved control of trade and goods production in the New World. The beads recovered from the Nueva Cádiz site, for example, were undoubtedly part of the pearl trade centered in Cabagua and Margarita Island. When the pearl beds were depleted, these expensive beads were replaced by cheaper, less complex styles (Dubin 1987: 258).

Nueva Cádiz beads have been discovered in burials in Peru and possibly looted from burials in Ecuador. I bought a string of them in the Otavalo market in 1985 because they were unusual and pretty, and was completely unaware of their identification and antiquity.

The white beads could have been clay, like those excavated by García and Pérez, bone or shell. Doña Lucia's pearls could have come from the Nueva Cádiz site, or they may have been local. Two Spanish travellers to Ecuador in the 1730s and 1740s, Jorge Juan and Antonio de Ulloa, wrote that, 'We have already seen that the beaches of Panamá and Manta have an inestimable treasure in the pearls which they nurture in the waves' (Juan & Ulloa 1826: 585, my translation).

In Peru, Spondylus shells are depicted on Chavín-style pottery dating between 900 and 200 BC (Burger 1992: Fig. 5). Spondylus shells and *mullu* have been found in many pre-Hispanic coastal burials, including dozens of complete shells in the tombs of the Moche lords recently excavated at Sipán, near Lambayeque. Spondylus shells and *mullu* were important ritual offerings made by highland indígenas to their holy places well into the colonial era. Sea shells of various kinds, because of their connection with water, are still used as fertility offerings in the highlands of Peru and Bolivia and continue to turn up in unexpected places. In the Chinchero, Peru, market in 1974 I bought a necklace or rosary of old trade beads with a small sea shell, a crucifix and other amulets attached, evidence of the continuing importance of shells.

High-altitude archaeologist Johan Reinhard excavated two little pre-Hispanic shell figurines at 19,855 feet in elevation on the summit of Mt Copiapó in central Chile. At least one of the offerings, a male icon, was carved from Spondylus (Reinhard 1992: 90). Among the offerings accompanying the 'ice maidens', young women sacrificed in Inka times at 19,200 to 20,700 feet in elevation on Mt Ampato in south central Peru, and discovered by Reinhard and Miguel Zárate in 1995, were three small figurines about 6 inches high made of gold, silver and Spondylus. At least one female statue had Spondylus bead pendants hanging from the ties of her miniature belt (Reinhard 1996: 77). The young women themselves were not wearing bead bracelets, necklaces or earrings, nor are the Inka women in Guaman Poma's drawings portrayed wearing beads. Bead jewellery has never been a part of highland indigenous women's dress in the southern Andes the way it has been in Ecuador.

Father Arriaga, in his campaign to extirpate idolatry in the Archbishopric of Lima beginning in 1610, forbade the ownership of Spondylus *mullu*: 'From now on no Indian, male or female, can have *mullu* . . . and anyone who breaks this rule will be given one hundred lashes and have his [or her] hair cut and proceedings will be initiated against him for lapsing into idolatry' (Arriaga [1621] 1920: 204, my translation). Judging from the seventeenth- and eighteenth-century evidence mentioned above, plus descriptions and paintings from the nineteenth century, such as Juan Agustín Guerrero's '*yndia de la capital*' (S. Indian of the capital), '*yndia que vende fruta en la Plaza Mayor*' (S. Indian who sells fruit in the Main Plaza), '*traje indiano de novio*' (S. Indian wedding dress) from around 1852 (Hallo 1981: 48, 58, 109), and an anonymous French print of an '*indienne de Quito*' (Indian of Quito) from the eighteenth or nineteenth century, no one in Ecuador ever paid much attention to Father Arriaga. All the women in the paintings mentioned above are wearing red beads. These beads were probably coral or glass rather than Spondylus, but they were worn because of their resemblance to the historically prized Spondylus *chaquira*.

Venetian, Bohemian and German beads on trade bead sample cards acquired by the British Museum in 1865 (Dubin 1987: 108–9) match those found in many old Ecuadorian necklaces, including necklaces from the Otavalo area and from Salasaca. Many of these beads were produced over a span of 400 years, making it impossible to date their arrival in Ecuador. Venice alone produced 2,280,000 pounds of glass beads in 1764 (Dubin 1987: 335), and some of those pounds ended up in Ecuador. From what we know of the African bead trade (Ibid.: 100), however, most of the antique Ecuadorian beads are probably from the nineteenth century. Black wound glass beads with white or polychrome dots are known as Alta Verapaz beads among collectors, and are still found on Ecuadorian necklaces.

In 1863, Friedrich Hassaurek, who was Abraham Lincoln's ambassador to Ecuador, visited Otavalo and described the Indian women's jewellery: 'The women . . . are very fond of bracelets and collars of red beads, to some which numbers of reals [coins] or half reals were suspended' (Hassaurek [1867] 1967: 155). As Joaquin Pinto's painting of a '*pastora* (S. shepherdess) *de Atuntaqui*' (c. 1900–1905) illustrates, red necklaces were worn in the Otavalo valley at the turn of the century (León Mera 1983: 107). Other Pinto portraits (Ibid.: 211, 243) show women in Quito with red bead loop earrings about three or four inches long and necklaces made of many strands of red beads, indicating that this style was common throughout the northern part of the country, and undoubtedly elsewhere. In none of the nineteenth-century paintings (or descriptions) do men wear beads.

Contemporary Bead Use in the Highlands

Today in Otavalo and Zuleta in Imbabura province and around Cayambe in Pichincha province females wear red or coral-coloured wristwraps and red, coral-coloured or gold glass necklaces composed of many strands of beads, sometimes with small, brass beads made in Cotacachi mixed in with the red or coral. Red necklaces are still worn around Lago San Pablo near Otavalo, however, and red, real coral or coral-coloured wristwraps are worn in all communities (Figure 7.3). Real coral beads are the most expensive and can cost up to US$100 for each wrist. Fine corals beads are now considered heirlooms and passed along from mother to daughter. Andean indígenas do not give dowries when young women marry; nor do the beads represent personal or family savings as does gold jewellery in India. There is prestige attached to wearing fine beads, however, especially to real coral.

Antique red and coral-coloured beads are still sold in the Otavalo market along with newer beads of all sizes and colours. Coral, *cornaline d'Aleppo* and other coral-coloured or red trade beads appear to have been valued in Ecuador because they resembled Spondylus and *carato*. In the past twenty years Spondylus, real coral, veintimilla (also known as *cornaline d'Aleppo* or white hearts), glass fake coral from India, and red and coral-coloured glass and plastic beads have been available for purchase in many Ecuadorian markets.

Red (or coral-coloured) necklaces were worn in Otavalo up through the 1920s, when gilded glass Czechoslovakian Christmas tree ornaments were introduced. More recently some gilded glass beads have also been imported from Japan. Beads of all kinds are sold at several kiosks in the Otavalo market, usually by the strand. It is up to the buyer to decide how many strands she needs to make a necklace of the desired size. She usually goes to another kiosk where notions are sold, buys a length of string or twine, preferably synthetic because these fibres are stronger than cotton, and strings the beads at home, holding them up to her neck to see how they hang. Each strand is strung on a separate string and is a little longer than the preceding one, with four or five extra inches left at each end for ties. The strings of all the strands are then braided together into one thick tie, and the necklace is ready for use.

Bead fashions are not static, and frequently there are generational differences. Up through the 1970s, masses of round, grape-sized, gilded glass beads were

Figure 7.3 Marta Conterón of Ilumán (near Otavalo), Imbabura province, with her son in the Otavalo market. She is wearing the newer style gilded glass bead necklace. (Photo: Lynn A. Meisch.)

popular in the Otavalo region. Then younger women and girls began buying and wearing smaller, gilded glass beads about the size and shape of a grain of rice. Not only are the beads themselves smaller, but the younger women wear fewer strands. These small, gilded glass beads have become popular with other ethnic groups and I have seen young women from Salasaca and various parts of Chimborazo province wearing these necklaces (Figure 7.1). The gilded glass beads are expensive; enough beads for the newer style necklaces (such as the one in Figure 7.3) cost at least US$70.

In Latacunga, Cotopaxi province and in Quizapincha, Tungurahua province, women wear necklaces in which large, round or oblong red beads predominate, but with other colours and shapes thrown in. In Chibuelo San Luis, west of Ambato, women wear red or coral-coloured necklaces and earrings with a few beads of other colours added to the strands. Chibuleo women especially prize real coral, and many of them wear extremely long, looped earrings made of coral beads.

This brings me to a feature of contemporary Ecuadorian bead use which is a survival of practices that were much more widespread in the past. This is the use of extremely long earrings (S. *orejeras*), up to 3 feet long in some instances. Formerly they were worn in Chimborazo, Tungurahua, and Imbabura provinces and possibly in other regions. A photo from Collier and Buitrón's *The Awakening Valley*, taken in 1946 shows an Otavaleña woman wearing these long earrings with a little hand at the end of the loop. She is also wearing a bead and coin rosary with a crucifix at the end. Carlos Conterón of Ilumán (near Otavalo) told me that through the 1950s for fiestas his grandmother wore *orejeras* that came down to mid-thigh. His wife Rosa Elena de la Torre put on for me the hat, necklace, and earrings she wore at their wedding in the early 1960s. These items, especially the earrings, are archaic today in Otavalo and I have never seen them worn together except this once by Rosa Elena.

Today *orejeras* from a foot to 3 feet long are worn daily by women in the Chibuelo communities west of Ambato in Tungurahua province. They make a resounding slap-slap when a woman walks, and if they get in her way she tucks them into the waist of her anaku. Chibuleo earrings also have an ornament at the end, either a coin or a decoration called a *jiga* (S. jig) made from a coin, and they frequently contain Cotacachi brass beads that resemble the pre-Hispanic gold beads from La Tolita. While I have no idea of the antiquity of this style in Chibuelo, long earrings are known in pre-Hispanic art styles from the coast. Many of these earrings were metal or shell edged with beads and this may be the origin of the long, bead loop earrings.

In Salasaca, east of Ambato in Tungurahua province, women value Venetian glass millefiori beads, which have multiple colours in one bead. Many of these Venetian glass beads date from the nineteenth century and were also popular in the African bead trade. The Salasacas, who have names for all the beads, give the glass beads with white or multicoloured dots the poetic name, *nina kuru* (Q. firefly). The beads with a black background and rather messy, mostly white dotted surface, are called *pisku kicha*, which translates, appropriately if less poetically, as chicken manure, and the *veintimilla* are called *china watchka*, meaning girl's beads or necklace (Laura Miller, personal communication).

India now supplies glass beads to Ecuador, including the beads called *pisku kicha* in Salasaca, as well as light green beads mottled with other colours, which are used in Chimborazo and elsewhere in Tungurahua. Salasacas buy Venetian glass beads from white-mestizo jewellers in Ambato; these are expensive (US$2 to $4 per bead) and highly prized. Because of their cost a few Venetian glass beads are usually strung along with a number of beads of different colours and sizes (including red and coral-coloured beads) to make one large necklace (Figure 7.4). In 1992, people in Salasaca requested that travellers bring them multi-coloured Fimo beads from the United States.

Chimborazo province has the greatest variety of bead necklaces, earrings and wristwraps. In San Juan and Nitiluisa, west of Riobamba, necklace styles include multiple strands of Otavalo-style small, gilded glass beads; strands of coral-coloured beads; yellow and blue strands worn together; or strands of white, mixed with strands combining yellow, white and green beads (Figure 7.5).

In Cacha Obraje, just outside Riobamba, women use coral-coloured, transparent, white, red, blue, black, yellow, green – virtually every colour bead, both in strands of a single colour and in strands of mixed colours. In Galti and Zulac farther south toward Caòar province women wear white beads mixed with other colours or many strands of solid white. In other communities around Guamote, women also mix strands of beads of one colour into a multi-coloured necklace (Figure 7.6). In the central sierra, many of the necklaces have one anomalous bead, a different colour or oddly shaped, perhaps to protect against the evil eye.

In the Licto area, southeast of Riobamba, women and girls wear necklaces and sometimes wristwraps. The classic Licto necklace consists of a number of strands of large (pea- to marble-sized) red or coral-coloured beads. One woman, who was wearing the old-style costume and hat, had a large silver or nickel crucifix attached to her red beads where they hung down over her chest. We also saw necklaces of other coloured beads: bright blue; or mainly red beads with a few blue and green ones mixed in. One woman wore wristwraps composed of many different, solid-coloured seed beads. Earrings ranged from inexpensive costume jewellery pieces inset with bits of coloured glass or fake pearls to fine, old silver earrings with coins and coloured glass, to foot-long loops of red glass beads. These latter were worn by older women and represent the older style.

Throughout Chimborazo province some women wear 4 to 7 inch-long multi-coloured seed bead earrings and wristwraps, some with many different coloured beads in a strand, others of only one colour. As I mentioned above, the red bead

Figure 7.4 Melchora Caiza of Salasaca, Tungurahua province. Her necklace includes red and coral-coloured beads, Venetian millefiori, and old trade beads. (Photo: Lynn A. Meisch.)

Figure 7.5 A woman in Nitiluisa, Chimborazo province wearing masses of white glass beads over strands of red beads. (Photo: Lynn A. Meisch.)

Figure 7.6 A woman in the Guamote market, Chimborazo province, wearing a bead necklace typical of this area. (Photo: Lynn A. Meisch.)

bracelets for babies also have a small charm for protection. Although the concept of the evil eye is middle Eastern and European, I think it is significant that in Ecuador these bracelets are always red or coral, which is the most common and preferred colour for beads.

Another archaic item is the coin bead necklace, which is called a rosary if it has a crucifix attached. The discussion of the coin bead necklaces worn by the Canelos Quichua brides in the 1920s and 1930s (below) suggests that their use was once widespread among rainforest Quichua women. Rosaries are European Roman Catholic introductions. In such sierra communities as Saraguro and Otavalo, rosaries were worn daily by women up through the 1940s or 50s, but today are used only on special occasions. In Saraguro the male and female sponsors of certain fiestas wear rosaries, and in the Otavalo area the groom wears a rosary at his wedding. In Chimborazo province women wore rosaries as necklaces through the 1970s and could be seen wearing them in the Riobamba market at that time. Now, however, rosaries are basically out of fashion except for special occasions, and are sold as antiques.

What remained a mystery until the summer of 1988 was the enormous number of coin and bead necklaces (with or without crucifixes) which are sold in antique stores and in markets throughout Ecuador, especially in Otavalo and Riobamba. The ones from Otavalo had red beads, like the necklaces described by Hassaurek in 1863, while the ones from Riobamba are a mixed lot. Many of these necklaces have dirty ties and have obviously been used, but nowhere in Ecuador did I ever see one actually being worn.

Chimborazo province has been a centre for Evangelical Protestant missionizing for several decades. Two Evangelical Christian indígenas in El Troje, Chimborazo, explained that rosaries and coin and bead necklaces were worn throughout the province until around 1979. But Evangelical missionaries forbade the wearing of rosaries because of their association with Catholicism and they also prohibited the use of coin and bead necklaces because they looked too much like rosaries. Thousands of indígena women converts to Evangelical Christianity stopped using these necklaces and many sold them. Others kept them '*guardado*' (S. guarded, put away) as keepsakes but do not wear them. Instead they wear necklaces with beads, but no coins.

This was a stunning and dramatic change, due entirely to ideology (or theology), and it took place within a very short period of time. I have found no coin with a date more recent than 1977 on any necklace I have examined, although the earliest coin is dated 1866. During two summers of research in Chimborazo province I finally spotted two women wearing coin and bead necklaces in the Guamote market, obviously from communities which are still Catholic. But while coins have disappeared from the necks of Chimborazo women, beads certainly have not, including red and coral-coloured ones. In several places in Chimborazo province including San Juan, we saw statues of the Virgin Mary that were dressed in the local traditional dress, complete with masses of bead necklaces, just like the local women.

In Cañar province, Cañari women and girls wear many strands of beads as necklaces which are worn as chokers, rather than as long strands. The beads range from antique European glass trade beads to more modern glass and plastic ones. No single colour or style predominates and usually there are several colours combined in a strand (Figure 7.7). Some strands are also strung with old coins. In the 1990s some Cañari women began wearing zig-zag necklaces from Saraguro (discussed below).

In Saraguro, Loja province, women and girls also wear bead necklaces. There are three basic kinds which are often worn together. One kind consists of several strands of glass beads. Until the 1950s females wore strands of finely carved wooden beads or beads made from *sacha achira* seeds (wild *achira*, Canna indica), and from a plant called San Pedro, which grow in the Amazon lowlands. Imported glass beads of various colours and sizes have now replaced seeds and wooden beads, The second kind of necklace, called *wallka tejido* (S. woven necklace), is made from tiny, glass seed beads (Q. *mullu*) imported from Czechoslovakia, the United States, and possibly elsewhere. The beads are joined in zig-zag rows (Q. *kingus*), and the number of rows and colour combinations indicate the wearer's community. The largest necklaces are worn by women from Gurudel and sometimes by women from Tuncarta. Smaller necklaces with only eleven rows of zig-zags with just two different colours are typical of Las Lagunas (Figure 7.8). One family I know in Tuncarta specializes in making necklaces to sell to other indígenas (Figure 7.9). They preferred to make them with monofilament nylon because of its strength and used fishing line if nothing else was available.

The third style appeared around 1990 and is called *colgante* (S. hanging, dangling). It is made from tiny seed beads in a looped chain which fastens around the throat. Hanging down in front from the looped chain are one to three small bead triangles from which are suspended bead fringes about two or three inches long, each one ending in a fake pearl. The *wallka colgante* can be worn over or under the necklace with zig-zag rows.

Rosaries have virtually disappeared, but several generations ago they were worn daily by indígena women in Saraguro, as well as by the sponsors of certain fiestas, and by brides on their way to church to be married. The rosary was made of wooden or glass beads, coins (representing the ten stations of the cross) and a silver crucifix. Originally the coins were silver Peruvian *soles* (old coins that were 900 parts silver), but in later years they were replaced by Ecuadorian coins. The only Saraguro rosary I have ever seen was from the community of San Lucas and has red and blue wooden beads (with the paint almost gone), 2½ and 5 cent coins from 1928, and one old silver coin with all its markings worn away.

Figure 7.7 Presentación Duy Tenesaca of Manzanapata, Cañar, province. (Photo: Lynn A. Meisch.)

Figure 7.8 Maria Macas of Las Lagunas, Saraguro, Loja province, and her son. (Photo: Lynn A. Meisch.)

Figure 7.9 Ashuca Losano of Tuncarta, Saraguro, making a wide zig-zag necklace, which she sold to other indígenas. (Photo: Lynn A. Meisch.)

Even in areas of the highlands where the women's dress is becoming increasingly Europeanized, as in Cotopaxi province, women still wear beads. They are a symbol of ethnicity to the extent that their inclusion on political murals in the town of Latacunga means the woman is an indígena and is, of course, an appeal to the indigenous vote. While highland Ecuadorian women use different colours, sizes, and styles of beads, there is still a marked preference for red or coral-coloured beads.

The Oriente

Today some indígenas in the Oriente wear beads, including males and females among the Cofán. The Cofán and the Siona-Secoya, all extremely small groups in the northern Oriente, are the only ethnic groups where males still wear beads. Beads worn by the Cofán as necklaces include small glass beads, usually strung in multiple, solid colour strands of blue, red and green, multiple strands of small, round, gilded glass beads like those used in Otavalo, and necklaces made from animal teeth and seeds. Shuar women, in the southern *Oriente* wear necklaces consisting of single coloured strands of small beads, with strands of white, red, dark blue, light blue and red in the same necklace.

Judging from old photographs and the commentary on them by rainforest Quichua (Chiriboga & Cruz 1992), bead use in the Oriente has declined since the rubber boom in the Amazon Basin between 1880 and 1914. In the black-and-white photographs mentioned above several Shuar and Achuar men and women (plates 7, 14, 53) are wearing choker necklaces of small, round, white, flat objects, that look like flattened cowry shells, sewn to a backing. These beads are too irregular to be white buttons; perhaps they are the bone *carato* beads mentioned in colonial times.

In these old photographs males of different ethnic groups, Achuar, Canelos Quichua, Chibasha Quichua, and Shuar (Chiriboga & Cruz 1992: plates 3, 5, 18, 31) are wearing long, multiple strands of beads crossed across their chests like bandoleers or over one shoulder and under the opposite arm in addition to multiple strands of small glass beads worn as chokers. As I argued above, it seems that the more contact Ecuadorian ethnic groups had with Europeans, the more likely they were to adopt European gender norms with respect to jewellery (and dress in general). In the Oriente since the early part of this century, males have gradually abandoned beads and adopted Euro-American styles of dress in general including shirts and pants instead of nudity, a lower body wrap, or a short tunic. The exceptions include the Huaorani and groups in the northern Oriente mentioned above, and even these communities are changing their dress. In November 1993, when Ecuadorian colonists in the Amazon basin and local indígenas filed a class action lawsuit in New York against Texaco for polluting in the Oriente, a Cofán indígena travelled to New York for the filing wearing traditional costume: a tunic, a bandanna around the neck, beads and a feathered headdress. He also wore shoes and white trousers, which are non-traditional, but made sense in terms of the weather in New York and American expectations of male dress, because the tunic worn without trousers would have looked too much like a dress and probably exposed him to ridicule. This photo appeared in colour on the front page of Quito's daily newspaper *El Comercio* (Friday, 5 November 1993), and in the American media as well. My point is that the Cofán was well aware of Euro-American norms with respect to the use of what we consider feminine dress and jewellery, but mixed his apparel to express his Amazonian origins without appearing too strange.

Because the photos of Amazon indígenas in Chiriboga & Cruz were reproduced from old and sometimes damaged plates or negatives and because they are black-and-white, it is difficult to determine what the above necklaces are made of. One bandoleer style necklace appears to be made from the iridescent green body of a beetle (Ibid.: plates 3, 18). The Cofán use these beetles to decorate headbands and to string on necklaces made for sale to tourists. Another bandoleer is obviously made of local seeds, including large olive-sized brown seeds, which are strung with the lower end cut off so they look like tiny bells (Ibid.: plate 5).

I have seen similar necklaces worn today by the Cofán, and photographs of these necklaces worn by the Secoya (Piaguaje 1990: various unnumbered plates between pp. 50–3). The three Chibasha Quichua men (Chiriboga & Cruz 1992: plate 18) are wearing masses of necklaces ranging in length from chokers to huge bunches of glass beads that hang to their waist or are worn as bandoleers, as well as necklaces of varying lengths made from animal teeth. Some males, for example a Shuar chief (Ibid.: plate 15) are pictured wearing only choker necklaces, in this instance made from what appear to be Otavalo-style round, gilded glass beads. Other Shuar and Achuar males were photographed wearing chokers consisting of one or more strands of opaque white or dark glass beads (Ibid.: plates 3, 31, 49, 50, 52, 53, 55, 68). A Napo Quichua man (Ibid.: plate 19) is shown wearing what looks like a rosary around his neck, with a small crucifix at the end. It is evident the glass beads were trade items in the Oriente as well as the *sierra* (S. highlands).

Women of different Oriente ethnic groups including the Shuar, Napo Quichua, Achuar, and Canelos Quichua also wore opaque glass bead necklaces, wristwraps, or both (Ibid.: plates 4, 6, 9, 17, 19, 27, 33, 37, 39). The necklaces consisted of multiple strands of opaque glass beads, frequently white, but also of darker colours, sometimes with strands of light and dark beads worn at the same time. The most stunning photos of bead use are those showing three young Canelos Quichua brides taken around 1930 and 1920 (Ibid.: plates 33 and 39). The young women are wearing masses of beads from their chins to their breasts. They include white and dark opaque glass beads, what look like gilded glass Otavalo-style beads and, hanging lowest, one strand of glass beads and coins. The bride in plate 39 must be wearing pounds of beads, white at her neck, dark in the middle, and light again over her chest.

The commentary by Napo Quichua indígenas on some of the above photographs, recorded in 1989 and translated from Quichua by Blanca Muratorio and Dolores Intriago (in Chiriboga & Cruz 1992) is especially useful for our understanding of the use of these beads, including gender differences.[3] The Napo Quichua call the bead wristwrap '*maquihuatana muyu*' (Q. wristwrap beads) (JAC: 198). One woman thought one man (Chiriboga & Cruz 1992: plate 19) was wearing a rosary (JAC: 204), but another said, 'No, that is called *canelos muyu* [Q. Canelos beads]; it is a necklace that they wore as decoration during celebration periods. They also wore necklaces made from animal teeth or toucan feathers' (FAC: 205). This same woman went on to say that, 'When we were girls we wore *maquicutun* [Q. blouse], *huallcamuyu* (Q. bead necklaces) and *maquihuatana muyu* (Q. wristwrap beads). It is only now that we dress differently' (Ibid.).

The Napo Quichua women and man also commented on the beads worn by a Canelos Quichua bride, whom they thought looked like an indígenas from the highlands. One woman observed that 'she has some *huallcamuyu* [Q. necklace beads] that must have belonged to her mother' (JAC: 213). All the women admired the necklaces, then one said:

> I used to have lots of beads like that but I lost them. They were white, green and red. All the women used to wear those beads, young and old. I also wore them. We had to wear them all the time, only taking them off to bathe. To sleep we only took off the longest ones. The necklace had to be very long, and it was also pretty when we put coins on them. Sometimes the cord would rot, the beads would fall off and we would have to remake the necklaces. It used to be a lot of work to wear those things (FAC: 213).

She also said that, 'It was pretty to wear the *pacha* [Q. for cloth, a garment that wrapped around the body and was tied over one or both shoulders] and the *huallcamuyu*. Besides the coins, we also used to put bird feathers, especially from toucans, and a kind of bead that was called *curimuyu* (Q. golden bead). That used to cost half a *centavo*' (Ibid.). The male in the group said that, 'Without having worn them I know what *curimuyu* are. Only women used to wear them . . . ' (AAC: 213). I suspect that these gold beads are the gilded glass beads that are now considered typical of Otavalo, and which also appeared there around 1920 (Meisch 1987: 54). Judging from the photos and the comments on them, bead use in the Oriente has declined considerably, especially among males, but not vanished. Note that even when both males and females in the Oriente wore beads, the use of certain styles was gender specific.

Summary

Beads continue to be an important part of traditional dress for female indígenas, especially in the *sierra*, and the general preference for red or coral-coloured beads is part of a centuries-old tradition based on the pre-Hispanic use of Spondylus jewellery. Today the use of certain kinds and colours of bead jewellery indicates indigenous ethnicity in general, but also the wearer's community or subgroup, religion, wealth, and most of all, gender. Beads are still such an essential part of indigenous female dress in the Ecuadorian *sierra* that bead merchants and vendors will have customers for years to come.

Notes

I began learning about and buying Ecuadorian bead jewellery during my first trip to the country in 1973. I have continued to pursue this interest on my own and during the course of field research on various topics funded by Fulbright fellowships, the Institute for Intercultural Studies, the Wenner-Gren Foundation, the National Science Foundation, the Stanford Center for Latin American Studies and the Stanford Institute for International Studies. Research on bead use in the highlands during the summer of 1988 was supported by Earthwatch and a grant from the Bead Society of Los Angeles. I am grateful to all these institutions and to the many people in Ecuador who taught me about beads and their importance.

1. Spanish words or terms are indicated by S.; Quichua (an indigenous language) words are indicated by Q.
2. Beads are called (S.) *cuentas* and (Q.) *mullu* or *muyu*, the latter glossed as a small, round thing. Beads are also called (Q.) *chaquira*, which originally referred to a particular kind of bead, but later came to mean beads in general. Beads are worn primarily by females in the Andean highlands in the form of a necklace composed of many strands of beads (S. *collar*, Q. *wallka, watchka* or *washka*, and as wristwraps (S. *pulsera*, Q, *makiwatana*), earrings (S. *sarcillus, aretes* or *orejeras* and as rosaries (S. *rosarios*). Quichua was not a written language until the arrival of the Spanish, and there are still disagreements about orthography. I give the original spelling in all quotations.
3. The Napo Quichua commentators include Juanita Andi C., Francisca Andi C., Helena Rebeca Cerda A., and Alonso Andi T. To avoid long and complicated citations, I will refer to the commentators by their initials and the page number of their comments in the English translation at the end of Chiriboga & Cruz 1992.

References

Adelson, L. & Tracht, A. (1983), *Aymara Weavings: Ceremonial Textiles of Colonial and 19th Century Bolivia*, Washington, D.C: Smithsonian Institution.

Alva, W. & Donnan, C. B. (1994), *Royal Tombs of Sipán*, Los Angeles: Fowler Museum of Cultural History, UCLA.

Arriaga, Pablo Jose de (1968 [1621]) *La extirpacion de la idolatria en el Peru, en Cronicas peruanas de interes indigena*, Madrid: Biblioteca de Autores Espanoles.

Barnes, R. & Eicher, J. B. (eds) (1992), *Dress and Gender: Making and Meaning in Cultural Contexts*, Providence and Oxford: Berg Publishers.

Bruhns, K. O. (1989), 'Intercambio entre la costa y la sierra en el formativo tardio: nuevas evidencias del Azuay', in J. F. Bouchard & M. Guinea (eds), *Proceedings of the 46 International Congress of Americanists*, BAR International Series 503, 57–74.

Burger, R. (1992), 'The Sacred Center of Chavín de Huántar', in Richard F. Townsend (ed.), *The Ancient Americas: Art from Sacred Landscapes*, Chicago: The Art Institute of Chicago, 265–8.

Caillavet, C. (1982), 'Caciques de Otavalo en el Siglo XVI: Don Alonso Maldonado y su esposa', *Miscelánea Antropológica Ecuatoriana*, no. 2, 38–55, Quito: Museos del Banco Central del Ecuador.

Chiriboga, L. & Cruz, S. (1992), *Retrato de la Amazonía, Ecuador: 1880–1945*, Bilingual Spanish-English edition. English translation by B. Muratorio and D. Intriago from commentaries on the photographs in Quichua. Quito: Ediciones Libri Mundi-Enrique Grosse-Luemern.

Cieza de León, P. de (1959 [1553]), *The Incas of Pedro de Cieza de León*. V. W. von Hagen (ed.), trans. H. de Onis, Norman: University of Oklahoma Press.

—— (1984 [1553]), *Crónica del Peru*, 3 vols. Lima: Pontifica Universidad Católica del Peru.

Collier, Jr., J. & Buitrón, A. (1944), *The Awakening Valley*, Chicago: University of Chicago Press.

Crespo Toral, H. & Holm, O. (1977), *Arte Precolombino de Ecuador*, Barcelona and Quito: Salvat Editores.

Deagan, K. (1987), *Artifacts of the Spanish Colonies of Florida and the Caribbean 1500–1800*, vol. 1: *Ceramics, Glassware and Beads*, Washington, D.C.: Smithsonian Institution Press.

Doyon-Bernard, S. J. (n.d. [1992]), 'La Florida's Mortuary Textiles: The Oldest Extant Textiles from Ecuador', Ms.

Dubin, L. S. (1987), *The History of Beads from 30,000 B.C. to the Present*, New York: Harry N. Abrams, Inc.

Eicher, J. B. (1995), *Dress and Ethnicity*, Oxford and Washington, D.C.: Berg Publishers.

García Galván, J. R. & Barriuso Pérez, M.A. (1986), 'Estudio de la chaquiras de Atacames (Ecuador)', *Miscelánea Antropológica Ecuatoriana*, no. 6, 61–80. Quito: Museos del Banco Central del Ecuador.

Guaman Poma de Ayala, F. (1980 [1583–1615]), *El Primer corónica y buen gobierno*, 3 vols, J. Murra & R. Adorno (eds), trans. J. L. Urioste, Mexico, D.F.: Siglo Veintiuno.

Hallo, W. (1981), *Imágenes del Ecuador del siglo XIX: Juan Agustín Guerrero*, Quito: Ediciones del Sol.

Hassaurek, F. (1967 [1867]), *Four Years Among the Ecuadorians*, C. H. Gardiner (ed.), Carbondale: Southern Illinois University Press.

Juan, J. & de Ulloa, A. (1826), *Noticias Secretas de America*, 2 vols, Facsimile of the David Barry edition originally published in London, Quito: Libri Mundi.

Kessler, E. & S. (1986), 'Ecuadorian Beads: Ancient to Modern', *Ornament*, vol. 10, no. 2, Winter, 48–52.

León Mera, J. (1983), *Cantares del Pueblo Ecuatoriano* [1892], Illustraciones de Joaquín Pinto, Quito: Museo del Banco Central del Ecuador.

Liu, R. K. (1978), 'Spindle Whorls: Part I Some Comments and Speculations', *The Bead Journal*, vol. 3, 87–103.

—— & Harris, E. (1982), *Nueva Cadiz and Associated Beads: History and Description*, Lancaster, PA: G. B. Fenstermaker.

Marcos, J. C. & Norton, P. (1981) *Interpretación Sobre la Arqueología de la Isla de la Plata. Miscelánea Antropológica Ecuatoriana*, no. 1, 136–54, Quito: Museos del Banco Central del Ecuador.

Meggers, B. J. (1966), *Ecuador*, New York: Praeger.

——, Evans. C. & Estrada, E. (1965), *Early Formative Period of Coastal Ecuador: The Valdovia and Machalilla Phases*, Washington, D.C.: Smithsonian Institution.

Meisch, L. A. (1987), *Otavalo: Weaving, Costume and the Market*, Quito: Ediciones Libri Mundi.

—— & Rowe, A. P. (in press [1997]), 'Introduction to Indigenous Ecuadorian Costume', in A. P. Rowe (ed.), *Costume and Identity of Highland Ecuador*, Seattle: University of Washington Press, and Washington, D.C.: The Textile Museum.

Murra, J. V. (1975), *El tráfico de mullu en la costa del Pacífico. Formaciones económicas y políticas del mundo andino*, Lima: Instituto de Estudios Peruanos.

Norton, P. (1986), 'El señorio de Salangone y la liga de mercaderes: El cartel spondylus-balsa', *Miscelánea Antropológica Ecuatoriana*, no. 6, 131–43, Quito: Museos del Banco Central del Ecuador.

Orchard, W. C. (1929), *Beads and Beadwork of the American Indians. Contributions from the Museum of the American Indian Heye Foundation*, vol. XI, New York: Museum of the American Indian Heye Foundation.

Piaguaje, C. (1990), *Ecorsa. Autobiografía de un Secoya. Shushufindi*, Rio Aguarico: Ediciones CICAME.

Reinhard, J. (1992), 'Sacred Peaks of the Andes', *National Geographic*, vol. 181, no. 3, March, 84–111.

—— (1996), 'Peru's Ice Maidens: Unwrapping the Secrets', *National Geographic*, vol. 189, no. 6, June, 61–181.

Salomon, F. (1986), *Native Lords of Quito in the Age of the Incas: The Political Economy of North Andean Chiefdoms*, New York: Cambridge University Press.

Silverblatt, I. (1987), *Moon, Sun and Witches: Gender Ideologies and Class in Inca and Colonial Peru*, Princeton: Princeton University Press.

Valdéz, F. (1992), 'Symbols, Ideology, and the Expression of Power in La Tolita, Ecuador', in R. F. Townsend (ed.), *The Ancient Americas: Art from Sacred Landscapes*, Chicago: The Art Institute of Chicago, 229–44.

Wilbert, J. (1974), *The Thread of Life: Symbolism of Miniature Art from Equador*, Studies in Pre-Columbian Art and Archaeology, 12–14, 5–112, Washington D.C.: Dumbarton Oaks.

8

African American Jewellery Before the Civil War

Helen Bradley Foster

Evidence

African American men, women and children wore jewellery, including beads, during the period of enslavement.[1] An excellent source of evidence for this would be jewellery predating the Civil War and passed down within African American families, but the chance of finding heirlooms of this type still in the possession of descendants of enslaved people seems unlikely at this date. The major social disruptions that occurred after emancipation left most Blacks destitute, so that their material possessions ordinarily were limited to those needed for daily survival. The Great Migration from the rural countryside into urban areas, particularly from the south to the northeast, also meant the loss of small personal items. Nonetheless, three other areas of investigation for documenting jewellery, particularly beads, exist: portraits, archaeological finds and first-hand accounts.

Portraits of African American women painted before the Civil War often show them with jewellery. In 1844, for instance, Adolphe Rinck painted an unidentified 'free woman of colour' in New Orleans (Figure 8.1). Some scholars believe the sitter to be Marie Laveau, the most famous American priestess of voodoo (Campbell & Rice 1991: xi). The sitter's left ear shows in the portrait; a drop earring attached to it appears to be either a flat, oval gold disk or perhaps a topaz bead. A necklace of threaded, round beads encircles her neck just above the collarbone; twenty large beads, each interspersed with a smaller bead of the same type, are visible. The orange-red beads could be either coloured glass or amber. A massive, elaborate red-and-yellow *tignon* (headwrap) in a madras pattern is tied in two places on the right side of the sitter's head. A cluster of small blue beads loops around and hangs from the lower knot and this tiny item may be the most significant piece of jewellery worn by the sitter. Teresa Singleton notes: 'the predominance of blue beads in the antebellum South . . . often comprise as much as a third of all the beads found at slave sites' (1991: 164). She refers to William H. Adams' proposition that this may relate to 'the widespread belief within the Muslim world, including many

177

Figure 8.1 *Woman in Tignon*, Adolphe Rinck, 1844, New Orleans, oil on canvas. Collection of the University Art Museum, University of Southwestern Louisiana, Lafayette, Louisiana.

parts of Africa, that a single blue bead worn or sown on clothing protected the wearer against the "evil eye"'. The blue beads worn on the headwrap of the New Orleans 'free woman of colour' are, quite possibly, linked to an older African belief in the protective power of such beads.[2]

More common than painted portraits are photographs of enslaved women, usually those who worked as domestics within white households. In these photographs, the women appear in 'better' clothes and often wear jewellery. I cite just three examples. A hand-coloured ambrotype, ca. 1855–60, portrays a seated Black woman wearing earrings and a necklace that is identified as 'African trade beads' by Jackie Napoleon Wilson (Figure 8.2).[3] A Black woman and child stand at Drayton's Plantation, Edisto Island, South Carolina, in the detail of a stereograph taken in 1862. Two long strings of beads hang around the woman's neck, dropping over her chest.[4] Lucy Edwards, photographed ca. 1850 in Virginia, apparently cared

Figure 8.2 *Portrait of a Seated Black Woman* wearing 'trade beads', artist unknown, 1855–1860, ambrotype, hand-coloured, 6.9 × 5.6 cm.
Reproduced with permission of the J. Paul Getty Museum, Los Angeles, California.

for white children as she is identified as a 'nurse'. Edwards wears a fancy plaid dress with lace collar, drop earrings, a beaded bracelet on her right wrist and a ribbon around her neck which threads a large medallion-type object.[5]

The monotone, occasionally hand-tinted, medium of early photography makes it difficult to identify specific jewellery materials. Furthermore, the jewellery may have been merely a photographer's prop used by many sitters. While painted portraits offer colour images, this is not always enough to ascertain the material, let alone ownership. After all, the artist might have supplied the jewellery as a fanciful detail. Nonetheless, the photographs and painted portraits do prove that it was not unusual for Black women to wear jewellery at the time.

Archaeological investigations concentrating on known African American sites yield a second type of evidence. Excavations at slave quarters on plantations and at Black burial grounds have been the most productive thus far. The archaeological context in which any artefact is found offers the first clues; but, in order to find meaning in the materials, the archaeologist must then refer to other sources, such as oral and written testimonies and visual images.

Archaeologists also compare new finds with similar materials to establish time and place of origin. Frederick W. Lange and Jerome S. Handler outline the means by which the enslaved people acquired their objects and the places from which they came: 'There are three principal categories: (1) brought from Africa, (2) commercial European, or (3) handmade in the New World' (1985:22). Lange and Handler agree with the usual assumption that Africans brought few possessions with them to the Americas, but to prove that this sometimes did occur they mention 'the burial of carnelian beads from India [and] Indo-Pacific Ocean cowries . . . on Barbados' (ibid.).[6] Today, carnelian beads are still common in West Africa and many Africans continue to use cowrie shells to decorate household and spiritual objects and they continue to sew cowries onto clothing and to wear them as beads.

Singleton illustrates several other examples of African-type jewellery material in her article, 'The Archaeology of Slave Life'. These include a cowry from the slave quarter at Bennehan plantation in North Carolina (1991: 157) and rings made of horn and ebony, along with faceted blue glass beads at Potici plantation, Virginia (ibid., 158, 162).

Mark Leone excavated the domestic work area of enslaved people in an eighteenth-century town house in Annapolis, Maryland (Wilford, 1996). Items of jewellery were found that may have been worn for their protective powers: 'brass pins, buttons and beads, disks pierced with holes, a brass ring' (Figure 8.3). Although the objects found in the Annapolis house probably are not from Africa, scholars credit their symbolic uses with customs found in West African belief. Cheryl LaRoche assesses the retention of African customs in bead finds at the African Burial Ground in New York City (ca. 1712–95), such as the beads worn for protection by African infants and children and found with two child burials at

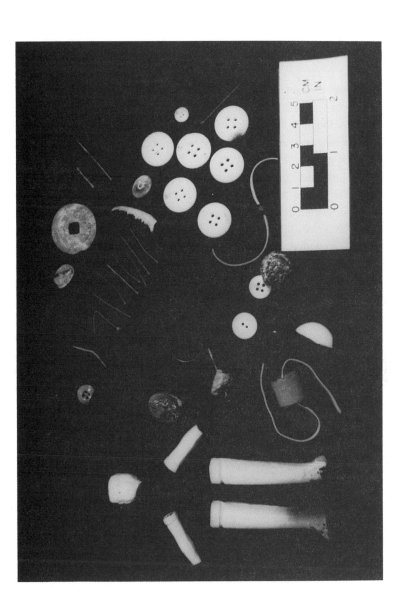

Figure 8.3 Jewellery-type objects recovered from the work area of enslaved people in a town house, Duke of Gloucester Street, Annapolis, Maryland. (Photo courtesy of Dr Mark Leone.)

the site (LaRoche 1994: 14) and the waistbeads worn by African females and found on the remains of an infant and an adult female at the cemetery (ibid., 13–14).

The small size of jewellery-type objects helps explain why they sometimes survived the passage from Africa to the Americas: they could be hidden on the person or could be considered by slave-traders as simply not of value. The total amount of beads uncovered at most sites, however, seems disproportionately small when compared to other forms of evidence for them. For example, only a single, blue glass bead was excavated at a Cumberland Island, Georgia, cabin inhabited by enslaved people for circa thirty-two years (Ascher & Fairbanks 1971: 8–9); while the artefacts found at the South Carolina Yaughan and Curriboo plantation sites yielded just twenty-four glass beads for an eighty-year occupation period (Wheaton & Garrow 1985: 252).

As elsewhere in American society at that time, burial places were strictly segregated by white peoples' concepts of 'race'. Because of this, cemeteries became one of the few places where Blacks could overtly decorate graves in a unique manner that retained the integrity of their homelands in West Africa.[7] From this, we might suppose that African Americans also continued to practise West African customs related to the body of the deceased. A number of societies, for instance, bury jewellery with the body; and there is evidence that beads have been important grave offerings in some West African societies. Of the artefacts associated with African American burials, however, beads are rare as a grave good.[8] For instance, there is no report of bead finds with the 140 human remains excavated at an African American cemetery in Philadelphia, in use from 1824 to 1842 (Parrington & Wideman 1986: 79–82). At the recently excavated 'Negroes Burial Ground' on lower Manhattan, in use from at least 1712 to 1790, only seven of the 400 uncovered graves held beads; that is, beads are associated with less than 2 per cent of the interments (LaRoche 1994: 16).[9]

There is, however, another profitable area for documenting the use of jewellery by the enslaved. This comes from the eye-witness testimony of African Americans themselves. In the 1930s, members of the Federal Writers' Program interviewed more than 2,000 formerly enslaved people about the conditions of racial slavery in the United States as they had experienced it.[10] Within these particular oral narratives, as well as in nineteenth-century travellers' accounts, people mention beads and other types of jewellery, hereby substantiating the material evidence found in archaeological contexts.

Functions

People have donned beads and other forms of jewellery almost universally since antiquity as an attribute of prestige and as a way to enhance physical appearance.

As well, people the world over and for millennia have worn certain beads and other types of amulets for bodily protection. Jewellery, therefore, possesses three main, often intertwined, functions. This was no less so for the West Africans brought in bondage to the Americas.

Markers of Prestige

Arab and European travellers give detailed accounts of the use West Africans made of clothing and jewellery as objects of prestige to mark status. Kings, chiefs, and other important male leaders owned and wore the most sumptuous items. They allowed people closely associated with them (wives, children and advisors) to wear the next finest dress and jewellery. From there, items of attire graduated downward in value relative to the individual's station in the social order.[11] A situation comparable to that in West African societies existed in the slave system of the American South where white people dressed better than did Blacks.

Clothing and other objects of dress also denoted status *within* American Black communities. Their understanding that bodily ornamentation marked one's status went back to Africa, but in the United States, whites determined what articles of prestige would be worn by whom. White social position, of course, was enhanced when house servants (those most often seen in public) appeared in better dress than did those working at agricultural tasks.[12] Allowing domestic servant women to wear jewellery for a photograph, along with finer clothing, also added to the slaveholder's own status. Some of these enslaved women, no doubt, did not own the jewellery they wore in photographs; rather, it most probably belonged to the white 'mistress' who loaned it to them for the occasion.

This supposition is not too far off the mark when we consider as one example the role white women played in attiring enslaved brides. From the testimony, we know that white women often supervised the brides' wedding gowns, either supplying fabric to the Black women to fashion bridal dresses or loaning them hand-me-downs. Matilda Pugh, enslaved in Alabama, reported: 'De dress I married in was one of her [mistress's] party dresses, hit was fine, made out ob white tarelton, wid a pink ribbon tied round my head . . .' (Rawick SS1, vol. 1: 109).[13]

For Beauty's Sake

As happens in many cultures, the wedding of an enslaved couple offers an instance wherein jewellery served to enhance the fashion statement of the wearer – in this case, the bride. The narratives of the formerly enslaved make clear that some African American brides actually owned the jewellery they wore on their wedding day. Among the finery that Eliza Hasty wore for her marriage in South Carolina shortly after the Civil War, she noted: 'Round my neck was a string of green jade beads . . .' (Rawick vol. 2.2: 255).

Ann Ulrich Evans, born 1843, enslaved in Missouri, also married just after the

Civil War, yet her experience suggests the importance which Blacks placed on beads as a form of personal adornment, particularly for celebratory events. In her narration, Evans describes how a man enticed her to marry him with presentations of gifts, including beads.

> I kept company with a nigger who worked for a man he didn't like. I was barefooted, so I asked Moses Evans to please buy me some shoes, my feet was so sore and I didn't have no money nor no home neither. So he said to wait till Saturday night and he'd buy me some shoes. Sure 'nough whe Saturday night come, he buyed me some shoes, and handkerchiefs and a pretty string of beads . . . Den in a few weeks me and him got married (Rawick vol. 11.7.8: 115).

Nevertheless, I surmise that, just as white women often oversaw the wedding gowns of their servants, in many instances white women might loan the brides jewellery to wear for the event, or even might give them jewellery as a celebratory gift. Toni Morrison describes just such a happenstance in her historical novel, *Beloved*, when Mrs Garner presents her servant, Sethe, with a pair of diamond earrings the day after Sethe's wedding (1987: 73–4).

We must not make too much of the largesse of white slaveholders in allowing their servants to wear finery. Racial slavery was, after all, a lawfully enforced system of class, and marks of class included bodily attire and adornment. Very early, several slave-holding states issued dress codes to that effect. A. Leon Higginbotham notes of South Carolina's 1735 code:

> when a slave managed to obtain clothing that might accord him some dignity or prestige, the act declared that when such clothing was 'above' that which a slave should wear, it could be taken from the slave by 'all and every constable and other persons' to be used for his or her own benefit (1980: 173).[14]

Moreover, the 1786 dress code issued by the governor of Louisiana (then a Spanish colony) forbade 'females of color . . . to wear plumes or jewellery' (Crété 1981: 80–1). In light of these early statutes, Southern whites certainly must have continued to curtail (if not by law then by entrenched custom) the type and value of the jewellery owned and worn by the Blacks in their midst. That is, while enslaved people wore jewellery, it is probable that they could not measure its value in ways necessarily associated with monetary worth.

The enslaved donned finery for all special events (Foster 1997: 176–99). This certainly included Sundays, the single full day that found them freed from routine tasks. Frances Kemble described the Sunday attire of enslaved people on her husband's Georgia plantation. Among the colourful and seemingly extravagant items with which the Black women bedecked themselves, Kemble writes they wore 'beads and bugles' (1865: 93).

African Americans acquired jewellery in several ways. As shown, some of it came their way as gifts. In rare cases, when they had money, they most often spent it on necessities; a few, however, purchased jewellery instead. Eda Raines, born 1853 and enslaved in Arkansas, remembered that at Christmas her master: 'generally gave usfo-bits to spend as we wanted to. Maybe we'd buy a string of beads or some notion' (Rawick SS2, vol. 8.7: 3223).

The enslaved also made use of found objects, particularly plant materials such as nuts and berries, to fashion jewellery. They usually describe threading these objects on strings and wearing them as necklaces. Alice Hutcheson, born 1862, enslaved in Georgia, said: 'Us used to string chinquapins [chestnuts] and hang 'em 'round our necks' (Rawick vol. 12.2: 285). The berries of the chinaberry tree offered a much used item for making beads. After flowering, the tree, naturalized in the Southern United States, develops yellow berries. Several people reported that they strung and wore these berries. Gus Feaster, enslaved in South Carolina, suggests that women donned them for the purpose of bewitching male onlookers: 'In dem days dey [de gals] dried cheney berries and painted dem and wo' dem on a string round dere necks to charm us' (Rawick vol. 2.2: 52). Feaster's statement further attests to the ingenious ways in which young Black women manipulated objects at hand to beautify themselves when no other kinds of jewellery were available to them.

As Protection

A number of narrators, however, stated that enslaved Blacks wore chinaberry beads not only to enhance their physical appearance but also as forms of protection. Martha Patton, enslaved in Texas, recalled: 'My mammy give me beads for my neck, china berry beads to keep me well. They'd pretty. I never had no other kind' (Rawick vol. 4.1: 137). Enslaved in another state, Rosa Washington of Louisiana told of the identical custom (Rawick SS2, vol. 20.9: 3981).

The formerly enslaved spoke of wearing many sorts of beads and other objects as jewellery because of their beliefs in these objects' protective powers. Victoria Taylor Thompson, enslaved in Oklahoma, recalled that her father: 'was a herb doctor, that's how come he have the name Doc. He made us wear charms. Made out of shiny buttons and Indian rock beads. They cured lots of things and the misery too' (Rawick SS1, vol. 12: 322). The interviewer paraphrased Amanda McCray, enslaved in Florida, who described herself as 'a grownup during the Civil War', writing that enslaved 'children wore moles feet and pearl buttons around their necks to insure easy teething' (Rawick vol. 17: 213).

Belief in the guardian forces of amulets (including beads) continued long after the end of enslavement. Pauline Johnson, enslaved in Texas, was six years old at the end of the War. Johnson wore a 'bronze medal of Our Lady of Mount Carmel' during her interview in the 1930s. When questioned about the other objects around her neck, she explained: 'W'at dese other t'ings on de string? O, dem's nutmeg. Dey's wo'n for de food of de heart. Bofe us [she and her sister] hab bad heart. Dey's 'spose to be two of dem togedder' (Rawick SS2, vol. 6.5: 2038).

People told about the protection offered by wearing a coin. Elisha Doc Garey, enslaved in Georgia, noted: 'Slaves wore a nickel or a copper on strings 'round dair necks to keep off sickness. Some few of 'em wore a dime; but dimes was hard to git' (Rawick vol. 12.2: 7).[15] Mark Twain, born in 1835 and a close observer of the institution of slavery, alludes to this custom among Blacks when he mentions that Jim, the enslaved man who escapes on the Mississippi with Huck Finn, wears a pierced nickel around his neck ([1876] 1948: 6). Ralph Ellison offers another literary glimpse at the custom when his narrator inventories the objects thrown into the street as an elderly African American couple are evicted from their apartment in Harlem. Among the items, the narrator sees 'a dime pierced with a nail hole so as to be worn about the ankle on a string for luck . . .' (1952: 206). Seventy years after slavery, Silvia Witherspoon, who was about ninety years old and had been enslaved in Alabama, continued to rely on the custom. In her case, she wore a coin as an apotropaic device to ward off the powers of a local magician. Witherspoon related: 'Sometimes I wears dis dime wid de hole in it aroun' my ankle to keep off de conjure, but since Monroe King tuk an' died us ain't had much conjerin' 'roun' here' (Rawick vol. 6.1: 431).

Africans displaced to the American south, of course, were not the only ones to wear certain objects in the belief that those objects protected their person. (Blue glass beads to protect from the evil eye and St Christopher medals to protect oneself on a journey, are but two modern examples.) The custom among enslaved Blacks, however, seems to be a retention of African cosmological belief. William Kelso, the excavator at Thomas Jefferson's Moticello slave quarters, reports: 'an African cowry shell, 'mojo' magic ring (?), and pierced silver eighteenth-century Spanish coins show that African tradition was very much alive within the Monticello community' (1986: 30). The ring is not a 'beaded' object, but the cowry shell and the pierced coin found at the site might well have been worn as beads. The cowry represents one of those instances of retention of an actual African object. The other items may have been acquired in the United States, but Kelso's description implies a continuity of African faith in the powers of those objects, even as the forms of the objects changed in the American setting. This points, as well, to improvisation, a dominant trait of West African and African American aesthetics, both in the ways the enslaved acquired objects and in the uses they made of them.[16]

References to a special type of earring worn by both men and women came from formerly enslaved Blacks who lived on the Sea Islands off the South Carolina and Georgia coast. (Known as the Gullah, communities of their descendants retain a remarkable number of Africanisms to this day.) We rarely get a thorough description of the earrings' form or the material from which they were made, but we may suppose that these earrings were metal and probably held no beads. Elsie Clews Parsons briefly noted in 1923 that among formerly enslaved Sea Islanders: 'Ear-rings, plain gold circlets, are quite commonly worn by women, the ears 'bo' (bored), and I saw a few older men with ear-rings' (1923: 204).

The following narrations from formerly enslaved people contain two important points about the Sea-Island earrings that Parsons does not mention. First, although lacking beads, the earrings are related to the strings of small objects so often worn for protective purposes; and, second, the particular use of a single earring was an African custom retained in the Americas. In the 1930s, Robert Pickney of Wilmington Island described the enslaved native Africans whom he had known: 'Doze Africans alluz call one anuddah 'countrymen' . . . [Some] weah eahring in duh ear. Some weahs it in duh lef eah an doze from annudah tribe weahs it in duh right eah' (Georgia Writers' Project 1972: 100). London Grayson, interviewed in 1939 on St Catherine's Island, more specifically demonstrates that earrings were another survival of the African belief in wearing jewellery as a form of self-preservation. Grayson, who wore a gold earring in his left ear, told the interviewer that the earring 'tended to improve his eyesight' (ibid: 73). On St Simon's Island, Ben Sullivan remembered an old African woman, enslaved on the Couper plantation, who 'weah one ring in he eah fuh he eyes' (ibid.: 171).[17]

A noteworthy final piece of evidence for the single-earring style comes from early nineteenth-century paintings of Haitian male dignitaries who are portrayed wearing gold loop earrings. Because most portraits show a three-quarter view of the head, it is impossible to determine if both ears contained rings. In his 1824 portrait, however, Citizen Jonathan Granville faces nearly straight ahead and wears a gold loop in just his right ear (Figure 8.4). The widespread custom among Blacks of wearing only a single earring, therefore, ranged from the Caribbean to the lower coastal Southern United States and ultimately back to Africa.

Conclusion

Bodily adornment affords a visible means of presenting one's personal style, and adornment includes wearing beads and other types of jewellery. Personal style thus became a method by which African Americans salvaged an identity of self worth and human dignity during the years of racial slavery in the Southern United States.

Enslaved men and women clearly enjoyed wearing jewellery. Many people wore it not only on special occasions but daily. They procured jewellery by various means. In some instances they received it as gifts; in some instances, they purchased beads with the rare cash that might come their way. Much of the time they made do with what was readily at hand, fashioning necklaces, bracelets and anklets out of nuts

Figure 8.4 *Portrait of Citizen Jonathan Granville* wearing a single loop earring, Philip Tilyard, 1824, oil on canvas, 50.8x48.3cm. Reproduced with permission of the Baltimore Museum of Art, Baltimore, Maryland, Purchase Fund BMA 1945.92.

and berries, coins and buttons, and shells and stones; and forging finger rings and earrings from metal.

Strung objects worn by children and adults and unadorned earrings worn by both men and women appear to be the most usual forms. Oral and visual resources offer descriptions of a few specific items, and a few items of actual material evidence recovered through archaeological investigation are available. Less discernible, however, is an accurate understanding of all the types of jewellery and their monetary value.

Jewellery served three important functions within the African American communities: as a way to enhance physical appearance and as a way to guard their bodies from harm. Of the third function, prestige, circumstantial evidence supports the notion that enslaved African Americans who worked in close contact with white slaveowners were allowed to wear better jewellery for the purpose of enhancing the masters' status. African Americans understood the principle perpetrated by whites because jewellery also had been a common prestige item in Africa. As of yet, however, no evidence verifies that the enslaved themselves purposely chose to wear such objects in order to mark their superiority over other Blacks. The peculiar institution forced the least-powerful members of that system to alter certain West African customs to meet the demands of accommodation to an environment that was, both physically and socially, harsh and new. Under the changed conditions, the material form of much of their African culture was lost or modified. Nonetheless, by wearing those small objects – which I have here labelled jewellery – the enslaved demonstrated an extraordinary ability to imbue the newer forms with a much older African spirit. This, then, is the outstanding message contained within the shreds of evidence about the beads and other jewellery made and worn by African Americans during their period of enslavement.

Notes

1. Throughout, I refer to citizens of the United States of America who claim African ancestry as either 'African Americans' or 'Blacks', spelled with a capital 'B'. I refer to Americans of European descent as 'whites', without capitalization. My discussion includes descriptions and analyses of a range of jewellery, not only beads, because they interrelate.
2. For extensive interpretation of blue beads in African American culture over time, see Stine, Cabak and Groover 1996.
3. The identification of the beads is in Wilson's label note to the photograph for its exhibition in 'Hidden Witness: African Americans in Early Photography', J. Paul Getty Museum, Los Angeles, 1995.
4. The photograph is in the Moore Collection, New Hampshire Historical Society, Concord.
5. The photograph is owned by The Museum of the Confederacy, Richmond, Virginia.
6. Cowry shells originate in the Indian Ocean, but smaller ones are found on the West African coastal beaches. Cowries served as an important form of monetary exchange throughout Africa.
7. For the African features of certain Southern American Black burial grounds, see Thompson (1984: 132–42) and Vlach (1990: 139–47).
8. Stine, Cabak and Groover discuss the Means Plantation burials at Parris Island, South Carolina, where 3,481 glass beads are associated with an African American graveyard. The authors note, 'In contrast to the Means Graveyard, most excavated African-American cemeteries do not contain very many beads' (1996: 62).
9. In her thorough and fascinating analysis of the beads from this site, Cheryl LaRoche notes that this cemetery is rather anomalous and 'is not directly comparable with other North American sites' (1994: 17). It is both the oldest and largest North American burial ground thus far found; and, because it is a colonial site, it contains the remains of some

who were born in Africa. See Fitzgerald (1992), Harrington (1993) and Allen (1995) for more general accounts of this site.

10. A few states published the narratives collected within their own boundaries. Benjamin A. Botkin edited an abbreviated book of the collection, *Slave Narratives: A Folk History of Slavery in the United States from Interviews with Former Slaves* in 1941. In the 1970s, George P. Rawick undertook the general editorship of the entire collection in a forty-volume compendium titled, *The American Slave: A Composite Autobiography*, 1972, 1977 and 1979; this includes two Supplement Series. My references to the narratives refer to the Rawick volumes; the abbreviation SS refers to the Supplement Series.

11. For eye-witness accounts and analysis, see Foster (1997: 21–43).

12. Norrece T. Jones describes the material benefits afforded enslaved people working at domestic tasks when compared to the lesser standards endured by field labourers (1990: 109–11). Elsewhere, I discuss the differences in the clothing that whites allotted to the enslaved in order to demark the status of Blacks according to their jobs (Foster 1997: 134–45, 158–9).

13. In spite of the awkward and sometimes offensive nature of the spelling used by the WPA interviewers (most of whom were white) in quoting their oral sources, I retain the original spellings. In so doing, I avoid misinterpreting the narrators' meaning; as well, the spelling gives a picture of the stereotypes by which whites depicted Southern Blacks at the time.

14. See Foster (1997: 134–5) for a summary of these regulations.

15. Sally and Richard Price note that Maroons, descendants of runaway African slaves in Suriname, continue to wear items such as cowrie shells and coins for protection against sickness, a practice that goes back to the early years of these societies (1980: 86).

16. Improvisation survived through the period of enslavement and remains a noticeable characteristic of African American culture to this day. See Thompson (1984), Vlach (1990) and Wahlman (1987) for extended commentaries on improvisation as a major component of African and African American aesthetics.

17. The shift in pronoun gender is correct in some African American dialects.

References

Allen, P. S. (November/December 1995), film review, 'African Burial Ground Revisited', *Archaeology*, 87–8.

Ascher, R. & Fairbanks, C. H. (1971), 'Excavation of a Slave Cabin: Georgia, U.S.A.', *Historical Archaeology*, vol. 5, 3–17.

Botkin, B. A. (ed.) (1941), *Slave Narratives: A Folk History of Slavery in the United States from Interviews with Former Slaves*, Washington, D.C.: Library of Congress.

Campbell, E. D., Jr. & Rice, K. S. (eds) (1991), *Before Freedom Came: African-American Life in the Antebellum South*, Richmond and Charlottesville: The Museum of the Confederacy and the University Press of Virginia.

Crété, Liliane (1981), *Daily Life in Louisiana 1815–1830,* trans. Patrick Gregory, Baton Rouge: Louisiana State University Press.

Ellison, R. (1952), *Invisible Man*, NY: Modern Library.

Fitzgerald, S. (October/November 1992), 'Negro Burial Ground', *American Visions*, 18–19.

Foster, H. B. (1997), *'New Raiments of Self': African American Clothing in the Antebellum South*, Oxford: Berg.

Georgia Writers' Project (1972), *Drums and Shadows: Survival Studies Among Georgia Coastal Negroes*, NY: Doubleday/Anchor.

Harrington, S. P. M. (March/April 1993), 'Bones and Bureaucrats: New York's Great Cemetery Imbroglio', *Archaeology*, 28–38.

Higginbotham, A. L. (1980), *In the Matter of Color: Race and the Legal Process*, Oxford and NY: Oxford University Press.

Jones, N. T., Jr. (1990), *Born a Child of Freedom, Yet a Slave: Mechanisms of Control and Strategies of Resistance in Antebellum South Carolina*, Hanover, NH and London: Wesleyan University Press/University Press of New England.

Kelso, W. M. (September/October 1986), 'Mulberry Row: Slave Life at Thomas Jefferson's Monticello', *Archaeology*, 28–35.

Lange, F. W. & Handler, J. S. (1985), 'The Ethnohistorical Approach to Slavery', in T. A. Singleton (ed.), *The Archaeology of Slavery and Plantation Life*, NY: Academic Press, 15–32.

Kemble, Frances Anne (1863), *Journal of a Residence on a Georgia Plantation in 1838–1839*, New York: Harper & Brothers.

LaRoche, C. J. (1994), 'Beads From the African Burial Ground, New York City: A Preliminary Report', *Beads*, vol. 6, 3–20.

Morrison, T. (1987), *Beloved*, NY: Knopf.

Opper, M.-J. & H. (1989), 'Diakhité: A Study of the Beads From an 18th–19th Century Burial in Senegal, West Africa', *Beads*, vol. 1, 5–20.

Parrington, M. & Wideman, J. (1986), 'Acculturation in an Urban Setting: The Archaeology of a Black Philadelphia Cemetery', *Expedition*, vol. 28, no. 1, 55–62.

Parsons, E. C. (1923), *Folk-Lore of the Sea Islands, South Carolina*, Memoirs of the American Folklore Society, NY: G. E. Stechert.

Price, S. & R. (1980), *Afro-American Arts of the Suriname Rain Forest*, Berkeley: University of California Press.

Rawick, G. P., general ed. (1972, 1977 and 1979), *The American Slave: A Composite Autobiography*, Westport, Conn.: Greenwood.

Singleton, T. A. (ed.) (1985), *The Archaeology of Slavery and Plantation Life*, NY: Academic Press.

—— (1991), 'The Archaeology of Slave Life', in E. D. Campbell & K. S. Rice (eds), *Before Freedom Came*, Richmond and Charlottesville: The Museum of the Confederacy and the University Press of Virginia, 155–75.

Stine, L. F., Cabak, M. A. & Groover, M. D. (1996), 'Blue Beads as African-American Cultural Symbols', *Historical Archaeology*, vol. 30, no. 3, 49–75.

Thompson, R. F. (1984), *Flash of the Spirit: African and African-American Art and Philosophy*, NY: Random House/Vintage Books.

Twain, M. ([1876] 1948), *The Adventures of Huckleberry Finn*, NY: Rinehart.

Vlach, J. M. (1990), *The Afro-American Tradition in Decorative Arts*, Athens: University of Georgia Press/Brown Thrasher Books.

Wahlman, M. S. (1987), 'Africanisms in Afro-American Visionary Arts', in *Baking in the Sun: Visionary Images from the South*, Lafayette: University Art Museum, University of Southwestern Louisiana.

Wheaton, T. R. and Garrow, P. H. (1985), 'Acculturation and the Archaeological Record in the Carolina Lowcountry', in T. A. Singleton (ed.), *The Archaeology of Slavery and Plantation Life*, NY: Academic Press, 239–59.

Wilford, J. N. (27 August 1996), 'Slave Artifacts Under the Hearth', *The New York Times*.

9

Beads and Breasts: The Negotiation of Gender Roles and Power at New Orleans *Mardi Gras*

Laurie A. Wilkie

Introduction

'**Throw** me something, Mister!', cries a child from the parade route, quickly grabbing the green plastic beads tossed in his direction by a float-riding masked krewe member. Behind him, a woman seated on her boyfriend's shoulders screams, 'Pearls! Throw me Pearls!', and catching the attention of a float rider, swiftly lifts her shirt and exposes her breasts. As reward, she is pelted with the bounty of *Mardi Gras* . . . plastic cups, underwear, aluminum 'doubloons', and significantly, the object of her desire, long strands of large plastic pearl beads. The 'best' of the beads (the longest strands with the biggest beads), she immediately places around her and her boyfriend's neck.

Interactions such as these are common place and multi-dimensional along parade routes and in the French Quarter (*Vieux Carre*) of New Orleans during Carnival season, particularly during the final weekend of Carnival, and culminating on *Mardi Gras* (Fat Tuesday). While the tossing of beads from floats has been a common feature of *Mardi Gras* parades during the last 100 years, the exposing of breasts (and less frequently, genitalia) by both men and women in exchange for beads has developed only in the last two decades. Interactions include the solicitation of women by men; women by women; men by women; and men by men. Through these negotiations, heterosexual and homosexual men and women use the freedom of carnival to stretch the boundaries of society's gender ideologies and power structures. The ethnographic data for this paper was drawn from five years of participant observation during Carnival in Louisiana, and through informant interviews and documentary research.

The History of Beads at *Mardi Gras*

It is not known exactly when bead throwing was incorporated into New Orleans Carnival ritual. 'Throws', or trinkets and candy tossed by maskers to parade watchers, have been a part of *Mardi Gras* tradition since at least the 1880s, when the Krewe of Rex threw peanuts and candy to the spectators (Huber 1977: 41). I have not, as yet, found published reference or documentary evidence to the origin of bead throwing at *Mardi Gras*, nor a reason for the introduction of these particular trinkets. Some native Louisianians have heard that the beads were somehow connected to rosary beads and to serve as a reminder of the spiritual during the height of Carnival. Whatever the earliest meanings of beads to Carnival goers were, they have been lost to modern Carnival participants.

By the early twentieth century, the practice of throwing beads was well established. In his account of a childhood *Mardi Gras* (around 1901), Lyle Saxon remembered while watching a parade, 'the maskers on the floats were throwing trinkets to the crowd in the street – beads, tiny bags of sweetmeats, metal ornaments' (Saxon 1928: 61). By this point in time, beads were popular throws. Saxon described the commotion among parade goers when he was tossed a strand of beads:

... the page with the bored smile tossed a string of green beads to me. It swirled through the air over the heads of the people between us and dropped almost into my outstretched hands; but my clumsy fingers missed and it fell to the ground. Immediately there was a scramble. Robert stooped, I fell from his shoulders, and I found myself lying on the pavement as though swept under a stampede of cattle. Hands and feet were all around me but somehow in the struggle I managed to recover those beads (Saxon 1928: 38–9).

Saxon's description of scrambles among parade goers to retrieve beads could be mistaken as an account of current Carnival parade behaviour. In 1938, the New Orleans City Guide, produced by the Federal Writers' Project, contained the following description of activities along a *Mardi Gras* parade route:

... Then – the first float of maskers. Hands wave and clap; people jump up and down, and everyone cries for the trinkets that the maskers carry in little bags or in their hands, shouting 'Mister – throw me something'. The trinkets are small, they are cheap, you can buy a dozen for a penny or so, but – a string of beads flies into the crowd, and the people go mad as they snatch for it. It is a belief in New Orleans that it is lucky to catch favors from passing floats. The maskers hold tight with one hand to the supporting iron pole; and with the other hand they throw gaudy necklaces and toss kisses from the mouths of their grotesque masks (FWP 1938: 66).

Writing a decade later, Robert Tallant observed,

As each float passed, the maskers aboard tossed their trinkets into the crowds lining the path of the pageant – a crowd who constantly yelled and begged, arms outstretched and hands waving for more and more of the bounty of King Rex, a crowd who struggled and fought with each other, sometimes sprawling to the street in an effort to seize a whistle or a string of beads, as often as not breaking and smashing and tearing apart the souvenir before any one person captured it, and behaving in general as if the junk were booty beyond price (Tallant 1948: 66).

Tallant's description of *Mardi Gras* bead frenzy was echoed in a 1981 newspaper article which appeared during Carnival season, 'The "throws" take on a magical quality in the air, and parade watchers leap to catch them. A month later, they wouldn't walk five feet for a wheel barrow full of doubloons or trinkets' (*Times Picayune* 1981).

Today, parade-goers carry away bags containing, literally, pounds of beads. These items are stored in boxes, packed in garages, and sometimes sold back to krewes for 10 cents a pound. The 'better' beads may be hung from rearview mirrors, hung from balconies, and saved to be worn as display items at the next Carnival.

It is important to note, at this juncture, that New Orleans's Carnival was a national tourist event by the late 1890s (Mitchell 1995: 94–5). The socially constructed value of beads during Carnival is reconstructed each year by participants not only from Louisiana, but also by national and international visitors to the event. The events and negotiations that take place in the bartering of beads which will be discussed here are not limited to residents of Louisiana. The negotiations of gender roles and ideologies that take place during *Mardi Gras* are acted out by a microcosm of larger society and are of relevance to audiences beyond the Louisiana borders.

Description and Perceived Ranking of *Mardi Gras* Beads

Until the 1960s, Carnival beads were made of cut glass. Immediately following the Second World War, glass beads made in Czechoslovakia were the most popular. The increasing costs of these beads, combined with concerns about political conditions overseas and the passage of a New Orleans safety ordinance, led to the replacement of the glass beads with cheaper plastic beads by the mid 1960s (Hardy 1991: 96). As will be discussed, shortly, plastic beads may be cheaper than glass beads, but the plastic beads most desired by Carnival goers can be quite expensive to purchase.

Informants generally describe beads as falling into one of three general categories: 'cheap beads', 'good beads' and 'pearls' or 'tit beads'. Beads are ranked by Carnival goers based upon several key attributes: size of beads in a strand, the length of a strand of beads, the shape of the beads, and the colour. Beads come in every colour of the spectrum, with transparent coloured beads the least desirable, and shiny metallic coloured beads and *faux* pearls the most popular. While beads are most commonly round in shape, oblong, cuboidal, and faceted spheres are also common. Some necklaces include beads in the shape of dice, *Mardi Gras* masks, gold babies or doubloons. These necklaces usually include gold metallic and *faux* pearl beads as well, and are by far one of the most popular *Mardi Gras* catches, considered to be of high quality or status. These bead necklaces are often broken by people fighting for possession of them. Throughout the parade routes and the French Quarter during Carnival season, scattered beads from these necklaces can be seen glittering in the gutters among the discarded beer cans.

The most highly coveted beads are those that combine the greatest number of desirable attributes (see Tables 9.1 and 9.2). For instance, large, round, medium to long strands of pearls are highly ranked beads, and are categorized as 'tit beads' by informants. Likewise, a long strand of small, transparent beads are not considered 'good enough' to be 'tit beads'. The relative ranking and desirability of different types of beads are quickly learned by Carnival newcomers, who witness the degree of begging, fighting and sexual favours that are employed to obtain different types of beads. The ranking of beads that exists today must have developed since the 1960s, when the plastic beads were introduced to Carnival goers. There are no

Table 9.1.   Ranking of *Mardi Gras* Beads by Bead Size and Strand Length

Ranking	Bead Size (diameter)	Strand Length
Low status	small <.6cm	22–30cm
Medium status	medium .7–1.0cm	30–60cm
High status	large >1.0cm	60–180cm

Table 9.2.   Ranking of *Mardi Gras* Beads based on Bead Shape and Colour

Ranking	Bead Shape	Bead Colour
Low status	round	transparent- red, blue, clear, yellow, green, orange, purple
Medium status	polygons, ovals	opalescent or metallic in any colour
High Status	babies, doubloons, dice, masks, medallions	pearls, any colour; pearls combined with metallic beads

available descriptions of 'pearl' coloured glass beads, and existing glass examples seen by the author were all translucent and multi-coloured.

Negotiation for Beads

Negotiations for beads (also referred to as the 'throwing game') take place as an interaction between people on the street and people on the floats, and people on the street and the balconies. Negotiations at parades take place primarily between the 'elite' of Carnival, the krewe members, and the street revellers, while the negotiations in the French Quarter are primarily between individuals not belonging to carnival social organizations.

Most Carnival participants learn the nature of bead negotiations during one of the numerous parades that occur during the last two weeks of Carnival. Parades are sponsored by Carnival krewes, which are exclusively male or female social clubs. The most popular parades, Zulu, Rex, Bacchus, and Endymion, are all male organizations. Krewe members pay annual dues to the krewes, and acceptance for membership is decided by the rest of the krewe. Costumed and masked, krewe members ride the floats and distribute throws during the parade.

Each krewe member pays for the throws they distribute. In 1991, it was estimated that the average float rider spent $400.00 on throws (Hardy 1991: 42). More recently, informants have heard of participants in some of the large krewes spending $1500.00, and smaller krewes around $700.00. High status beads, which are curated to a greater degree than 'cheap' beads, and therefore, less likely to be sold back, are purchased new. A bundle of twelve *faux* pearl necklaces, 60 cm long with a .7 cm diameter are selling for between three to four dollars. Long strands with large beads or ornate necklaces often can range in price from five to eight dollars a piece.

On each float, the beads are displayed to the on-lookers, hanging in large bunches, out of reach. To incite the crowd, the maskers (krewe members) will pull long strands of pearls from the hangers, twirl them like a lasso, dangle them, or pretend to throw them. They may make eye contact with someone in the crowd and throw that person the beads, or they may throw cheaper strands of beads, and keep the long strand for later . . . such a person is often called a 'bead tease'.

When the parades are running smoothly, the floats move too quickly for bartering or negotiation of any form to be possible. Eye contact or random luck lead to the acquisition of beads. One woman remembered as a child, she would call 'Uncle Henry' to each of the floats . . . once in a while, a Henry with a niece would be on a float and throw her beads, either appreciating the ploy, or in the blur of movement, thinking his niece was really there.

As carnival goers quickly learn, however, *Mardi Gras* parades rarely run smoothly. Float engines overheat, children jump too close to the floats, marching bands slow their pace, and a hundred other things happen to slow, and even stop, the parades. If the beginning of the parade moves far ahead of the rest of it, the front section will stop until the gap is lessened. When the floats are at a standstill the maskers and parade goers have the opportunity to barter.

In the parade context, bartering for sexual favours is, based on observation of over twenty parades, exclusively between male maskers and female parade goers. Typically, negotiation begins with a women asking for a throw. Often, pleading for an extended period can ultimately lead to reward, with the masker throwing something to the asker as the float begins to move away. In other instances, the masker may request a favour in return for beads.

While maskers have been observed soliciting kisses from women for beads, most commonly, they ask the women to show their breasts. The maskers rarely speak to the parade goers, so the request is usually stated on a sign that is held by the masker, or the masker communicates his desire by mimicking the action lifting or pulling open a shirt, or he may cup or tug his own breasts. The woman may consent or continue to beg. At this point the masker may repeat his request or decide to ignore her. A masker may decide to throw the woman beads anyway, even though she has not complied with his request.

A woman can comply with the request in several ways. If she is close to the float, she will most probably pull open her shirt at the neck so that the masker, situated above her on the float, can see her breasts down her shirt. Women showing in this manner are able to minimize their public exposure, so to speak. Often, the masker will drop the desired beads directly into her open shirt. A woman further from the floats can comply from atop a companion's shoulders, or sometimes, from a balcony above the parade route. In this position, women expose themselves by lifting the shirt up. Because this kind of display is visible to a wider audience of maskers, the woman in this situation is usually rewarded with a larger number of throws than the former woman.

A popular bead-gathering strategy at parades is to stand by a woman who is exposing herself while seated on someone's shoulders. She is sure to be thrown a large number of desirable objects, and due to her precarious position, is unlikely to be able to catch many of her throws. Due to this foraging strategy, when negotiations begin between a masker and a woman, the crowd around her is likely to try to encourage the woman to consent. Alcohol is a common part of *Mardi Gras* festivities, and a woman may unexpectedly find herself being surrounded by a group of drunken male parade goers who are trying to intimidate her into exposing herself. A woman who denies the request may find herself being booed by the crowd around her, and sometimes grabbed and jostled by disgruntled onlookers. In such a context, the parade quickly becomes frightening.

Not all negotiations are begun by the maskers. At any parade, there are women who arrive with full anticipation of exposing themselves. Like the woman in the introduction to this chapter, these women attract the attention of a masker, flash their breasts and hope that their offering will be rewarded . . . most often, they are, but women have been observed to go unrewarded for self-initiated shows. In contrast, I have not witnessed any masker-initiated display that went unrewarded.

Displays in the French Quarter

While negotiations for beads between maskers and parade goers are almost completely unidirectional (maskers ask for displays of nudity in exchange for beads), prior to parades, along the parade routes and in the French Quarter, bartering takes place between individuals on the street and between individuals on balconies and on the street, with any party being able to purchase nudity with beads.

Many residents in the French Quarter take advantage of their balconies to watch the street festivities. The balcony crowds purchase high quality beads, which they offer to passer-bys in exchange for a display of nudity. The dynamics of these negotiations are of a different tenor than those in the parade setting on several levels. First, while females are overwhelmingly more likely to expose themselves than men, men as well as women are solicited. Some women on balconies will ask men to show their 'tits', a request that is readily accommodated in most instances because it represents no risk on the part of the exposer, and only serves to reinforce society's image about the acceptability of bare-chested males.

Perhaps some of the more intriguing interactions, however, are in the well-known Gay section of Bourbon Street. Given the fluidity of gender boundaries, and the prevalence of Transvestites, Transsexuals, Bisexuals, Gay and Lesbian populations during Carnival, it is not always easy to understand the dynamics of the throwing game in this section of the French Quarter. For the sake of description, I am referring to men or women who I observed only in homoerotic acts, either on the balconies or streets, as Gay or Lesbian, individuals only observed in heterosexual acts as Heterosexual, and individuals observed in bisexual acts as Bisexual. Outside of the Carnival context, the observed individuals may perceive themselves to be of a different sexual orientation. However, like myself, the participants of Carnival define each other by our acts in that setting.

It is not uncommon to observe instances when Gay men on balconies will use beads to solicit men (in many cases, men who appear to be heterosexual) to expose their penises, or Lesbian women who use beads to solicit other women. The nature of these negotiations have very different dynamics. The negotiation between homosexual men and apparently heterosexual men are often marked by extreme tension and bullying on both sides. I observed an interesting negotiation in 1994. A young man wearing a Greek fraternity shirt, one arm around a woman, the other holding a large beer, was solicited by a man to 'show his dick'. The man offered a very good strand of pearl beads as an enticement – the strand was a least 120 cm long and the individual beads were around 2 cm in diameter. The young man had a number of strands already around his neck, suggesting he or his companion had already been involved in bartering. The beads offered were obviously of extremely high status, and of better 'quality' than the ones worn by the man being solicited. The young man, in response to the request, pulled up his shirt, exposing his chest, and demanded to be given the beads (perhaps this is how he obtained his other strands).

The man on the balcony grew angry and said he couldn't have them because he had not exposed the proper body part, 'No dick, no beads', he yelled. By this time, a crowd had gathered to watch the interaction. A number of people on the street were Gay males who encouraged the young man to expose himself, as did his female companion. Ultimately, he did not expose himself and was met with numerous jeers as he slunk away. It is only in this kind of setting that males encounter the intimidation and hostility that women cope with as a result of undesired solicitations. I have observed at least ten interactions that involved males soliciting apparently heterosexual males; only in one instance did the solicited male expose himself. Between Gay men, negotiations tend to be flirtatious and lacking implied aggression.

For Gay men, Mardi Gras is a time for activism and demonstrations of Gay pride. Many members of the community dress in studded leather teddies, thong pants, chains and so on. In the context of Mardi Gras, normally conservative heterosexual Louisiana finds these displays less intimidating, and may, eventually, be developing greater tolerance towards the Gay community. This is not to suggest that Gay-bashing is not a component of Carnival festivities. I have witnessed instances of verbal abuse directed at Gay men, as well as potentially violent confrontations between drunk party-goers. The bead negotiations of Mardi Gras provide another means of forcing the heterosexual community to acknowledge their presence, and gain a sense of empowerment.

Beads, and throws in general, can also be a means of educating and protecting the Gay community. In the age of AIDs, condoms have remained popular throws in the Gay section of Bourbon Street, as well as in other settings. In 1991, beads with medallions advocating safe sex as a means of fighting AIDs were distributed. The purple beads sported a green medallion. The medallion bore the inscription 'Play Safe/No AIDs Task Force' around a safety pin. These beads are still worn annually by some Carnival goers. Erasers shaped like erect penises and homoerotic trading cards have also been seen used as throws.

The Lesbian participants of Mardi Gras are not as visible as Gay men, in dress or action, although solicitation of women by women has reportedly become noticeably more common over the last two years. I was able to interview two heterosexual women about the negotiations. Both agreed that the women they had displayed for (the displayers perceived these women to be Lesbians) had been more pleasant and respectful in the negotiations than the men with whom they had interacted. One woman stated that the women she had 'shown' for had been polite during negotiations, and she had felt as if she was being asked to do a favour for someone. In negotiations with men, however, she felt she was being bullied and was not respected. Both women also thought they had received better beads for their efforts than they had from men.

People on the balconies not only provide beads for nudity, but will also solicit beads in exchange for nudity. I have only witnessed females engaged in this form of interaction. The person, or their agent, on the balcony requests beads from the crowd below. When a proper amount of quality beads are perceived to be obtained, the exposure will take place. After the exposure, the person will often begin requesting beads again, thus renewing the cycle. Female breasts are the most commonly exposed body part, but buttocks, and less commonly, genitals, are also exposed.

Unlike the women on the street, who can be harassed and molested by people around her during negotiations, the individuals on the balcony can expose themselves from a secure place, and if they become bored with the crowd, can go inside the residence. Individuals on the street, however, must contend with people on the ground who have watched them expose themselves, and who may interpret their willingness to expose themselves as willingness to provide other services as well. Women on the street do not usually risk exposing themselves unless accompanied by a number of males. I have witnessed women on the street level who, after or while exposing themselves were grabbed and molested. One woman stated that when displaying, she waited until the ground crowd's attention was focused elsewhere before showing. In such a way she limited the audience for the display to herself and the solicitor. She was careful about displaying only when she felt that she was not in risk of physical harm from other Carnival goers.

It is not my intention to suggest that quality beads are only obtained through the bartering of nudity or sexual favours. Many 'quality' strands of beads are thrown randomly to parade audiences, and males do obtain a number of these. Height is definitely an advantage in parade settings for obtaining throws: people seated on ladders, sitting on someone else's shoulders, standing on a balcony or hanging from a tree, are all likely to obtain a number of quality bead strands. Such a strategy is dependent upon random acts. Additional strategies for the acquisition of beads do exist. Alcoholic beverages can sometimes be successfully traded for good beads. As mentioned previously, standing near someone who is exposing themselves can be an excellent bead foraging strategy. In addition, being accompanied by an obviously pregnant woman, a young child or a very aged person can also incur bead tribute. I have also, on one occasion, witnessed a person steal a strand of beads from around the neck of an unconscious drunk on Bourbon Street, in the French Quarter. Several of these alternate strategies will be discussed shortly.

Display of Beads

Once obtained, it is important that beads are displayed, for in the Carnival setting, beads are a form of wealth, and those people who control beads have the potential to use them to control other people. Cheap beads are stuck in pockets, given to children or dropped on the ground. Good beads and pearls are worn around the neck. No matter how long a strand of beads, it is never doubled, for to do so would shorten its length and lessen its visual impact. Carnival goers stroll through downtown New Orleans with a thick band of beads looped around their necks and long strands of beads hitting their knees and getting wrapped between their legs as they walk; the soft clicking of the beads knocking together can be heard.

A popular New Orleans *Mardi Gras* saying is 'beads go to beads', thus emphasizing the importance of display. Beads are power . . . power to purchase sexual favours and power to control the sexual behaviour of others. Beads send strong visual messages. A Carnival participant with many beads around his or her neck may be solicited by other Carnival goers for gifts of beads. Kisses, pinches, gropes, displays of nudity, or exchanges of other items (alcoholic beverages, a number of lesser quality bead strands, other desirable throws such as underwear or Zulu coconuts) may be bartered for good beads.

To maximize the visual impact of display, individuals wear what are referred to as 'seed beads' to the festivities. Seed beads are high quality beads that were obtained from previous Carnivals or purchased. Veterans of Carnival are able to display a broad diversity of quality beads. For out-of-state newcomers, many of the New Orleans hotels provide guests with quality strands of beads to wear. Many individuals use the parades to expand their bead bounty with the intention of using these newly acquired beads to initiate bartering in the French Quarter. Although no parades are routed through this Quarter, Bourbon Street is perceived to be the centre of Carnival festivities, and the vast majority of bead negotiations take place in this part of the city.

Intrinsic to the interpretation of the beads' meanings by other Carnival goers, however, is a gender bias. While men with large numbers of quality beads are perceived as having potential power and sexual access to woman through beads, women with large numbers of beads are perceived as being sexually available, for the assumption is that they have exposed themselves to obtain their beads. Women with large numbers of quality beads are more likely to be solicited by balcony observers to display their breasts, while their male counterparts are more likely to be solicited for beads.

The Negotiation of Gender Roles through Carnival

Despite growing scholarly interest in Gulf Coast Carnival celebrations, little mention or serious consideration has been given to the role of displays of nudity in the negotiation of gender ideologies and power. Authors who do discuss this aspect of carnival activities fail to recognize the significance of the act or to consider why women choose to engage in this activity. Consider Kinser's 1990 description of female nudity at *Mardi Gras*:

> This is springtime sex, the sex associated with loose women, sex which is seductive and titillating. It is not reproductive sex, heavy and grand with autumnal fruit. Women are here to be gawked at, tasted, tossed aside; they are here to be taken in excess, like Carnival food. Not many genitals, lots of mammaries. Sex is gay in every way in *Mardi Gras*. It revolves around male bonding. Sexual revolution or not, positivization or not of male bodies, most of the skin parts [sic.] being exposed in today's Carnivals are female (Kinser 1990: 266).

Kinser emphasizes that the majority of nudity at *Mardi Gras* is female, and therefore, **must** be solely for the benefit of male enjoyment; women exist at *Mardi Gras* only to be 'gawked at, tasted, tossed aside', as if the women have no control over their bodies and behaviour. His short description, with its obvious androcentric view, fails to consider what statements women may be making through Carnival celebrations. Likewise, Kilburn (1992), a sociology student who wrote a master's thesis on incidence of public nudity at New Orleans *Mardi Gras*, did not once consider the social implications of the displays; instead, he spent a large portion of his study defining what constituted a display (nipples had to be visible for his research team to count the incidence as a display), and how many displays could be recorded over the final four days of Carnival. Despite the shallow consideration of female nudity provided by these men, *Mardi Gras* celebrations have long served as a time and place for negotiating gender roles.

Gender and Carnival

De Caro and Ireland write (1988: 58): 'Public celebrations and public performances are enacted because they have "meanings" for those who enact them. They communicate ideas, beliefs and feelings and may often constitute complex symbol systems designed to interconnect attitudes and emotions.' Carnival is a time for society to act out its stresses and tensions through an inversion and satirization of social roles and stereotypes. The begging of gifts by the commoners (Carnival goers) from the elite (krewe members or balcony-standers) can be seen as an exaggeration of the socioeconomic relationship that exists between these individuals outside of the Carnival context. Zulu, the African-American Krewe formed in 1916 as a satire of race relations in New Orleans, represents a reversal of the traditional krewe royalty, with African warriors in black-face representing Zulu's royalty. For women, now and in the past, *Mardi Gras* has represented an opportunity to rebel against standards of behaviour imposed upon them by the patriarchal power structure of society. While rebellion did not always take the form of public nudity, it is apparent in several historically documented *Mardi Gras* traditions of the past.

During the 1850s, Tallant (1948: 107–8) reports, '*Mardi Gras* became a time for drunkenness, violence (particularly of the Irish towards African-Americans with whom they competed for employment on the wharves) and the antics of prostitutes, who openly displayed their wares.' Cross-dressing, a behaviour still common, particularly to men, during *Mardi Gras*, was popular among women as early as the mid 1800s. In 1857, two women were arrested during Carnival for impersonating men. By the early twentieth century, many prostitutes rented carriages and drove through the city dressed as men and smoking cigars (Mitchell 1995: 135). Women dressed in men's clothing during street parades in the early twentieth century were often perceived as prostitutes, for, in a circular way of reasoning, it was thought (by male authors) that only prostitutes engaged in the practice. Prostitution was legal in New Orleans until 1917, and prostitutes were visible players in *Mardi Gras* celebrations, whether selling their wares or parading through the streets as dressed up 'Baby Dolls', in small, frilly, inviting, costumes (Saxon et. al. 1991). Through their parades, the prostitutes forced the city to confront not only their sexuality, but also the fact that they were self-supporting women, whose behaviour could not be controlled by the men who paid for their services. In emulating the cross-dressing of the prostitutes, other women could also challenge notions about female behaviour and sexuality.

Military style costumes were popular for women after the First World War, as was the practice of smoking cigarettes and cigars (Mitchell 1995: 138). In addition to cross-dressing and smoking, in the early twentieth century, women would crowd into the famous bars of the French Quarter, for only on *Mardi Gras* were they allowed into the saloons. Women also danced in the streets during Carnival, adopting popular dances of the time, including sexually provocative dances such as the 'Black Bottom', a dance of African-American origin (Mitchell 1995: 132–3). Lyle Saxon described a dance similar to the 'Black Bottom' which he witnessed in an African-American saloon during *Mardi Gras* of 1903:

> To the center of the floor came a woman, a thin quadroon. She began to shake in time with the drumbeats, first a shoulder, then a hip. Then she began to squirm and lunge. At each beat of the drum her position would change, and as the measured beating continued she moved her body with each beat. At last she was shaking all over, head wagging, hips bobbing back and forth (Saxon 1928: 48).

Women engaging in these dances often danced alone, the provocative nature of the dance emphasizing their identity as sexual individuals, apart from and independent from men. Women's acts of Carnival rebellion did not go uncontested. As mentioned above, women were sometimes arrested when cross-dressing. Likewise, police officers, even when prostitution was legal in New Orleans, have been described trying to remove prostitutes from the streets during Carnival. The krewes, as patriarchal communities of the upper class, also tried to impose order on the presentation of women during *Mardi Gras* through the introduction of women into the royal courts in 1886.

The court image of the woman as debutante, dressed in virginal white, was in sharp contrast with the alternate image of the woman dressed in masculine attire that characterized Carnival on the streets. By the rules of Carnival hierarchy, the most for which a man could strive was to be a Carnival king, and the most for which a woman could hope was to be a Carnival queen. A man became king when he was mature, at the height of his power and ability; the honor crowned his career. A woman became a Carnival queen when she was a girl, queenhood ended her childhood. After she was queen she might go on to become a woman, a wife, a mother (Mitchell 1995: 105).

Through the introduction of young women into their courts, the Carnival krewes strove to impose their ideal of womanhood on the Carnival canvas. Their ideal women were to provide a contrast to the women participating in the street parties. The contrast was to be the contrast of purity versus sin; the future mother versus madam; beauty versus ugliness.

While female cross-dressing may have been considered within the realm of 'lowborn' women's activities, male cross-dressing has not appeared to have any stigma attached to it. 'The man disguised as a woman poses less, not more, of a threat than a woman asserting her sexuality would have' (Mitchell 1995: 140). Perhaps, it is this acceptance of male cross-dressing that has allowed the Gay male population to claim a unique share of Carnival festivities. By the 1960s, New Orleans had attracted a large resident Gay population. A number of Gay krewes exist, with some sponsoring parades of over-the-top transvestite maskers. On *Mardi Gras*, men wearing very scanty leather thongs, teddies, and other revealing inventions can be seen strolling along Bourbon Street. Leather shops throughout the quarter begin stocking large selections of leather lingerie in December. Studded collars, whips, assorted harnesses and masks can be found in abundance and will be worn for display and shock value during Carnival. These costumes are stocked almost exclusively in men's sizes, with little selection being available to women. Kinser (1990: 262), regarding the Gay population, argues:

The informal tolerance habitually granted the gay community and the fascination directed toward them on *Mardi Gras*, however, are not just demographic effects. They also reflect shifts in the meaning of sexuality, private and public. Open display of a semi-nude male body, revealing its capacity for sexual ambivalence, attractiveness, and beauty, has become possible because of the decline of patriarchal roles for men.

Yet, if patriarchal roles for men have declined, why then, does the negotiation of displays of female and male nudity for beads persist?

Gender Tensions in the 'Throwing Game'

The origin of the current displays of nudity for beads is unclear. Kilburn (1992: 11) claims that the ritual can be traced back to the 1975 Carnival season, when a group of women on a balcony showed their breasts, and then held a sign stating something along the lines of 'We'll show our tits if you show your dicks'. Kilburn does not cite a reference for this story, but if true (or as much folklore, based upon a perceived truth), then it is important to note that the activity was initiated by women who were attempting to solicit *male* nudity. The act is not simply a means of providing pleasure for men, but a means of procuring a sexual thrill for the women and men alike.

The earliest newspaper account of nudity in the French Quarter that I was able to locate dates to 1986:

> The clientele of Lafitte's in Exile Bar on Bourbon Street did not let the cold put a stop to a more recent tradition probably peculiar to the French Quarter.
>
> In fact, the people who were willing to drop their drawers or lift their shirts – depending on their gender – for long strands of expensive cut glass and fake pearl beads, did not seem to notice the cold at all.
>
> The beads were offered by a group of young men who collect on the balcony of the bar to dangle the coveted beads over the head of potential exhibitionists (*Times Picayune* 1986).

Again, note that this description includes slightly different gender dynamics than are seen currently during Carnival. Men are enticing both men and women to expose themselves. Several important questions, for this analysis, are left unanswered by this news item. First, we have no idea of the sexual orientation of the men soliciting the nudity, although it is clear that they were soliciting acts of nudity from both men and women. We also get no feeling for whether males or females were more likely to comply with the requests. Today, requests for nudity displays are over-whelmingly directed towards women. The phrase 'show your tits!' is as commonly heard as 'throw me something, mister' during celebrations, while the phrase 'show your dick' is often seen as a play on the breast theme, rather than something that may have been introduced at the same time.

The only quantitative data on public displays of nudity that I have been able to locate were contained in Kilburn's (1992) sociology thesis, which aimed to study the structure of balcony/ground and float/street interactions and nudity. Using video cameras located throughout the French Quarter, his research team spent four days (February 9–12) during Carnival 1991 season and filmed displays of nudity, which he later analysed. His data records 409 breast exposures, sixty-three penis exposures, forty-seven buttocks exposures and one exposure of female genitalia. Unfortunately, it is unclear from Kilburn's data whether it is male or female breasts and buttocks that are being shown. However, since Kilburn takes a great deal of time explaining that bra and non-nipple views did not count as true 'shows', we may be able to assume that his focus was on collecting video-footage of female breasts. Even given his suspect numbers it is clear that by 1991, displays of nudity were biased towards female participation.

Why do women participate in public displays of nudity during Carnival? Answers to this question from participants generally group into several set answers: 'Why not?', 'It seemed to be okay to do,' 'I don't know why,' 'It's *Mardi Gras* and I wanted to let loose,' 'I was drunk,' 'I can't believe I did that,' 'I felt pressured,' and 'What's the big deal, guys go topless all of the time.' My informants were mainly college-aged women, who were attending school in Louisiana, but did not necessarily live permanently in the area. Several felt that they would never consider such an act outside of the Carnival context, but would again participate at Carnival, while others were embarrassed by what they had done and said they would not participate again. Still other informants used the opportunity to complain about the double standard that finds it acceptable for men to go topless or urinate in the street without punishment, whereas women are punished for the same behaviours.

Women who said they were unlikely to expose themselves again at Carnival cited peer pressure as the reason for their participation while women with no regrets were most likely to have made the decision to expose themselves before entering the Carnival atmosphere. The decision to expose oneself, or to provide oneself with the option, includes going to the festivities braless, and wearing a shirt conducive to display and to receiving solicitations. Tight-fitting, low-cut, stretch-knit shirts were popular among participants. Those women who had exposed themselves did not consider themselves to be sexually loose or in any way morally deficient, but instead saw themselves as controlling their bodies. Women who did not expose themselves, although solicited, were often embarrassed, and or insulted by the request, stating that they were not 'just a piece of meat', or a 'sex object'. Other women I have spoken with were disgusted by what they perceived to be the preference of male solicitors for certain 'types' of women. Many women perceived that blonde, thin, well-dressed, heavily made up women were the most likely to be solicited, and the most likely to receive 'good beads' without exposing themselves.

The negotiation of beads for displays of nudity is not a fully accepted behaviour, even within the Carnival setting. In Baton Rouge, in 1989, a local television reporter was removed from the air by her station after she exposed her breasts from a *Mardi Gras* float. The same television, in 1995, tried to cover up the arrest of their married male news anchor who had a voracious appetite for prostitutes. Only after a rival news programme broke the news of his arrest was the anchor reprimanded, asked to publicly apologize and removed from the air. Clearly, the female reporter had, in the eyes of the station management, committed the greater moral offence. In 1995, two women were arrested in Houma, Louisiana, for the offence of displaying their breasts. The following news blurb ran in the *New Orleans Times Picayune* (1995) under the title 'Beads for Breasts Brings Arrests':

> HOUMA A deputy sheriff jailed two women who allegedly bared their breasts in order to win the favors of bead throwing float riders.
>
> Breast baring for the colorful but nearly worthless beads is a common Carnival practice in New Orleans, particularly in the French Quarter. And its not unheard of in Houma, a smaller city about 40 miles to the southwest.
>
> Usually authorities look the other way. But on Monday night, Robin Lottman, 31 and Lisa Allen, 33, both of Houma, were charged with obscenity, a felony in Louisiana. Both have since been released on $3000 bail from the Terrebonne Parish Jail.

The article goes on to state that the arrests were made because other members of the crowd had complained to police that the women had bared their breasts while children were in the area. The mother of one of the defendants complained to the reporter that 'If you are going to pick up the girls for doing it, they should get the float riders for asking'. The float riders were not identified, nor were any charges brought against them. Charges against the two women were eventually dropped. In this, and the case of the news reporter, the actions of these women were perceived as a threat to the broader fabric of societal order, even within the context of Carnival celebrations.

Discussion and Conclusion

Throughout its history, Carnival has provided a forum for society to negotiate the boundaries that separate and define the genders. In particular, women have used public *Mardi Gras* celebrations as an opportunity to express and celebrate their sexuality, thereby contesting society's gender ideologies and power structures of a patriarchal society. When these women protesters were perceived as pushing society's boundaries too far, even if only within the context of Carnival, they could be punished with fines and imprisonment.

In the nineteenth and early twentieth centuries, prostitutes used Carnival as a time to confront society's internal conflicting and hypocritical views of femininity.

Dressing as men, wearing pants, smoking cigars and travelling in open coaches, both mocked their male clientele while also symbolically stating that they 'wore the pants' in their household, and were independent from the domestic drudgery that characterized the married woman's domain. At risk to their social reputation, women who were not prostitutes also donned the dress and behaviour of men for Carnival.

Likewise, in the early twentieth century, prostitutes paraded as 'Baby Dolls' through the French Quarter (Saxon et. al. 1991). Their small frilly costumes, styled after the dresses of young girls, also mocked the dual expectations that were placed on women by society. On one hand, the patriarchal society expected women to be innocent, 'little girls', of high moral standing, who would embrace the domestic sphere, and dutifully tend to their husbands and children. At the same time, as the prostitutes' livelihood so clearly illustrated, women were also used to fulfil the sexual needs of men. While men were allowed by society to be sexual beings as well as fathers and husbands, women's sexuality was to be suppressed. The sexually titillating 'Baby Doll' costume both mocked this double standard while also affirming, symbolically, women's sexuality.

Today, through the 'throwing game', the same tensions between men and women, and the nature of human sexuality are expressed. The bartering for beads that takes place at Carnival is complex. Through the solicitation of women, men on the floats attempt to exert control over female sexuality. The solicitation of a woman can create an atmosphere of intimidation, as other onlookers bully her to comply, which may ultimately lead her to reluctantly submit to the request. Still other women go to *Mardi Gras* with the expectation of being solicited and complying to both obtain beads, but also as an expression of their independence and control over their sexuality. Enticing the men to solicit them becomes a form of sexual control for the women. Displays are undertaken with the intention that payment will be offered for the display. Women at parades expect to receive the highest 'quality' of beads in exchange for displays of nudity. While some women perceive the display of breasts to be merely a transaction to earn beads coveted within the Carnival atmosphere, men may perceive this willingness to mean that the women are symbolically for sale, that their bodies can be purchased. Likewise, women are just as likely to perceive men as easily manipulated into providing bead wealth. Through the control of her body, a woman can exercise sexual control over men. Displays of large numbers of good beads on a woman may be interpreted to mean that she is sexually loose, but at the same time, communicates that she is a successfully powerful being. As such, the woman, as an individual is making a statement against societal norms which perceive women's sexuality to be dangerous.

Society, both within and beyond the context of Carnival, has attempted to reign in women's sexuality, and reinforce male control of it. Women who are obviously pregnant, and conforming to the socially acceptable role of woman as mother, are rewarded with bead wealth, as are women who are conforming to male ideals of female beauty. Older women, in their seventies or eighties, are also commonly rewarded with bead wealth, perhaps as tribute to their age, their status as perceived grandmothers, or perhaps for their perceived nonsexual status. While women who comply with male wishes and display their breasts after being solicited (even if the women may have intentionally dressed to attract the solicitation) are always rewarded with bead wealth, sexually aggressive women, who initiate unsolicited displays, are not always rewarded. In exposing themselves uninvited, these women are denying male control over the negotiation. Finally, society may punish women for their Carnival-world behaviour by imposing penalties from the 'outside' world upon them, such as the arrests and job suspension discussed above.

Women standing on the balconies of the French Quarter also attempt to assert their sexual control over men through the 'throwing game'. Women ask men to either show their 'dicks' or their 'tits'. Kilburn (1992) recorded 63 observed instances of penis exposure in his study of 1991 Carnival, but did not record whether these exposures were by men to other men, to women, or to mixed groups. I have witnessed two penis displays, one of which was a male displaying to a male, in the second instance, to a female audience. As a ground level participant, it is likely that I have missed other displays of this nature. I have observed far more instances of men exposing their chests to women, in exchange for beads. Unlike the negotiations between men and women over the display of women's breasts, which involves the breaking of a societal taboo regarding female nudity, the male display of a bare chest is within societal norms. In other words, women on balconies often reward men for staying within the boundaries of their prescribed gender norms. Society already acknowledges men's sexuality, it is not an issue to be negotiated during Carnival.

Like women, the Gay population of New Orleans also use the context of Carnival to express their sexuality and sexual power, both through dress and parade and through the bartering of beads. Soliciting males, be they Gay or straight, to expose their penises, provides a means of exerting sexual control while also expressing male identity in the same way as the float maskers. Like women, who may be intimidated into displaying their breasts reluctantly, heterosexual males are placed in the situation of being intimidated into displays of nudity by Gay men. In many ways, this Carnival activity plays upon the stereotypical homophobic fear of being 'hit on' by a Gay male, and the implications that may have for one's 'maleness'. The bead negotiation directly confronts this issue. Lesbians also participate in the 'throwing game', negotiating with women to display their breasts, yet these negotiations seem to lack some of the tension inherent in the men's negotiations.

It is not possible within the scope of this chapter to address all of the nuances of bead bartering at Carnival and the gender implications. Sexual access and control of sexuality, whether it be male or female, are just two aspects of the social, racial and economic issues that are expressed through the acquisition and wearing of beads during Carnival celebrations in New Orleans. Historically, women have used Carnival as an opportunity to cross gender lines set by society. Cross-dressing, once a scandalous *Mardi Gras* behaviour, is not a remarkable event, as women have successfully appropriated the garments of men as their own. The acceptance of the female body, and the broader issues of women's sexuality and right to control their own body, is still a much contested issue in today's society where domestic violence, prostitution, movements to restrict abortion and abolish sex education, sexual harassment and rape are all too common. An activity which was once apparently more gender-balanced, the solicitation of beads in exchange for a display of nudity, has become a means through which women and men negotiate control over themselves and one another with fake pearl beads.

References

De Caro, F. A. & Ireland, T. (1988), 'Every Man a King: Social Tension and Carnival in New Orleans', *International Folklore Review*, vol. 6, 58–66.

FWP (1938), Federal Writers' Project of the Works Progress Administration for the City of New Orleans, *New Orleans City Guide*, Boston: Houghton Mifflin.

Hardy, A. (1991), *Mardi Gras Guide*, 15th annual edition, New Orleans: Arthur Hardy Enterprises.

Huber, L. V. (1977), *Mardi Gras: A Pictorial History of Carnival in New Orleans*, Gretna: Pelican Publishing.

Kilburn, J. C. Jr. (1992), 'Ritualistic Exchange at *Mardi Gras*: An Examination of a Contemporary Urban Bacchic Ritual', unpublished Master Thesis, Baton Rouge: Louisiana State University.

Kinser, S. (1990), *Carnival American Style: Mardi Gras at New Orleans and Mobile*, Chicago: University of Chicago.

Mitchell, R. (1995), *All on a Mardi Gras Day: Episodes in the History of New Orleans Carnival*, Cambridge: Harvard University Press.

Saxon, L. (1928), *Fabulous New Orleans*, New York: The Century Co.

Saxon, L., Dreyer, E. & Tallant, R. (1991), *Gumbo Ya Ya*, Gretna: Pelican Press.

Tallant, R. (1948), *Mardi Gras*, Garden City, New York: Doubleday.

10

Beads, Prestige and Life Among the Kelabit of Sarawak, East Malaysia

Monica Janowski

The visitor to the Kelabit Highlands in Sarawak on the island of Borneo is immediately struck on landing in Bario by the beads worn by the women. Bario is nowadays the focal centre of the Kelabit Highlands and the only place to which the national carrier, MAS, flies. It is by far the largest settlement in the Kelabit Highlands, and receives outside visitors regularly. Perhaps because of the public gaze which the size of the settlement and the presence of outsiders puts them under daily, practically all women in Bario wear bead necklaces nearly all of the time when they are in a public place outside the longhouse, and very many of them – probably all those who own them – also wear bead caps (*petaa*) made up of the most highly valued beads (see Figure 10.1).

My fieldwork (twenty months 1986–8 and four months 1992–3) has been carried out in a small community about twelve hours' walk from Bario called Pa' Dalih, which now consists of three longhouses and a few individual houses, and which has a population of about 100. In 1987 I took photographs of all the beaded items in the possession of individuals in that community and the neighbouring tiny community of Batu Patong, which now has a population of about twenty. There were, in total, sixty-nine beaded items – necklaces, caps and belts. Most of my data comes from Pa' Dalih, although some is from short visits to Bario and discussions with Bario people visiting Pa' Dalih and some was collected in town. Although beads are worn less in Pa' Dalih than in Bario, their ownership is of great significance and beads are restrung, examined and discussed very often.

There are dozens of named varieties of beads in the Kelabit Highlands. I shall not here give an exhaustive description of all of these; I shall rather give an overview of the most important varieties, and I shall explore what I see as the rationale behind the possession and wearing of them. Bario, which is today the major Kelabit centre in the Highlands, has a population of about 1000 most of whom live in six one- or two-longhouse communities within less than an hour's walk from each other but separate in jural and administrative terms and in terms of land use. A small number live outside the immediate Bario area there are a further seven longhouse

213

Figure 10.1 *Petaa* or bead cap with *ba'o rawir* beads in a broad band across the front. (Photo: Monica Janowski.)

communities, three within a few hours' walk of Bario and four in the southern part of the Highlands at a day's walk or more away, one of which is Pa' Dalih, my field site. Each of these communities has a population of no more than about 100 people; thus the total population of all of these Kelabit longhouses is no more than 1500. There are about an equal number of Relabit living in towns, mostly in Miri. These are in regular contact with the Highlands; there are daily flights from Miri up to Bario. Town life in Sarawak revolves to a large extent around ethnic identity, and, at least among the Kelabit, social life is expected quite explicitly to be based largely on networks based on this kind of identity. For the Kelabit, these networks include not only Kelabit, but also, to some extent, Lun Bawang from the Fifth Division, who speak a closely related language and who belong to the same Christian church, the Sidang Injil Borneo. Maintenance of Kelabit identity in town is through social practices and also through material culture. The possession of varieties of beads valued among the Kelabit is a very important part of this. While beads are rarely worn in town, except by older people visiting or living with their children or grandchildren, it is considered important for status for a woman to possess a good collection of old beads.

The Kelabit in the Highlands and their Relations with Neighbouring Groups

The Kelabit Highlands is part of an inland tableland at about 3000–3500 feet above sea level which spans Kalimantan, which is part of Indonesia, and Sarawak and Sabah, which are part of Malaysia. A number of rivers originate in the Highlands which is quite clearly separated from other areas by mountains and difficult terrain. The part of this tableland which forms the Kelabit Highlands is in Sarawak, and is at the headwaters of the Baram, which drains to the sea near Miri, also in Sarawak. It is isolated from the lower reaches of the Baram, however, because the river becomes unnavigable many days' walk below the Kelabit Highlands.

The term Kelabit is one which came into currency early this century (Harrisson 1958). It is not clear to what extent the ancestors of the people who now call themselves and are called 'Kelabit' had any unity – politically, culturally or economically – at that time. Now, however, they do think of themselves as a group which has cohesion vis-à-vis non-Kelabit, even if there are other closely related people living in other parts of the tableland.

In the past the Kelabit were dispersed in a larger number of longhouse communities, mostly within the area which has come to be known as the Kelabit Highlands. The present configuration of settlement derives from the confrontation with Indonesia in the early sixties when, because of the proximity of the border, the majority of communities resettled in the Bario area. This was partly through encouragement from the government, which was concerned with security near the border, and partly because of the expectation which has been borne out that Bario would become a centre for government services, including health services and an air link with the coast. There does exist a rivalry between Bario and other settlements even nowadays, however, and there is a resistance on the part of many people, like those in Pa' Dalih to move to Bario.

The Kelabit Highlands is separated from the rest of the tableland of which it forms a part by ranges of mountains, which are however easily crossed by a number of passes. Most of the rest of the tableland area is inhabited by people closely related linguistically and culturally to the Kelabit, who have been variously called Murut, Lun Dayeh and Lun Bawang and who speak languages belonging to what Hudson has called the Apo Duat language group (Hudson 1977). Jayl Langub (Langub 1987) has suggested that the term Lun Bawang is the most appropriate for this group, and I shall use this term. The Lun Bawang to the east of the Kelabit live in Kalimantan in Indonesia, since the border follows the range of mountains separating the Kelabit Highlands from their area. Those to the north, in the Ba Kelalan and Long Semadoh area, are in the Fifth Division of Sarawak.

Kin, social and trading relations between the Kelabit and the Lun Bawang are quite close at the present time, and in the past it is likely that this was also the case, although broken by periods of feud. The Kelabit did not, however, until the introduction of a regular air service, have very significant trading relations with areas outside the Highland area. Travel to places further down the Baram was very difficult in the past, involving a journey of some weeks in many cases. On the west and south the Kelabit Highlands are separated from areas inhabited by other tribes by very rugged terrain. In this direction were nevertheless traded, although probably on an infrequent basis, items in demand outside the Highland area but in the production of which the Highlands were specialized. This included damar resin, the salt produced in the Highlands from salt springs and tobacco. Such items were traded for manufactured items such as cloth and for prestige items – Chinese jars, gongs and beads.

Material Culture and Beads: Influences from Outside

In the course of trade outside the interior tableland area the Kelabit came into contact with the cultures of the Kenyah and Kayan living further down the Baram in a way which related Lun Bawang living in the interior did not. Due, it would appear, to this exposure, Kelabit crafts bear many similarities to those of the Kenyah groups, particularly in the decoration of such items as baskets and beaded items made of machine-made beads: the Kelabit use many of the animal and anthropomorphic images which are used by the Kenyah. However, it would not appear that

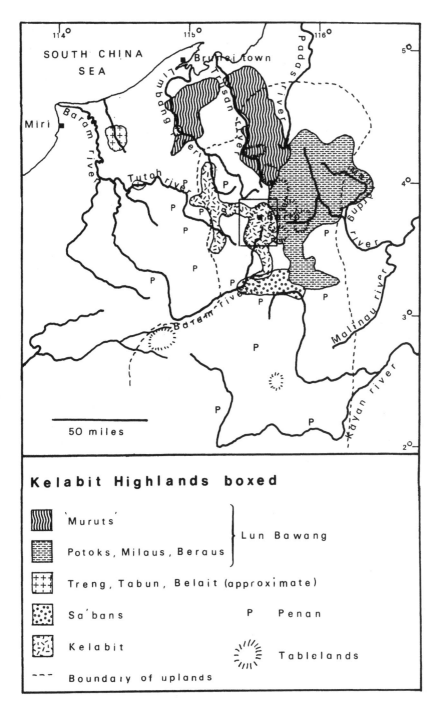

Distribution of speakers of *Apo Duat* languages

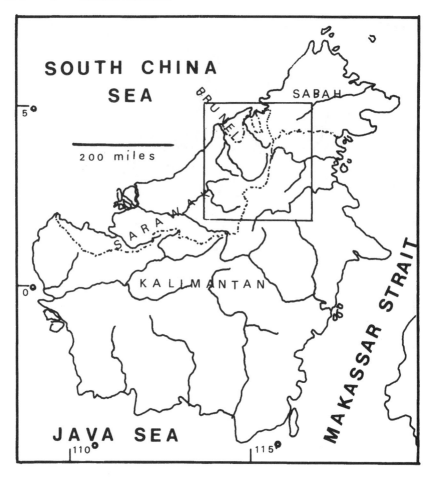

Borneo with *Apo Duat* area boxed

this goes very deep: the Kelabit do not seem to attribute much significance or symbolic value to these images while the Kenyah certainly do (Whittier 1973).

As far as old beads are concerned, however, the Kelabit were until recently influenced in their tastes only to a very limited extent by peoples outside the Highland area. The beads which have been valued by the Kelabit are almost all different from those valued by peoples further down the Baram and appear to be very similar to those valued by the Lun Bawang. Recently, with the enormously greater exposure of the Kelabit Highlands to outside, down-Baram influences, the Kelabit have begun to acquire more beads of kinds valued by the Kenyah and Kayan who live down river, but these are still not considered to be of the highest value. The beads most esteemed nowadays are still beads which appear to be peculiar to the Kelabit and Lun Bawang of the Highland area.

What Makes a Bead Valuable?

For the Kelabit, probably the most important point about a bead, in terms of assessing its value, is its age. The most valuable beads are all considered to be *ma'on* ('ancient'). There is very little information about beads in Borneo, and only few references to Kelabit beads (although see Sarawak Museum 1978, Mumam 1991, Harrison 1950, Jamowski 1993b.) There is a good collection of Kelabit beads at the Brunei Museum, however, judging from what I have learnt from Heidi Munan in Kuching and from Professor Ian Glover of the Institute of Archaeology at the University of London, the Kelabit estimate of the relative ages of different beads appears to be fairly accurate – they do not make an absolute estimate in terms of years or any other measure of time, simply judging relative ancient-ness – and it seems that many of those they consider really ancient may in fact be a couple of thousand years old.

However, age is not the only quality which a bead must have to be valuable. A major point about very valuable beads is that they are said to derive 'from our ancestors', *let tetepo*. Beads are a form of heirloom (*pusaka* in Malay) as are dragon jars and gongs. Their value is not only in themselves but is related to who has owned them in the past. I shall return to this later.

Bead Fashions and Ways of Wearing Beads

It is possible to retrieve data on which beads were worn most and were considered most valuable back to about the beginning of this century, and it is clear from this that fashions have changed considerably during this time – and presumably did before that too.

The two major ways of wearing and displaying beads are the necklace (*bane*) and the bead cap (*petaa*). While necklaces are worn by both men and women, bead caps are worn only by men. The Kelabit are constantly undoing and remaking necklaces and bead caps, combining and recombining beads in different ways according to changes in fashion (see Figure 10.2).

The *petaa*, or bead cap (see Figure 10.1) is the highest concentration of value. There is both documentary and verbal evidence of such caps existing back to about the beginning of this century, and there is no reason to suppose that they were an innovation then. *Petaa* contain two varieties of beads: one valuable and a number of much less valuable varieties, with the valuable variety displayed in a broad band across the front of the cap. An interesting point about these caps is that fashion dictates which variety is displayed at the front. In the course of the century this has changed, but whichever variety is in fashion – and this was probably true also in the past – practically all bead caps are based on that variety.

It appears that in the early part of this century the heavy cornelian beads known

Figure 10.2 Making a bead cap. (Photo: Monica Janowski.)

as *ba'o burur* (see Figure 10.3) in the Kelabit Highlands were placed at the front of the cap. As far as I know there are no caps left containing these beads, only necklaces, and these are rarely worn. Later the green and blue glassy beads known as *let* or *ba'o bata'* (see Figure 10.4) displaced *ba'o burur*; no examples of these caps remain either. More recently, from about the 1950s onwards, the small elongated orange beads called *ba'o rawir* have become particularly sought after for bead caps, and all those that I know of except one have these beads at the front, including that shown in Figure 10.1.

The fact that a certain variety is fashionable for bead caps does not mean that it becomes more valuable, at least not in theory. The Kelabit say that *ba'o burur* and *ba'o bata'* are as valuable as *ba'o rawir*, since they are equally ancient. However, people are not, at least at the moment, interested in buying *ba'o burur* and *ba'o bata'*. Their theoretical value is maintained by the fact that they are not normally sold at all. When I managed (with difficulty) to persuade certain Kelabit ladies to sell me some of these unfashionable varieties, there was considerable difficulty establishing what price I should pay.

There is a standardized pattern to the choice of beads used for the Kelabit bead cap, and this appears to have been the case with previous caps based on *ba'o burur* and *ba'o bata* as well as with the present-day cap. Not only are the high-value beads at the front the same, but the rest of the beads – which for the current cap based on *ba'o rawir* are of little value and may even be machine-made – are placed in a standardized order (see Figure 10.5). There is a little room for innovation, but only in the cheapest and most unimportant of the constituent beads – for example, while it is usual to use one type of small red bead in one part of the cap, other types, including modern ones, may be used. Also, the width of the band of high-value beads at the front of the cap varies, and it is obviously more prestigious to have a wider band. However the general pattern hardly varies at all.

The high-value beads at the front of the cap account for by far the greatest part of its value. They are, nowadays, valued in money terms, and in these terms each bead is worth about M$20, which means that the cap is worth from M$4000 to (I have been told) M$8000. These sums are equivalent to £1000 and £4000 respectively and indicate the enormous repositories of wealth which the caps represent.

Ba'o burur, ba'o bata' and *ba'o rawir* are not the most valuable beads, however. The variety called *alai* (see below) is one of these. The other extremely valuable category is the small number of multichrome, European beads (*ba'o barit*, literally 'painted beads') which the Kelabit possessed until recently (when multichrome beads have entered the Highlands in greater numbers, coming from downriver tribes like the Kenyah and Kayan who presumably had more contact with outside traders).

It would seem that the reason these very valuable beads are not made into bead caps is simply that very few people have enough of them to do this. There was one elderly lady called Mata Bulat (literally 'Eyes Wide Open') with whom I was

Figure 10.3 String (*bane*) of *ba'o burur* beads, which are still considered valuable but are no longer fashionable. (Photo: Monica Janowski.)

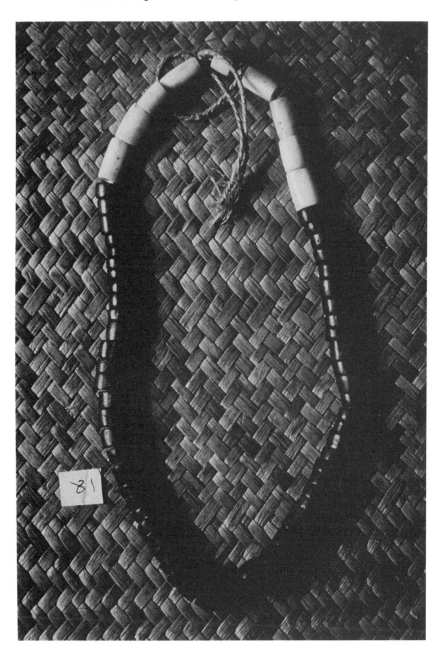

Figure 10.4   String (*bane*) of let or *ba'o bata'* beads, which are still considered valuable but are no longer fashionable. (Photo: Monica Janowski.)

Figure 10.5 *Petaa* or bead cap from the side, showing the order in which beads are placed in the cap, which is fixed. (Photo: Monica Janowski.)

acquainted but who died in 1992 who owned a bead cap based on the very valuable *alai* (Figure 10.6 shows Mata Bulat wearing her *setaa*). She was renowned for her bead wealth. She also owned a bead cap based on *ba'o rawir*.

All beads, including those of high value, may be made into necklaces, *bane*. Young men often wear strings containing beads considered valuable some decades ago – the *ba'o burur* and *ba'o bata'* mentioned above. Figure 10.7 shows a young man wearing his necklace, which contains such beads, as well as a high-value multi-coloured bead in the centre.

In the past it appears that bead aprons and jackets in the Highlands were made by the Kelabit. These are no longer made and I have never seen one. Belts (*brit*) are sometimes made from the smaller beads, mostly the less valuable ones, and in the last couple of years in particular this has become fashionable (see Figure 10.8).

The Material and Colour of Beads

Most Kelabit beads are made of glass, except for the cornelian *ba'o burur* and a variety called *ulub*, made of shell, which formerly were used at the side of *ba'o bata'* and *ba'o burur*-based bead caps and at the back of necklaces based on these beads (Figure 10.4).

Almost all of the glass beads which the Kelabit possessed until recently were monochrome. However, the Kelabit can see differences in colour between beads which appear to me to be the same. Thus, there are two kinds of *alai*, although I could not see the difference between them. The more prestigious Kelabit ladies who owned necklaces made of *alai* had no trouble at all distinguishing between the two kinds. The more ancient type may be worth as much as M$150 (about £43) for each bead, while the less ancient type may be bought for M$30 (about £7.50). Mata Bulat's *alai* bead cap (Figure 10.6) which was made of the more ancient variety, would have been worth perhaps M$80,000 (£20,000). Most *alai* are opaque yellow (see Figure 10.9), although there are blue *alai*, which are not worth much less.

Very few Kelabit traditional beads are multichrome. The few that exist are of high value, however, and their ownership history is well known. The beads at the centre of the necklace seen in Figure 10.10 are called *labang kalong* and are said to have been worth a human life each. Multi-coloured beads, described in general as *ba'o barit*, literally 'painted beads', are presumably of European, probably Venetian, origin and must have entered the area later than the monochrome beads, which are of Indian, Middle Eastern and perhaps Chinese origin (Mumam 1991).

Recently, multi-coloured beads have been entering the Highlands in greater numbers. Most of these derive from the Kenyah and Kayan. Some of these newly

Figure 10.6 *Petaa* or bead cap with *alai* beads as the beads placed across the front in a broad band. (Photo: Monica Janowksi.)

Figure 10.7 String of beads (*bane*) worn by a young man. It is made up of beads which are no longer fashionable, although some are considered valuable. (Photo: Monica Janowski.)

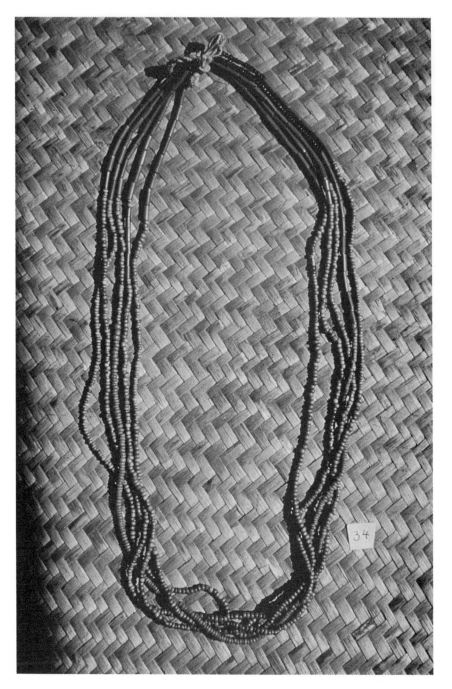

Figure 10.8 Belt (*brit*) made up of beads of little value. (Photo: Monica Janowski.)

Figure 10.9 String of beads (*bane*) with yellow *alai* beads at the sides. At the top are beads from the Bead Shop in Covent Garden, London. (Photo: Monica Janowski.)

Figure 10.10 String of beads (*bane*) with very high value beads in the middle called by the Kelabit *labang kalong*, which in the past were considered to be worth a human life each. (Photo: Monica Janowski.)

arrived multi-coloured beads are particularly popular, especially among some of the young ladies in Bario. They are not favoured by older women, however. The prices which are given for them do not compare with those given for the most valuable of the high-value Kelabit beads, never exceeding M$20 (£5) per bead and usually ranging between M$5 (£1.25) and M$10 (£2.50).

Besides old handmade beads, the Kelabit also have some machine-made beads. They have been doing beadwork of the Kayan/Kenyah type for some time, using the tiny town-bought glass beads. Such beading is still practised, although it may have diminished somewhat in importance. Centres for sun hats, beaded decorations for rattan baskets and beaded necklaces are made (see Figure 10.11). These may be made entirely of tiny beads. They may also be made partly of tiny beads strung and then wound into a bunch and partly of valuable old beads (see Figure 10.12). The tiny beads used for beading are still quite sought after in the Highlands and prices given for them exceed considerably their value in town. There are few ladies who are able to do beadwork, and their work as well as the beads themselves are priced very high.

The Kelabit also buy the larger machine-made glass and plastic beads which are available in town nowadays. These are sometimes mixed with old beads in necklaces, usually with beads of little value. In addition, they make beads themselves out of lead, cast in small-bore bamboo (see Figure 10.13). These are used in the present-day bead cap as one of the minor beads at the sides.

Innovation in Beads

The Kelabits are quite innovative in their interest in beads. Although they place the highest value on those which they consider ancient and 'from their ancestors', they are always interested in any beads. When I showed them a catalogue from the bead shop in London's Covent Garden enormous interest was shown and everybody wanted to order some, being willing to pay quite high prices. In the end, not knowing to whom to give the beads which I eventually received from the shop, I gave them to the church in Pa'Dalih to be auctioned. Giving items to the church for auction is very usual; every week at the main church service on Sunday there is an auction of such items, which include vegetables, rice, valued gathered items (e.g. honey) and things bought in town. This is a recognized way of donating money to the church and also of generating prestige. The auction was not only a way out of my difficulty but provided an interesting way of assessing how much these new beads were valued and how the assessment of their value developed over the course of the auction. My Covent Garden beads fetched quite considerable prices in the auction, more than they cost in London, although much less than old Kelabit beads. Interestingly, their value rose quite a lot over the course of the auction, due, I think, to people

Figure 10.11 Beaded necklace made up of tiny town-bought beads. (Photo: Monica Janowski.)

Figure 10.12 Man's string of beads (*bane*) which used to belong to Penghulu Miri, leader of the Kelabit of the southern part of the Highlands during and after the Second World War, which contains high-value beads and also tiny town-bought beads wound into a bunch. (Photo: Monica Janowski.)

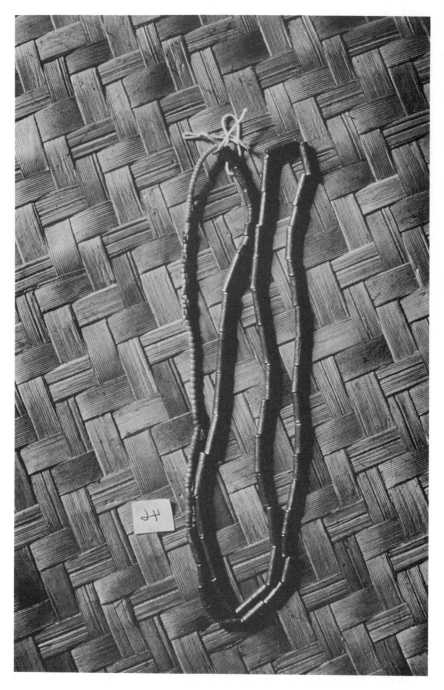

Figure 10.13 Collection of beads including lead beads cast by the Kelabit in small-bore bamboo. (Photo: Monica Janowski.)

seeing how interested certain prestigious ladies were in buying them. They began immediately to be incorporated into necklaces, often together with high-value beads (see Figure 10.9), and their value rose even more.

Beads and 'Big People'

The Kelabit longhouse is divided up into residential units which cultivate, cook and consume rice together, and which I have called hearth-groups (Janowski 1995); these are headed by a couple termed its *lun merar*, literally 'big people', who are those who direct the rice-growing of the hearth-group. It is the *lun merar* of a hearth-group who buy, keep and wear most beads, and certainly those of high value. In a given hearth-group there may be more than one couple, although only one in each generation, as is usual for Sarawak tribal peoples. However there is normally one focal, decision-making couple, and these are the *lun merar* of the hearth-group. Older and younger couples, who are not so actively involved in rice-growing, are subsidiary and follow the decisions made by the focal couple.

Beads and Gender

It is nowadays mainly *lun merar* women who wear beads, particularly high-value beads. Although Kelabit men do wear beads (see Figure 10.14), many *lun merar* men do not wear any. However, in the past *lun merar* men did wear valuable beads. I have seen necklaces consisting of very valuable beads belonging to the leader of the southern Kelabit, Penghulu Lawai, who lived in Pa' Dalih and whose widow is still there (see Figure 10.12), and photographs taken by Tom Harrisson at the time of the Second World War (Harrison 1959) show men wearing necklaces containing valuable beads. It seems probable that the fact that men wear beads less nowadays may be due to exposure to a town culture which discourages the wearing of beads by men. However, beads appear to have always been more of a female business, as jars and gongs used to be male business. Beads are inherited through females, just as jars and gongs are inherited through males. It is women who know about beads – and who discuss them endlessly. Their interest in beads is, in fact, catching; as a female myself, I too became interested in beads to the point of attempting to buy as many as possible. However, although I managed after a good deal of effort to buy some *ba'o bata'*, some *ba'o burur*, and a number of odds and ends, I was simply unable to buy any *ba'o rawir*; the Kelabit women were certainly not selling them and they always beat me to it when Lun Bawang people came to sell them. I was unable to buy *alai* and traditional Kelabit multichrome beads for the same reasons; but I would not have been able to afford many in any case!

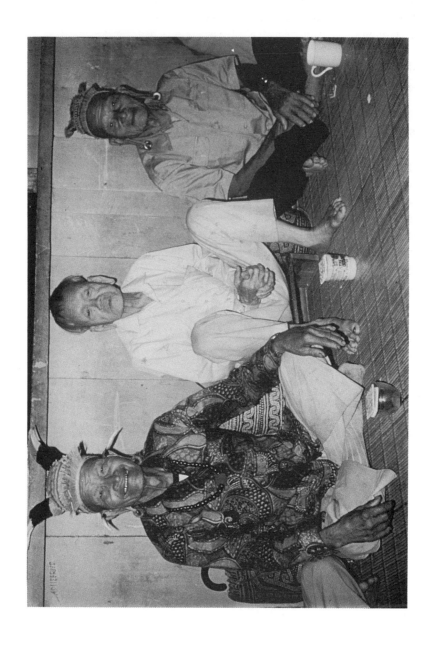

Figure 10.14   Group of Kelabit men at an *irau* feast. One is wearing a string of beads (*bane*). (Photo: Monica Janowski.)

Among the young, beads are worn by both sexes. Children up to their teens may have necklaces belonging to their mothers placed around their necks, but usually the beads are not valuable. Teenage boys, as has been mentioned already, often wear old-fashioned but theoretically valuable beads, which they make up into short chokers (see Figure 10.7). Teenage girls wear valuable and fashionable necklaces belonging to their mothers, and as they grow older will be given necklaces and even bead caps for themselves.

Beads, Status and Status Mobility

Beads are a prestige marker, as gongs and jars used to be. The Kelabit system of prestige differentiation is based on how 'good' (*doo*) a person is considered to be, as I discuss elsewhere (see Janowski 1991: Chapter 8). It has been argued that the Lun Bawang group, including the Kelabit, used to have a system of 'stratification' similar to that of the Kayan and the Kenyah (Crain 1970: 183; Deegan 1973: 86; King 1978: 21; Rousseau 1990: Chapter 7). I would disagree with this, and would argue that the lack of distinction between named 'strata' among the Kelabit is not a degeneration of a previous system but an inherent part of the way prestige is constructed. Kelabit scholars writing on their own people also argue that what they term 'stratification' used to exist but has diminished or vanished since the Second World War (Lian-Saging 1976/77: 115–25; Talla 1979: 76–90; Bulan, n.d.). However, their designation of classes does not agree, and the labels which they appear to be loan words from Kayan and Kenyah.

How 'good' a person is, is in turn, based on the status of *lun merar*, or 'big person'. It is as a member of a married couple that an individual is a 'big person' and a 'good person', and all successful couples, heads of hearth-groups, may be described as such. However, heads of longhouses and groups of longhouses are 'bigger' and 'better' and there is a sense in which only they can be described as 'good people' – in some contexts they are described as *lun doo to'oh*, or 'really good people'. An equivalence between adults, literally 'big people' and those of high status appears to exist in the 'stratified' societies of Borneo as well (see Rousseau 1974: 343–4 and 403–4). In the past, I was told, only such 'really good people' had the very valuable beads. The other two major markers of status of this type were Chinese dragon jars and gongs. Of the three markers, however, only beads are still actively sought and displayed. People proudly display the very valuable varieties as proof that they are 'really good'.

The link between beads and status has developed a new twist nowadays, which arises from the very fluid situation with regard to status mobility due to the pattern of cash influx. Since the Second World War, and especially since the early sixties, when an airstrip was constructed in Bario, MAS, the national carrier, has allowed a special rate for rice and this, coupled with the demand for Bario rice in towns on the coast in Sarawak such as Miri and Kuching has led to a great deal of rice being sent down for sale. In addition, many Kelabit go temporarily or permanently to work in town and some send money back, although this is a less important source of wealth. There is a positive mania for buying beads, because these are markers of prestige and it is hoped that the possession of them will legitimate status mobility. Those that can afford to buy them do so at every opportunity. It is practically impossible for an outsider like myself to buy any beads, even beads of little value. Kelabit nowadays practically never sell beads to each other, because they avoid selling any beads at all. However Lun Bawang from over the border, where there are similar bead tastes, bring beads into the Kelabit Highlands to sell, particularly the high-value ones which are so much in demand for bead caps, *ba'o rawir*. There are more opportunities for earning money in Sarawak, and thus the Kelabit have money which the Lun Bawang want. Therefore it is possible for the Kelabit to satisfy their hunger for beads without buying from each other.

The money which has entered the Highlands has not been spread out evenly, however. It has hardly reached the communities in the southern part of the Highlands such as Pa' Dalih, since it is too far for them to carry much rice to Bario to send down by MAS. Even within the Bario area, access to land suitable for making permanent wet rice fields for growing *pade adan*, the small-grained rice in demand on the coast, is restricted and is not evenly distributed. When resettlement took place in the early 1960s, land was allocated in such a way that some hearth-groups have access to more and better land than others. Those hearth-groups with more land are able to work it with the help of hired labour from over the border in Lun Bawang areas – indeed the people of those areas are especially skilled in wet rice cultivation, even more so than the Kelabit. The hearth-groups which have benefited are in some cases those already considered to be of high status, but in many cases they are hearth-groups which may have previously been of low status.

Although those who have acquired wealth try to legitimate it by purchasing beads, there is a good deal of private gossip about whether or not individuals are really 'good'. In the Kelabit Highlands status traditionally derived from success in rice cultivation, and the sale of rice in town could be seen as part of the same tradition. Thus the status being advertised through beads appears to a certain degree to be legitimate. Nevertheless, the status acquired through successful rice cultivation was much harder won and was carried out with only minimal help from non-hearth-group labour, since there was no corvée and there were few slaves. The present rapid – and, some might say, unfairly distributed – acquisition of wealth is therefore seen as in some sense contentious.

The Rice Meal, *Irau* Feasts, Beads and Status

Status is advertised not only in the display of prestige heirloom items such as beads, but also in the holding of lavish *irau*, feasts, where the host hearth-group provides the whole of the Kelabit population with a rice meal. The rice meal is focal in the generation of prestige, of 'goodness', as I discuss elsewhere (see Janowski 1991: Chapter 8; Janowski 1995). It is this which generates the status of *lun merar* and of *lun doo*. The rice meal occurs at different levels: at the basic hearth-group level, where it is provided by the 'big people' of the hearth-group, at the longhouse level, where it is eaten together by all members of the longhouse, and at the multi-longhouse level, where it occurs at *irau* (see Carsten 1987 for an analysis of the constitution of 'houses' at different levels through the rice meal in Langkawi off Peninsular Malaysia). In the provision of *irau* the host hearth-group puts itself in the position of provider for and parents/grandparents of the whole of the Kelabit population; *irau* are essentially huge rice meals.

Irau are one of the most important occasions at which beads are displayed. Women take out their best beads to display and all who have them wear bead caps (see Figure 10.15). There is, especially in Bario, considerable competition in the holding of *irau*; although all hearth-groups hold them, the most lavish and well-attended generate the most prestige. They are very public events, often hosting thousands of guests, and thus are important fora for the display of prestige through beads.

Kelabit Notions of Life Force

Beads, then, are associated with being *lun merar* and *lun doo*. The point about being *lun merar/lun doo* is that a successful couple is the source of human life (*ulun*) for one's dependants – whether these are only the members of the basic hearth-group or, for the leader of a group of longhouses, all the inhabitants. *Ulun* is what differentiates proper humans from all other forms of life, including hunters and gatherers. In the traditional setting it is only through rice-growing that it is possible to generate *ulun*. However, the generation of *ulun* is also based on harnessing and domesticating raw life force from the forest, *lalud*. The relationship between rice and this raw life force is played out at the rice meal, which consists of wild foods (vegetables and meat) and rice.

Life Force, Gender and Prestige

The rice meal as a whole is the achievement of the *lun merar* couple. It is described as *kuman nuba'* ('eating rice') and this is indicative of the way in which rice is

Figure 10.15 Line of women dancing at an *irau* feast. They all belong to the same longhouse, and are wearing a 'uniform' and a *petaa* (bead cap) with a broad band of *ba'o rawir* beads across the front. (Photo: Monica Janowski.)

often made to stand for the whole meal. In the same way, rice is associated with the couple as a unity. However, it is also associated with the female, as wild foods and *lalud* are with the male. While females know more about the subtleties of rice-growing and used to have personal relationships with the rice spirit, Deraya, males are more associated with the bringing in of the most important of wild foods, meat. Males go hunting in the forest on almost a daily basis in Pa' Dalih, while females normally never go into the primary forest unaccompanied – although they gather in young secondary growth.

I have discussed elsewhere the subtle way in which both the separateness and the unity of the two genders are significant among the Kelabit (Janowski 1995). There is no straightforward association between *lalud* and men, just as there is not between rice and women. Although rice is associated with women, it is also associated with both men and women as *lun merar* couple. In the same way wild foods, and *lalud*, are associated with men but also with the couple.

Both *ulun* and *lalud* are prestigious, because both are associated with the provision of life for dependants, and this is the source of prestige for the Kelabit. And both are associated with the *lun merar* couple, who accumulate *lalud* and, as a unity, bring it together with rice and generate *ulun* for their dependants.

Living Beads, the Natural Environment and Life Force

I would suggest that beads, and in the past other heirlooms such as jars and gongs, represent a crystallization of this raw life force, *lalud*. This is the reason for their prestige, and for their association with the *lun merar* couple.

Beads, and in the past other heirlooms, are treated as though they were in some sense alive. Thus jars, especially very valuable ones belonging to people of high status, were said to roar and to be potentially malevolent (Harrisson 1959). The very high value beads – *alai* and the varieties of multichrome bead (*ba'o barit*) which have been in Kelabit possession since before the recent influx of multichrome beads – are talked of in ways which suggest that they reproduce. I witnessed a man from the Lun Bawang Kerayan area over the Indonesian border attempting to sell a huge yellow bead which he called *pun alai* (grandparent of the *alai* beads) to a Kelabit lady. He was asking several hundreds of dollars for this bead, and no one was willing to buy it. However it excited great interest, and his claim that it was *pun alai* was taken seriously. These valuable varieties generally exist in both male and female form: small but suggestive differences between two beads which are called by the same name are indicative of gender. The difference is often between an oval male bead and a round female bead. Small varieties of valuable beads are called *anak* or 'children' of the larger beads. Figure 10.16 shows a necklace containing 'male', 'female' and 'children' beads.

Figure 10.16 String of beads containing beads described by the Kelabit as 'male', 'female' and 'children'. (Photo: Monica Janowski.)

As far as the Kelabits are concerned, beads do not have a human origin, but a natural one, and it seems probable that this was the attitude to jars and gongs too in the past. There is no knowledge in the Kelabit Highlands as to the source of any of the beads which are in the possession of either the Kelabit or other tribes. Even nowadays, although Kelabit living in town may know that beads are manufactured, those living in the Highlands are unaware of this fact and many express the opinion that beads are of natural origin.

It would seem, then, that the Kelabit believe that beads carry a life force. It seems clear that if beads are considered to have a life force, this is *lalud*; only humans – and only rice-growing humans, at that (see Janowski 1990) – have *ulun*. The Kelabit exhibit a considerable interest in stone; they used to keep luck stones called 'thunder stones' (*batu perahit*) in rice storage, in the belief that this would make the amount of rice increase, and until the 1950s they erected megalithic stones at *irau* feasts to commemorate prominent leaders. Other Borneo peoples keep small luck stones which, like Kelabit beads, are believed to reproduce. It may well be that the Kelabit regard beads as equivalent in some sense to stones.

Beads, Life Force and the Inheritance of Prestige

It is the 'very good people' (*lun doo to 'oh*) who, at least until recently, owned the most valuable and most ancient beads (*ba'o ma'on*), the ones which reproduce and seem to carry life force from the forest (*lalud*). These beads are considered to have been in the possession of 'very good' people for many generations.

The Kelabit appear to believe that the potential to be 'good' is inherited. They place emphasis both on ancestry as a predictor of achievement and on actual achievement. There is, however, a tendency for the former to be a self-fulfilling prophecy; those who believe themselves to have 'good' ancestry and who are believed by others to have it appear to be the most likely to be successful rice growers and providers for others. Those whose ancestry is not believed to be so 'good' have to make an effort to overcome their own and others' scepticism about their ability to succeed.

To a large extent, 'good' ancestry is legitimated and proven through the possession of beads, and, in the past, jars and gongs, which have been inherited from 'good' ancestors. It is 'very good' people who own beads described as being 'from our ancestors' (*let tetepo*), as I mentioned earlier. It might be argued that such beads have proved their possession of strong life force (*lalud*) over the generations by enabling their owners to fulfil the potential which they were born with, through their 'good' ancestry, to be successful in rice-growing and the provision of rice, particularly at feasts. On the other hand, it is also possible that they are seen as depositories of the *lalud* accumulated by their owners.

It is in this light that the emphasis on the history of the ownership of beads should be understood. The drive to purchase beads as part of a bid for upward mobility should also be understood in this light. If the Lun Merar of a hearth-group own beads classed as 'ancient', this legitimates their claims to be 'good', which cannot only be based on performance but need to be founded on 'good' ancestry – which is traditionally proven by bead ownership. It remains to be seen whether beads will go the way of gongs and jars and cease to be a marker of status.

Conclusion

In this chapter I have given some information about the types of beads which the Kelabit value and wear. I have analysed the association between beads, adulthood and prestige and have suggested that beads are strongly associated with *lun merar* ('big people'), as married couples heading hearth groups are termed, and with high status or *lun doo* ('good people') a status, which, as I have argued elsewhere (Janowski 1991: Chapter 8), are equivalent. 'Big people' are responsible for providing the rice meal for dependants; this is the basis of their prestige. I have also pointed out, however, that beads are associated with *lun merar* women more than with *lun merar* men.

Beads appear to be seen as having a life of their own. They may be regarded as repositories of *lalud*, either in and of themselves or through the depositing of *lalud* accumulated by their owners over generations. *Lalud*, as I have pointed out here and elsewhere, is associated with the male rather than the female (Janowski 1992, 1993a, 1994). However, the links between gender and the generation of human life (*ulun*) through the rice meal is a complex one (Janowski 1995). There is no one-to-one association between the two components of the rice meal and the two genders. As rice stands for the whole process in many contexts, so, I would suggest, can *lalud*. Where it is made to stand for the whole process it necessarily becomes associated with the couple as a unity, male+female undivided – the prestigious 'big people' couple as a seamless entity.

I have pointed out that because of changes in agriculture, the sale of rice to the coast from Bario and income from town, there have been profound changes in the distribution of wealth (in the form of both rice and money), especially in Bario itself. Because of this, bids for upward status mobility are being made. Concurrently, and I would argue as part of the same phenomenon, there is a very strong interest in buying beads, which are brought in for sale from across the Indonesian border by the closely related peoples there, who belong to the same Apo Duat language group. The beads which are bought are those varieties traditionally valued in both areas and which are seen as 'ancient', and 'from our ancestors'. I have argued that the buying of these beads is part of an effort to legitimate bids for upward status mobility.

References

Bulan, L. (n.d.), A Kelabit discourse, unpublished manuscript.

Carsten, J. (1987), 'Analogues or Opposites: Household and Community in Pulau Langkawi, Malaysia', in C. Macdonald et les membres de l'ECASE (ed.), *De la hutte au palais: societés 'á maison' en Asie du Sue-Est Insulaire*, Paris: Editions du Centre National de la Recherche Scientifique.

Crain, J.B. (1970), 'The Lun Dayeh of Sabah, East Malaysia: Aspects of Marriage and Social Exchange', Ph.D. thesis, Cornell University; published by University Microfilms.

Deegan, J.L. (1973), 'Change among the Lun Bawang, a Borneo people', unpublished Ph.D thesis, Washington University.

Freeman, D. (1955), *Report on the Iban*, London School of Economics Monographs on Social Anthropology no. 41, London: The Athlone Press.

Harrisson, T. (1950), 'Kelabit, Land Dayak and Related Glass Beads in Sarawak', *Sarawak Museum Journal* 5, 201–20.

—— (1958), 'The Peoples of Sarawak: The Kelabits and Muruts', *Sarawak Gazette* 84, 187–91.

—— (1959), *World Within*, Oxford: Oxford University Press.

Hudson, A.B. (1977), 'Linguistic Relations among Borneo Peoples with Special Reference to Sarawak: An Interim Report', *Studies in Third World Societies*, 3, 1–44.

Janowski, M. (1991), 'Rice, Work and Community among the Kelabit of Sarawak, East Malaysia', unpublished Ph.D. thesis, London School of Economics.

—— (1992), 'Forest, Rice and Life: An Attempt to Understand how the Kelabit of Sarawak see Themselves', unpublished paper presented at the Department of Social Anthropology, University of Cambridge, 23 October 1992.

—— (1993a), 'Kelabit Names and Kelabit Titles: Grandparenthood, Prestige and Kinship', unpublished paper presented at the Institut de Recherche sur le Sud-Est Asiatique, Centre National de Recherche Scientifique, Aix-en-Provence, 6 July 1993.

—— (1993b), 'Kelabit Beads', in V. H. Sutlive (ed.), *Change and Development in Borneo*, Selected Papers from the First Extraordinary Conference of the Borneo Research Council, Kuching, Sarawak, Malaysia, 4–9 August 1990, Williamsburg, Virginia, USA: Borneo Research Council.

—— (1994), 'Gender, Siblingship and the "Big Person" – Kinship among the Kelabit of Sarawak', unpublished paper presented at the Department of Social Anthropology, University of Cambridge, 27 May 1994.

—— (1995), 'The Hearth-group, the Conjugal Couple and the Symbolism of the Hearth-group among the Kelabit of Sarawak', in J. Carsten and S. Hugh-Jones (eds), *About the House. Levi-Strauss and beyond*, Cambridge: CUP.

—— (1997), 'The Kelabit Attitude to the Penan: Forever Children', *La Ricerca Folklorica* 34, 55–8.

King, V.T. (1978), 'Introduction', in V.T. King (ed.), *Essays on Borneo Societies*, Oxford: Oxford University Press.

Langub, J. (1987), 'Ethnic Self-labelling of the Murut', *Sojourn*, vol. 2, no. 2; Reprinted *Sarawak Gazette* 60, 3–17.

Lian-Saging, R. (1976/77), 'An Ethno-History of the Kelabit Tribe of Sarawak. A Brief Look at the Kelabit Tribe before World War II and after', unpublished Graduation Exercise submitted to the Jabatan Sejarah, University of Malaya (Kuala Lumpur) in partial fulfilment of the requirements for the degree of Bachelor of Arts, Hons.

Munan, H. (1991), 'Beads', in L. Chin and Mashman (eds), *Sarawak Cultural Legacy, A Living Tradition*, Kuching: Society Atelier Sarawak.

Rousseau, J. (1974), 'The Social Organization of the Baluy Kayan', unpublished Ph.D. thesis, Cambridge University.

—— (1990), *Central Borneo. Ethnic Identity and Social Life in a Stratified Society*, Oxford: Clarendon Press.

Sarawak Museum (1978), *Beads*, Kuching: Sarawak Museum Occasional Paper No. 2.

Talla, Y. (1979), *The Kelabit of the Kelabit Highlands, Sarawak*, edited by C. Sather. Report No. 9, Social Anthropology Section, School of Comparative Social Sciences, Universiti Sains, Penang.

Whittier, H.L. (1973), 'Social Organization and Symbols of Social Differentiation: An Ethnographic Study of the Kenyah Dayak of East Kalimantan (Borneo)', unpublished Ph.D. dissertation, Michigan State University.

11

Greek Beads of the Mycenaean Period (ca.1650–1100 BC): The Age of the Heroines of Greek Tradition and Mythology

Helen Hughes-Brock

The Mycenaean Civilization

As an archaeologist contributing to a largely anthropological volume, I must point out certain problems specific to archaeology in general in the study of beads, but like my fellow contributors I focus upon a particular time and place. I have chosen a society whose beads are an exceptionally rich source of information about some aspects, but rather disappointing with regard to information on the relation of beads to gender.

To start with a confession – the heroines of my title are not as firmly rooted in the Mycenaean age as the title implies. In fact some lively disagreement exists as to whether the 'real' backgrounds to their stories belong to the Late Bronze Age (and thus not after ca.1100 BC) or to the very different world of the Early Iron Age, the earlier part of the first millennium BC. Nonetheless, the garbled and embroidered stories of these ladies contain enough Bronze Age-looking elements to justify my using them both to provide some small islands of familiarity for readers likely to be somewhat at sea with the archaeology, and also to give a human face to some otherwise rather drily archaeological observations.

The 'Mycenaean' civilization of mainland Greece (also called 'Late Helladic' in archaeological literature) is so designated from the spectacular finds first made in 1876 at Mycenae, the seat of the powerful King Agamemnon, leader of the Greek army in the war over the abduction of Helen of Troy. In Crete the period is known as 'Late Minoan', the final half-millennium or so of the distinctive 'Minoan' culture (the archaeological name, from the legendary King Minos, who kept the fearsome Minotaur in the Labyrinth at Knossos), which had been evolving on the island since the Stone Age. In the middle portion of the second millennium the Minoans were at their peak, highly skilled and exceptionally imaginative craftsmen and artists, enjoying relations of one kind or another with the peoples of the Aegean

247

islands and the surrounding kingdoms of Egypt, Anatolia, the Near East and Mesopotamia. It was at this point that their cultural orbit was entered, in some relatively sudden way which causes much speculation and puzzlement, by the less advanced and somewhat unadventurous Greeks, who had settled some centuries before on the mainland. The contact with the Minoans, whatever brought it about, seems to have acted as a sort of 'shot in the arm' on these earliest Greeks and was the principal impetus to the development of Mycenaean civilization, the first of Greece's periods of cultural greatness. A Minoan background is apparent in various aspects of some Mycenaean materials, technology, forms and uses of beads.[1]

Who Wore Beads?

Beads occur archaeologically in deliberate deposits in building foundations, religious places and buried hoards, and are found on workshop sites and as stray finds in settlements, but by far the richest sources are of course graves. The Mycenaeans buried their dead with plenty of finery and equipment, but unfortunately for us they had a preference for burial in (presumably family) groups. The commonest tomb type, well suited to a hilly country, is a chamber dug back into the slope of a hill, sometimes elaborated as a beehive-shaped stone-built half-subterranean vault. (An exceptionally magnificent example of the 'beehive' type is the misnamed 'Treasury of Atreus' visited by every tourist at Mycenae.) The chamber was closed with a temporary stone wall and reopened at the successive funerals of several, even as many as twenty-odd, individuals. The Mycenaean Greeks seem to have had no qualms about disturbing their dead (certainly after the flesh had gone, if not before: their beliefs can only be guessed at) and on each occasion earlier burials were swept aside, finery and other grave goods were removed for reuse or recycling, and objects were mixed up, kicked aside and trampled underfoot. This activity was hardest of all, needless to say, on beads. Only the latest burials can be found undisturbed, and as often as not even they will have been spoilt by later tomb-robbers. The result is that in most cases we find beads and skeletons only in a scattered mess and cannot tell which beads belonged to which individual. The less common single burials ('simple graves') provide evidence for people with less wealth, less sense of family tradition, or different beliefs (Lewartowski 1995). We will certainly never know as much as we should wish about any distinctions of material or type, but one thing we know for certain, both from the occasional intact burial and from portrayals, is that beads were worn by men, women and children alike. Aegean archaeologists therefore do not fall as easily as some for the assumption that beads in a grave mean it is a woman's.[2]

How Were Beads Worn?

These unobliging burial customs have also left us with only sparse evidence for such things as the order of stringing and the length of necklaces. Some beads were strung in graduated sets. Other surviving sets consist of beads of the same shape and material but in two or three size-groups. There is a justifiable temptation to illustrate these as attractively made-up necklaces, but the arrangements are only modern conjectures. Some intact assemblages of a dozen or more quite miscellaneous beads represent an individual's heirlooms or choice of favourite trinkets, including exotica like Egyptian scarabs – a practice with good ethnographic parallels. Intriguing cases of a lone bead in an intact burial include a significant number of cornelian, a stone which probably had amuletic or symbolic properties (see below), but we cannot know whether the red bead really was worn alone or was combined with beads of perishable materials (Hughes-Brock 1995: 115).

There are, however, some useful portrayals of necklaces on wall-paintings, carved ivories, terracotta figurines and gold signet rings (e.g. Warren 1975: 123, 41, 131 colour illustrations; Demakopoulou 1988: 195 no.170, 192 no.168; 1996: 35; full treatments in Kilian-Dirlmeier 1980 and Younger 1992, especially pp. 261–9). In all these media most of the figures shown are females – mostly human, but also the occasional sphinx, which in the Greek version had a woman's head (the solving of her riddle by Oedipus led to his marrying his mother Jocasta). We see, for example, small globular beads alternating with long drop beads, both kinds alternating in red and yellow. (Figure 11.1 from colour illustration Warren 1975: 123; Demakopoulou 1996: 35) or small globular beads spacing out flower-shaped 'relief beads' (of which more below). Often two or more strands are worn together (as Xenaki-Sakellariou 1985: pl.28; Demakopoulou 1988: 192–3). The colours of the wall paintings are limited, however, and their interpretation uncertain (Younger 1992: 257). Yellow must certainly mean gold. Red may portray the popular cornelian. (Red jasper, imported from Egypt for making sealstones, was not in the bead repertory [Hughes-Brock 1995: 111–12], and beads of red painted wood or dough would probably have been beneath the ladies and goddesses portrayed.) Blue will stand for the very common blue glass and faience beads as well as for the rare lapis lazuli and possibly silver. The fresco painters had no pigment which could accurately reproduce the purple and lilac shades of amethyst, for example, although amethyst beads imported from Egypt were certainly worn and attractive beads were also made of local purple soft stone. Nor had they greens to depict the green and greenish soft steatites and serpentines which were even commoner than the purple and reddish varieties.

The materials used for stringing do not survive in the Greek climate. Woollen or linen thread was probably the commonest. Animal hair, single or plaited, is dependably strong.[3] Leather thongs are a possibility for large-holed and heavy beads.

The tiny disc beads, made mostly of faience like the examples found by the thousand in Egypt, required something fine (Demakopoulou 1988: 216 no.198). I once used a strand of my own hair to string a little set of these for the dig photographer. It worked beautifully – much better than the fine sewing thread I had tried first, which was uncooperatively floppy.

For both these questions, who wore beads and how they were worn, Mycenaean practice and climate put us at a disadvantage, in great contrast with Egypt (to name the best example). The tightly wrapped mummies of the bead-loving Egyptians preserve intact the elaborate beadwork collars as well as the conventional positioning of particular amulets at particular spots on the body at particular periods (Andrews 1990; 1994 passim). After the Mycenaean era single burials were the general fashion, and moreover they were of a less conspicuous form than the chamber tombs and so got less attention from grave-robbers. They give us a little more information. (They hint, for example, that white beads made of bone, a cheap and ubiquitous material, may have been associated with women and children. See below.) We can be thankful, however, that the Mycenaeans did at least bury goods with their dead. Archaeologists like such peoples, just as on settlement sites (as the late Dame Kathleen Kenyon, excavator of Jerusalem and Jericho, once remarked), they like untidy housekeepers.[4]

Various Uses of Beads

It is generally assumed that most beads were used on necklaces, and no doubt this is correct. Bracelets can be thought of in the same category. Too many arch-aeologists, however, make the mistake of stopping there. My male colleagues, I am tempted to say, are the worse offenders, but a worthy exception is Peter J. Francis, Jr., the Director of the Center for Bead Research in Lake Placid, N.Y., whose article 'When is a bead not a bead?' (1988) is the only specific treatment I know of. Beads, as Francis points out (after usefully asking what 'bead' means in the first place), can function as pendants, seals, amulets, spindle whorls, tools, net weights, burnishers, touchstones. Most, if not all, of these uses have sometimes to be considered with regard to Mycenaean beads.

Seals in the Mycenaean context are a special case, as I indicate below. Amulets are a foggy matter. Whereas the ancient Egyptians had a large repertory of amulets, the names and functions of which are well known from their writings (Andrews 1990: 171–85; 1994), Mycenaean amulets are less easily identified as such. A rare case of an amulet mentioned in ancient literary sources is the crescent moon, which was widely used throughout antiquity and has obvious associations with women's fertility and so also with children (Wrede 1975). The Greek lexicographer Hesychius describes it as worn by children. Of the few Bronze Age burials with crescent amulets, a nice example is the grave of a child buried with its mother in the Mycenaean cemetery at Eleusis (Wrede 1975: 248), the principal seat of the worship of the corn goddess Demeter, whose daughter Persephone returned from Hades every spring. Whether the crescent was specific to girl children we do not know. A terracotta figurine with painted features appears to show a crescent as centre-piece of a bead necklace worn around a woman's neck (Kilian-Dirlmeier 1980: 33–4, fig.2:20).

Two bead types which probably had amuletic value are a shield of the standard Aegean figure-of-eight shape and an opium poppy (see Figure 11.1; Hughes-Brock 1995: 115). These might appear to belong among the 'relief-beads' (v.infra) but there are differences. For one thing, they are often made of red stone, usually cornelian; the colour in itself probably had symbolic value. The shield is purely Aegean and probably associated with a goddess (Warren 1985: 204). The poppies occur all over the eastern Mediterranean, possibly connected with trade in opium as a commercial enterprise and thus a different kind of exchange from the high-level 'gift'-giving on the one hand and the long-distance exchanges with Europe on the other, both to be discussed below.[5] The lively Mycenaean contacts with the Levant are attested by widespread finds of Mycenaean pottery there and may have brought in the myth of Europa, carried away to Crete by Zeus in bull disguise from her native Tyre. (They did not, however, bring in writing. The Mycenaean 'Linear B' syllabic script was adapted from a Minoan invention. The Semitic alphabet came later.)

Spindle whorls v. beads is a perennial problem in accounts of Mycenaean excavations. Women must have taken up their spinning at any odd moment they had their hands free, just as until very recent times the Greek countrywoman side-saddle on her ass, spinning as she rides, has been a familiar sight to travellers and a favourite subject of postcards. Even queens spun, involved as they were with responsibilities for cloth production. (Odysseus's faithful wife Penelope, unpicking her weaving every night, is the most famous illustration of this, but Helen of Troy has a silver work-basket on wheels for her spinning, a gift from an Egyptian lady: Odyssey IV, 120–35.) Small terracotta balls, cones and bicones, left lying about everywhere, are one of the commonest finds on Mycenaean sites, the Mycenaean equivalent of present-day ring-pulls. The shapes are bead shapes, but some are too large and heavy to be beads (Barber 1991: 43, 51–5). With smaller, lighter specimens we cannot be certain. Most are unpainted and thus, we might think, too dull-looking to be decorative, but ethnographic parallels might caution against making too much of that argument.

A specifically Mycenaean and Minoan problem concerns so-called 'steatite conical whorls', 'buttons' or 'conuli', small, neatly shaped cones (or variants of the cone shape) mostly of soft stone or terracotta, of diameter usually between about 3 cm and 1.25 cm (see Figure 11.1; Demakopoulou 1996: 67 nos.58–9).

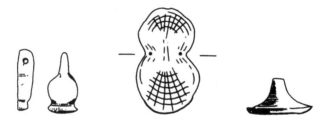

Figure 11.1 Woman offering a necklace: fragment of wall-painting of a cult scene at Mycenae. Poppy-head; shield; 'conulus'.

The biggest would be uncomfortably heavy for beads. The smallest would be ineffective as spindle whorls, and moreover some of them are made of pretty, brightly coloured stones and are found in numbers in graves, pointing to use as beads. It was not until Mycenaean archaeology was one hundred years old that a Greek archaeologist, calculating from sizes, find-spots, the hugely varying numbers found with burials and the curious little projections sometimes shown at the bottom of skirts in fresco and sealstone scenes, set forth the arguments for a third possibility, that a principal use of these 'conuli' was as dress-weights on hems to make heavy woollen skirts hang well (Iakovidis 1977; cf. Younger 1992: 273–4). Although they sometimes seem to be shown on men's hems, their use as hem-weights was no doubt more a women's matter. The 'simple' graves contain fewer on average, implying a simpler costume (Lewartowski 1995: 107). A few specimens found threaded on fancy pins were probably used for the fancy coiffures seen on court ladies in frescos. On necklaces they could have been used by men as well, and both sexes could also have used them as cloak-buttons and as tassel-gatherers, e.g. on belts.

Tassel-gatherers, indeed, as well as hair ornaments (on pins or nets), drawstring finials and decorative knob-handles on the lids of baskets or wooden boxes are among bead uses not generally borne in mind, because the associated materials have perished, but all are plausible. Some beads were pinheads, but we only know this when the shaft of the pin is of a material which survives, like the bronze shafts with magnificent large rock crystal pinheads which would otherwise have been taken for unusually shaped necklace beads (Demakopoulou 1988: 80; 1996: 86). On a famous vase from Minoan Crete, a *tour de force* in rock crystal from the sixteenth or fifteenth century, fourteen rock crystal beads on bronze wire form the elegantly curved handle (Warren 1975: 40, illustration). For bead decoration sewn onto leather or cloth, or woven in, the evidence has perished, of course, but in one tomb near Mycenae some 40,000 tiny yellow, brown, black, blue and white disc beads were found lying in position, forming a multiple chevron pattern perhaps from a bead-net dress of a kind known from Tutankhamun's tomb (Barber 1991: 172). An intriguing find was made at Troy (but from the third millennium, long before Helen and the Trojan War), where a fire destroyed a room where someone (probably a woman) was working at a loom. Near the loomweights lay a scattering of tiny gold beads. The excavators suggested that the weaver had removed and hung up her necklace to keep it out of her way as she worked, or had lost it as she fled. Elizabeth Barber's equally plausible, and more interesting, suggestion is that she was weaving the little beads into her cloth (1991: 171–2; 1994: 212–14).

Materials and Their Sources; Beads in Long-distance Contacts

The numerous materials used for beads reflect a variety of social and economic phenomena. (For what follows see generally Harding 1984; Bouzek 1985; Cline 1994, 1995a; Hughes-Brock 1995, forthcoming.) Gold was certainly of high value, but silver is less commonly used for Mycenaean artefacts of any kind (ancient business documents show it sometimes circulating at a higher value than gold). Bronze was in heavy demand as the standard metal for tools and vessels and of course for the weapons and armour described in loving detail by Homer; relatively few bronze beads survive. When mourners re-entering a chamber tomb retrieved previous corpses' grave gifts, bronze was eagerly removed for reuse or recycling. Even allowing for this practice, bronze seems not to have been popular for beads. Its heyday as a bead material came in the first half of the first millennium, when bronze had given way to iron for practical uses. At that period northern Greece and Macedonia in particular have a rich repertory of heavy bronze beads and pendants, including some shapes such as jugs, birds and spoked wheels (probably a sun symbol) which seem to have religious associations, and some which occur over a broad band stretching as far as the Caucasus and may (as noise-makers?) have had associations with shamanism (Kilian-Dirlmeier 1979; Bouzek 1987: 92–100). Vital copper and tin were not used on their own for beads but only in alloy as bronze. The long-distance exchange processes which brought them to Greece are apparently reflected, however, in other bead materials.

Of these reflections the most striking is amber. Many amber beads from Mycenaean sites have been analysed by infra-red spectroscopy at the Amber Research Laboratory at Vassar College and nearly all display a pattern peculiar to the enormous (and still very productive) deposits of amber on the shores of the Baltic (Hughes-Brock 1985: 257–8). This, then, is a proven case of very long distance contacts. But the contacts were not direct. At the very beginning of the Mycenaean period (and of Mycenaean archaeology) the 'Shaft Graves' dug at Mycenae by Heinrich Schliemann yielded quantities of amber beads originally strung on several strands held apart by amber 'spacer-plates', rectangular plates between about 3.2 cm and 3.8 cm long and a little less wide with decorative perforations forming X and Y patterns (Bouzek 1985: 54–8, fig.22; Demakopoulou 1988: no.280). These belong to the Wessex Culture of south-central England, which produced the later elements of Stonehenge. Moreover, a gold-framed amber disc found in a tomb at Knossos in Crete so closely matches Wessex examples that it could be from the hand of the same goldsmith (Hughes-Brock forthcoming). The raw amber from the Baltic could easily have reached England without human agency, since it can be found washed up on English shores, but how and why did the finished products reach faraway Greece?

One possible, but controversial, answer is the search for Cornish tin. Several generations have debated on the nature of the Mycenaean link with Wessex and such questions as whether there was 'directional' or 'down-the-line' trade, whether some prestige was attached to the making of the journey itself and the contact with the special lore of the exotic megalithic monuments (such as Stonehenge), and the degree of what an earlier generation would have called 'civilizing influence' which Mycenaean contact might have had on the Wessex Culture (Hughes-Brock 1993: 219–20; forthcoming). What cultural baggage or 'ideological content' may have travelled with amber is another puzzle. An association of amber with women apparent in Britain (and still flourishing today around the Baltic) was lost on the way. Whether its ancient Greek name *elektron* preserves some ghost of an old awareness that amber had associations with sun cult is unclear (Hughes-Brock 1985: 260). In northeastern Europe amber played a vital role throughout prehistory in bringing in metals (not locally available) and general foreign contacts.[6]

Tin sources in both Britain and Bohemia may be reflected in the find-places of amber beads as well as of beads of faience and glass, which provoke another, related, debate: are the beads local or imported, and was the vitreous technology learnt from the south or invented independently (Harding 1984: 87–104)? Access to the all-important tin supplies has been suggested as one explanation for the wealth which brought about the revolutionary Greek exposure to Minoan culture, the 'shot in the arm' which helped to produce 'Mycenaean' civilization. Tin might thus be compared to Saudi Arabian oil, although of course the resultant process of social and economic change was not so dramatically sudden and swift. Metals and metal technology (particularly involving iron, at the transition to the Iron Age) were also sought in the Black Sea area. Helle, who fell into the Hellespont (Dardanelles), the Golden Fleece (perhaps connected with the search for gold?), Jason and the Argonauts and his sinister foreign queen the infanticide Medea – all these may reflect Greek involvement with that region. At the approach to it, in a highly strategic position, stood Troy. The Trojan War, whatever it really was, may have been more about metals, access to metallurgical know-how, or even fishing rights, than about the abduction of the beautiful Helen.

The other remarkable long-distance material is lapis lazuli. The generally accepted source for this is the Badakhshan mines in Afghanistan, explored by Georgina Herrmann's expedition of 1964 (Cline 1994: 25; see general survey Clark 1986: 67–9). From at least ca.3500 BC it was reaching Mesopotamia (Müller-Karpe 1985: pls.9, 10). The palace at Thebes yielded a cache of seventeen Mesopotamian engraved lapis lazuli cylinders of the kind used for sealing documents, and a workshop connected with the palace (excavated beneath the present-day Oedipus Street) contained several dozen pieces of the blue stone (objects finished and half-finished, and scraps) alongside beads, other objects and scraps and fragments of other materials, accumulated there for working, reworking or repair. The origin of the seal cache has been interpreted in a number of ways – as casual arrivals, an individual's trinket collection, the stock of a foreign or local craftsman or a 'gift' from a foreign ruler to the King of Thebes (Cline 1994: 25–6). Lapis lazuli figures in the correspondence about 'gifts' between Egyptian and other kings (e.g. on necklaces and a beaded fly-whisk sent by King Tushratta of Mitanni in Anatolia to Nefertiti's father-in-law Amenhotep III [Moran 1992: 78]); recipients sometimes complain about the quality or even question its genuineness. Some of the Mycenaean finds probably arrived as such 'gifts', the polite word for exchanges which in reality had political and economic motives (the politeness sometimes wears amusingly thin). Any anthropologist will think of Malinowski and Mauss, who indeed are cited by Wright (1995: 68–9) and in Cline's lively paper on these collections of letters and the degree of Mycenaean involvement in royal exchanges detectable in them (since no such letters survive from the Greek side, alas! [Cline 1995a; cf. 1994: 85–6]). The Theban cache has been interpreted (attractively, but unproveably) as an attempt by a particular Assyrian king, hard pressed by a neighbour's embargo, to solicit help from Thebes. Prestigious 'gifts' in the other direction included fine many-coloured textiles (a long tradition in Crete), probably produced largely by women. Not all such gifts, beads included, arrived directly from their country of origin. Some went the rounds, accumulating value as they built up a distinguished pedigree of ownership, like some items mentioned by Homer.

These personal diplomatic relations between royal individuals (queens as well as kings), carried on in writing and by high-ranking ambassadors, cemented by marriages and even on occasion by visits made in person like the Queen of Sheba's, are a different matter from whatever processes brought amber to Greece from illiterate, barbarian Europe. During the early Mycenaean generations amber is concentrated in the tombs of two rich centres, Mycenae and the southwestern district around Pylos (well placed to receive goods from the Adriatic, the probable route of amber), whereas the prosperous Thebes region, home of Oedipus's wife-mother Jocasta and his brave daughter Antigone, has yielded only a handful for the whole of the Mycenaean era. This does suggest that, in the case of the earliest shipments at least, only particular ruling families were at the receiving end (this is well before the adulterous Clytaemnestra was Queen at Mycenae and Homer's garrulous old Nestor ruled Pylos), but we know nothing of who had handled them before.[7]

Much commoner fine bead stones (on which see generally Younger 1979; Hughes-Brock 1995) came from less faraway regions. Rock crystal was local. Amethyst probably came from Egypt, where it had a long history as a bead stone. Contacts between Egypt and Crete went back to the third millennium. Mycenaean contacts at royal level seem to find some reflection (garbled, one hopes!) in the fifty daughters of 'Danaos' (one of the early words for 'Greek') who married the sons of 'Aigyptos' and massacred their husbands on their wedding night. A well-known series of frescos from fifteenth-century tombs of Egyptian nobles (some of whom belonged to families which had a tradition of specializing in the Aegean branch, so to speak, of the Pharaoh's diplomatic service) shows processions of men in colourful Minoan or Mycenaean dress carrying 'tribute' to the Pharaoh, including strings of beads painted in red, yellow and blue but, alas, not of otherwise identifiable material (Hughes-Brock 1993: 220). Some finds at Mycenae of faience objects with Egyptian royal inscriptions probably reflect embassies in the reverse direction. Egyptian contacts evidently reached further down the social scale, however, for Mycenaean pottery occurs at a variety of Egyptian sites and Egyptian trinkets found their way into Mycenaean tombs. How far mercantile activity was independent or was under royal control is debated (Sherratt & Sherratt 1991; Gillis 1995), but it clearly brought Egyptians and Greeks into contact. Some degree of conscious choice is discernible in the matter of trinkets: Egyptian beads are common enough in Mycenaean tombs, but amulets (except scarabs) are very rare. Perhaps Egyptians, devoted as they were to their amulets, did not wish to part with them, or were afraid to do so. Or perhaps Mycenaeans liked the Egyptians' beads but did not care for their amulets – found them too exotic, or unpleasing to look at, or best not meddled with, or just meaningless. To what extent the 'ideological content' of Egyptian imports was understood, adopted or adapted is a matter of conjecture.

The very popular cornelian probably arrived from several sources, not yet determined – some even possibly from the ancient and still active industry in Gujarat. Agate was liked, particularly for seals; Younger (1979: 42) suggests an Indus Valley origin for some, imported as finished beads and recut. Anything originating in India probably came via Mesopotamia, like the lapis lazuli.

Colours

All of these stones, except the transparent crystal (and translucent cloudier quartzes), have obvious colour interest. Red and green may have had symbolic value – blue possibly too, but glass and faience were blue anyway for technical reasons (Hughes-Brock 1995: 115–16). The local soft steatite and serpentine are less bright but come in various blue-green-grey shades, and occasionally purple-red, which are quite attractive. Conspicuous by their absence are white materials, except for a few white shells. Greece has plenty of white stone (one thinks of the later marble statues!), elephant and hippopotamus ivory were available from Egypt and Syria for luxury articles, and animal bone was everywhere and was used happily enough for tools and pins. One gets the impression that either white beads were strongly felt to be not decorative or some sort of taboo was at work – an association with death or mourning, perhaps? (Cf.Carey in this volume on diviners' white beads in southern Africa.) Possibly considerations of skin colour came into play. As in Egypt, women in the frescos conventionally have light skin, men reddish-brown, and Homer's epithet 'white-armed' for the goddess Hera and other females probably bore the same implications of ladylikeness that light skin had for our grandmothers. White beads against the skin might have produced an undesirable contrast.[8] (Will our own white summer jewellery go out of fashion when suntans do?) This would not explain, however, why we do not find white beads with men either. At the end of the Mycenaean period a few bone beads do begin to appear – plain discs easily made by slicing cattle leg bones. In intact individual graves of the Early Iron Age (early first millennium) in Macedonia they have been found mostly in women's graves of the poorer sort, with few other grave gifts. The present evidence on this subject is thin and hard to assess; perhaps future excavations will produce more (Hughes-Brock 1983: 293–4).

Glass and its much older cousin faience account for vast numbers of blue and blue-green beads of many shapes, including the characteristic Aegean 'relief-beads' of which more below. The technology had been developed in Egypt and in Mesopotamia, and Mycenaean glass manufacture may have remained to some extent dependent on the Near East for material. (The raw materials are cheap, but the original fusing process requires skilled firing at very high temperatures, so that glass and faience are only a cheaper alternative, not a cheap substitute, for lapis lazuli or turquoise. Reworking of glass cullet can be done at lower temperatures, as in the present-day industries all over the Near and Middle East which recycle Coca-Cola bottles and other glass.) The fourteenth-century shipwreck off Ulu Burun in southern Turkey, which contains the most important international Mediterranean assortment of material, included in its cargo ingots of blue glass, destined for working somewhere. So far neither their origin nor their destination is entirely clear (Bass 1987: 716–18; Cline 1994: 100–1, 235–6).

Bead Makers, Seal Engravers and Craft Organization

Of humbler finery only shell beads survive, particular the tube-shaped dentalium, a ready-made bead which required no working but was occasionally painted red. The huge missing element is the perishable materials – unbaked clay, wood, dough/ paste, seeds. It is hard to believe these did not exist. What did poorer people wear, after all? Although there is absolutely no proof, one might guess that home bead making was a women's and children's occupation.

Other bead makers have left little more trace. The numerous beads of semi-precious stones and of faience and glass were clearly made by specialists. Workshops for luxury goods such as fine stone vases and ivory items have been found at or close by the palaces of Mycenaean rulers, and some bead making went on there too, but the skimpy palace records on clay tablets (in the script called 'Linear B', the earliest Greek writing), which survive sporadically only when the buildings they were stored in burnt down, do not happen to tell us much about the workers. That women worked for the palaces we know, because the tablets do mention women, including foreign captives, involved in cloth production, providing the background to Agamemnon's heartless description of a Trojan girl's fate as his captive, ending her days at his palace in Greece pacing endlessly back and forth working at the upright loom (as well as serving him in bed: Iliad I, 29–31; see Chadwick 1976: 78–83 on women slaves in the palace at Pylos, 150–2 on textile production).[9] Possibly women had some hand in palatial bead making, but we have no evidence. Beadwork on cloth, woven in or sewn on, was probably a sub-department of textiles and thus likely to be women's work.

Related to bead production in some aspects is the production of engraved sealstones, the rubber stamps of the ancient world. These had been in use since the third millennium in Minoan Crete, where they shed valuable archaeological light on art, religion, foreign relations and Minoan administration systems. (Indeed it was Minoan seals, commonly worn by Cretan peasant women as milk charms, which led to the discovery of the Minoan civilization in the 1890s.) The Mycenaeans took over the idea and eventually used them in their own palace administration systems (alongside the Linear B written records on clay tablets), as well as apparently fancying them as collector's items and possibly using them at a lower social level for sealing such things as merchandise and containers of household stores. Most at this period took the form of a lentil- or almond-shaped bead 1.5–2.5 cm in diameter or length. Frescos show bead-seals worn on a string on the wrist, looking like a wristwatch. Certain nondescript specimens made of inexpensive local soft stone may have been worn by people who had nothing important enough to warrant real sealing but wanted to show off, like watches worn nowadays in a society where precise time-keeping does not matter. High seal-holding officers probably included women, particularly in religious functions. Egypt had women 'sealers' even in private households (Ward 1989: 36–7).

Workshops for both beads and seals are frustratingly scanty in the archaeological record. Premises in some cases may well have been shared, since the techniques for shaping and many of the tools and stones used were the same. Certain stones, however, seem to have been confined almost entirely to seals, e.g. jasper (common in Egypt), milky blue-white chalcedony, certain rare breccias and tufas with coloured bands or spots, and silvery-black haematite. Haematite seems to have a rather specialized repertory of engraved motifs, perhaps implying that it was the speciality of a particular workshop or workshops; or perhaps it had some symbolic reference, or it was easier to work to the flattish seal shapes than to globular or fluted beads. Garnet was used to some extent for beads in Egypt but it occurs there only in little pieces too small for seal making. It is not in the Aegean bead repertory at all. One gets the impression that there was some division between the makers of seals and beads and that the seal makers, whose products served palace officials of high rank, got first choice of fine and imported stones and so to some extent determined which stones were imported. If a stone was good only for beads, like garnet, it was not of interest (Hughes-Brock 1995: 112–13). Glass and faience, on the other hand, were overwhelmingly bead materials. Glass seals are rare. Some were cast in stone moulds by a mass-production method, which of course negates the very point of a seal.

Relief-beads and Symbolism

Moulds bring us to relief-beads, the Minoan and Mycenaean speciality (see Note 1). Made in gold and faience, but principally in glass, these have a flat back and often two parallel perforations to secure them on two strings, creating a broad band of identical mass-produced beads strung side by side. The front bears a relief design from a repertory which includes such motifs as cockle and cowrie shells, marine creatures, papyrus heads, lilies, rosettes, 'ivy' leaves, altars, jugs and hair curls, all in a form highly stylized but clearly intended to be recognizable as something, even if their prototype is stylized almost beyond recognition (see Figure 11.2; Higgins 1980: 65,76–82, figs.10,13, pls.9B, 10A–C; Harden 1981: 39–49, pls.II–VI; Xenaki-Sakellariou 1985: 300–8, pls.*passim*; Sargnon 1987: figs.102–14; Demakopoulou 1996: pls.*passim*). Rare types are the woman-headed sphinx (Harden 1981: pl.IV no.46) and a tiny woman (Xenaki-Sakellariou 1985: pl.84). A set of eleven in gold, cornelian and lapis lazuli shaped like a woman's breast being squeezed or held in a hand are unique and early and perhaps were conceived as amulets more than as real relief-beads (see Figure 11.2, bottom from Higgins 1979: 34, fig.33; Sargnon 1987: fig.174; Gates 1989: 223, pl.LI, b, discusses this as a fertility motif, possibly interpreted with a sense of humour). Shield-shaped beads too may have functioned more as amulets (v.supra), probably representing not men's armour but some aspect of a goddess (Warren 1985: 204). One unique gold bead from Pylos is shaped like a helmeted head (Higgins 1980: fig.13 no.30), likely to be male but one cannot be entirely certain, since no beard is shown and since goddesses can have warrior associations, like the classical Athene in armour. Otherwise no beads have a specifically masculine motif.[10]

These motifs are a mixed bag. The cowrie shell has an old history and in Egypt was worn on women's belts with the fertility implications suggested by its supposed resemblance to the vulva (Andrews 1990: 140,143; 1994: 42; Clark 1986: 23–6 gives comparanda from other ancient societies). Since the stylized version which the Aegean borrowed looks more like a kind of wallet and the cowrie is not a familiar Aegean shell, one wonders how far its original significance can still have been in mind (see Figure 11.2, bottom, from Xenaki-Sakellariou 1985: 302). A like case is the papyrus head, associated in Egypt with the lush Nile-Delta-like landscape of the Afterworld. The altar and the libation jug, on the other hand, were local types, instantly recognizable. Sea creatures had an association with Minoan religion; bivalve shells and shells of the rare and elegant paper nautilus or 'argonaut' (*Argonauta argo*; Figure 11.2, middle) are found in Minoan shrines alongside female figurines of goddesses, votaries or priestesses (like King Minos's daughter Ariadne, who helped the Athenian prince Theseus to escape from the Minotaur by leading him out of the labyrinthine palace of Knossos with a thread). Curiously, the choice of sea creatures on relief-beads overlaps only partly with those in other media. For example, the octopus and cuttlefish are common on pots but rare on beads, the argonaut is a favourite on both, while fish and dolphins appear mainly in frescos and on a certain class of sealstones. Bucranium (bull's head) beads or pendants refer to a prominent element in religion, well known from

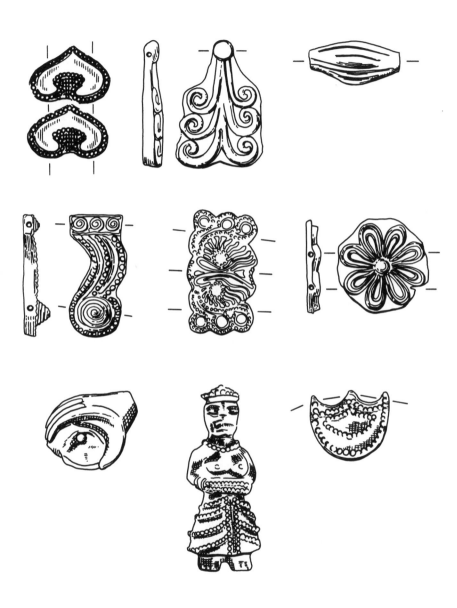

Figure 11.2 Top: 'sacral ivy'; lilies; grain of wheat. Middle: hair curl; pair of argonauts; rosette. Bottom: hand grasping breast; woman (holding box or tray); cowrie shell.

pots, seals, figurines and frescos and reflected somehow in the terrible half-bull, half-man Minotaur, but an equally important religious motif, the sacrificial double axe, is not a relief-bead subject. There may have been a sense that some motifs were more 'serious' than others, as the crucifix is more serious than a cross. The double axe was perhaps too strong to wear on a string of beads, or it belonged to a different 'department' of religion.

Sets in the several versions of the hair-curl shape have been found in position near skulls and were apparently worn sometimes on headbands (see Figure 11.2, middle, from Harden 1981: fig. 3; Sargnon 1987: figs.102–4). Their meaning is not easy to see, unless cutting a lock of hair was part of some mourning or status-altering rite. Motifs which look like a chrysalis, a bee and a butterfly may suggest new life after death (Hughes-Brock 1992: 628). The 'rosette' (Figure 11.2, middle) appears so commonly both as relief-beads (as Müller-Karpe 1985: 93 fig.46b) and in other media that it might be thought virtually secular and ornamental, but it has a long history of use by women as a protective sign, e.g. to bring back one's man safely; perhaps Homer intends peculiar poignancy when he makes Andromache weave it for her husband, the doomed Trojan hero Hector (Iliad XXII, 438–72; Barber 1991: 372–3; 1994: 155). The stylized 'ivy-leaf' and 'lily' (Figure 11.2, top), like the papyrus, probably had some connexion with a goddess, fertility or the afterlife – or perhaps with gynaecological medicine (Warren 1985: 201–4)?[11]

Among ordinary beads very common shapes are stylized wheat or barley grains and gourd seeds (see Figure 11.2, top, from Xenaki-Sakellariou 1985: 297 types 47–9; Demakopoulou 1988: 216 no.198). These may convey something or perhaps just go back to the simple ancient idea of using real seeds as beads. The only 'messages' conveyed by Aegean beads are pictorial ones. Writing, used only for limited purposes, never appears on them, in contrast to Mesopotamia and Egypt (e.g. Andrews 1990: 197 fig.183).

Workshops and Manufacturing Processes

Relief-beads have been found in several dozen types and from tombs all over the Mycenaean world. The stone moulds for producing them are known from only about twenty examples, and the find-places are instructive (cf. Hughes-Brock 1992: 627–8). None comes from a tomb and the great majority come from the major centres of Mycenae and Knossos. The chief, or even only, places of production, then, were the workshops attached to palaces. The Linear B tablets refer to goldworkers and workers of something blue, doubtless blue glass and faience. Some moulds were used for both. They are blocks of soft stone with several matrices per face and were a valuable piece of equipment, recut, not discarded, if something went wrong with a matrix (Demakopoulou 1988: 218–19 no.204; 1996: 117 no.61).

Carving the matrices required the same skills as seal engraving and may have been done by the same personnel, in workshops which probably produced other luxury items too, such as finger rings, inlays and elaborate relief-decorated stone and metal vases (Laffineur 1995). Using the find-places of mould-made products as an argument for itinerant craftsmen is a recurrent temptation but risky, since bead wearers, as well as makers, can travel (Laffineur 1995: 191; cf.Hughes-Brock 1992: 627–8). The moulds could last for years and were either not the personal property of the craftsmen or else either too valuable or too workaday to be buried in their owners' graves. The origin and status of such craftsmen are not well understood, although the story of Daedalus, the Leonardo-like all-rounder (even aeronautical engineer) of Knossos, suggests that the best of them enjoyed royal respect. The written documents of neighbouring societies speak of skilled craftsmen being given, lent and captured – a far cry from Oxfam or Peace Corps workers going abroad to teach well-digging, but still a contribution to what we nowadays call 'development'.

Beautifully fashioned gold granulated beads (Figure 11.2, bottom; Demakopoulou 1996 *passim*) also came from palace workshops, but we do not know whether all goldsmiths, or all supplies of gold, were under royal control. The Oedipus Street workshop at Thebes contained, alongside the lapis lazuli mentioned above, granulated beads and scraps of gold, oddments of other stones and some tantalizing remains of tools – bronze instruments which may have been a knife and an engraving tool, and an iron point, which must have been a 'state of the art' instrument in the thirteenth century (Symeonoglou 1973: 63–71, figs. 263–74). A detailed account of tools and techniques of bead making is given by Evely (1993, esp.146–71, 195–206; cf.Andrews 1990: 67–96), who draws on the much better evidence for the processes from sites in Iran and India (p.202). The important study by Kenoyer, Vidale and Bhan (1991) uses evidence from both prehistoric Indian sites and the very instructive surviving bead industry of Khambat (Cambay) in Gujarat to discuss the relevance of ethnographic accounts to the interpretation of archaeological data such as location and layout of workspace and to raise fundamental questions about craft specialization and evidence for state control. (Cf.Heltzer 1996: 278–83, Eyre 1987: 192–3 on Egypt.) In the Mycenaean case we cannot tell whether the valuable and imported materials got into the hands of independent or part-time specialists or if so, how – as raw material or as odd or broken items acquired from the owners for making up, repair or reworking. An individual, intact burial of unusual type in Athens is interpreted as an 'artisan's grave' because it contains a stone mould with globular depression and pouring-channel, a celt and two bone objects, one perhaps a tool handle, the other with four small depressions (to hold beads during polishing or stringing?) – things possibly used for bead making (Immerwahr 1971: 110, 231–2, pls. 55, 77). The only other grave gift was a modest undecorated jug. If this grave really was a bead maker's, then he or she may have been an independent worker, not necessarily working full-time at the craft but perhaps doing it on the side and at 'free' times, like the Khambat bead makers. Whether there were families or 'guilds' of bead makers, as around Venice and Khambat, we cannot know. Egypt gives us detailed pictures of bead workshops, with men using multiple bow-drills, making up elaborate wide collar necklaces, etc. and making remarks to each other in hieroglyphs (Andrews 1990: 68–81; cf.stocks 1989, whose experiments recreate techniques shown); the workers portrayed are always men (cf.Robins 1989: 106).

How local raw materials were gathered is unknown. Possibilities range from gathering by local men, women and children, whether free-lance or hired for the purpose, as in present-day Gujarat (Kenoyer et al. 1991: 49), to organized profess- ional operations as in Egypt (though of course on a far smaller scale than the Pharaohs'). That Minoans and Mycenaeans understood the properties of the materials they worked, e.g. the fracturing habits of various stones, is clear from their finished products (Hughes-Brock 1995, passim; for a good parallel study see Barthélemy de Saizieu and Bouquillon 1993). Some imports probably arrived with specialist processes already completed nearer source, e.g. preliminary removal of the crust of Baltic amber and sometimes the colour-enhancing heat treatment of cornelian and agate. The properties of certain working materials were well known from Neolithic times: abrasive emery sand from Naxos and obsidian, good for blades and drills, from Melos. The making of purposeful voyages specifically to these two Cycladic islands is an early proven factor in Aegean 'development'.

Social and Economic Aspects

Many social aspects of bead behaviour within Mycenaean society, and their relations to gender, are elusive. Younger's thorough survey of the evidence from portrayals (1992: 261–9) succeeds to some extent in relating beads and other jewellery to the social and religious contexts of the people portrayed, but much of the evidence is problematic and a good deal of it comes from Crete or the island of Thera and may not reflect specifically Mycenaean situations. He concludes that bead necklaces were perhaps not often worn by men. They are regularly shown worn by women, as well as in scenes where a woman holds or fingers a necklace as though to draw attention to its value (Figure 11.1), a gesture appropriate when the necklace was to be offered, as we know they were from the beads found in shrines and from portrayals of strings of beads hung on them.[12] In religious scenes women predominate (see e.g. Müller-Karpe 1985; 104 fig.56 nos.1–6; Sargnon 1987: figs.199–216 passim; Demakopoulou 1996: 93–5 nos.15–18).

The relief-beads may have been insignia of some kind of religious or other office or social status. This is suggested not only by their religious or symbolic motifs but also by the fact that they were not exported. Thus when found in the Ulu Burun shipwreck they were taken as a virtual badge of ethnicity, not trade goods but personal property indicating that a Mycenaean individual was on board (Cline 1995b: 274). Relief-beads in the tomb of a group of women and children in Cyprus may also prove Mycenaean identity. Interestingly, both tomb and wreck also contained a few beads of amber, which again are more likely to have belonged to Mycenaeans than to anyone else in the eastern Mediterranean (Bass 1987: 722; Hughes-Brock 1993: 223). Whether or how rank and offices, and their insignia, were passed on we do not know,[13] but it is a fact that whereas some cultural elements (e.g. pottery styles) show continuity into the Iron Age, the relief-beads stopped dead with the end of Mycenaean society. Perhaps they were always buried with their owner,[14] or production stopped when the palace workshops stopped functioning, or the ceremonies or offices or beliefs associated with them were abolished or died out.

Indeed we cannot know how *any* beads were passed on, or changed hands, within Mycenaean society – whether, for example, Mycenaean women (and men) were 'curators' (who pass on a string of beads whole) or 'splitters' (who distribute them among their children) (Francis 1992). We do not know whether beads bore any relation to marital status. (The documents from other societies mention princesses marrying foreigners, like the disastrous Danaids. Sent abroad along with their accompanying treasures, these brides and their attendants doubtless brought their own beads with them.) Amber beads have a distinctive chronological distribution: at first huge quantities but in few burials, then more burials but fewer and fewer beads with each. This has been taken to suggest a trickling down the social scale through gifts of a few beads at a time as rewards from lord to vassal, marriage gifts, heirlooms, robbers' loot, the salvaging of beads from tomb floors at funerals and so on (Hughes-Brock 1985: 259). Presumably at some levels of society beads changed hands in exchanges of an ordinary buying and selling (bartering) kind. There is no reason to think that they served as currency.

In Mycenaean society, as in others, beads had more to do than make people look nice. In an age without money they probably served to some degree for the storage of wealth, though not necessarily on any generally agreed scale. Their symbolic or relative exchange value is unknown. Their display function is obvious from the quantities laid out with the dead. How exactly the Mycenaeans measured these concepts is not clear, of course. Assessing them archaeologically is not so simple as it might be thought and is a question Mycenaean specialists have been rather slow to address (but see now perceptive treatments, drawing on anthropological models, in Voutsaki 1994 and 1995 and Wright 1995). Do we measure the number of goods in a grave, the number of different kinds, the weight of the metal in them, the number of people and the time and skill involved in making them, the difficulty of access to the raw materials, or what else? Access to materials, control of such access, control of labour, familiarity with admired foreign (or merely foreign) cultures – all these things help to create power and status, and then go on to legitimate it (Peregrine 1991). That beads were deeply embedded in all this is more than clear. Small in size, they played no small part in the formation of Mycenaean states and the development of a distinctive Mycenaean culture.

Notes

The drawings are by Lyn Sellwood, to whom go my warmest thanks.

1. For good general accounts see Vermeule 1964; Warren 1975: 41–6, 119–36; Chadwick 1976. On the problem of the genesis of Mycenaean civilization and the Minoan role in it see Wright 1995. Müller-Karpe bases a chapter on the tomb of a Mycenaean 'queen' and 'princess' (1985: 90–110). On beads, with illustrations of many types, see Xenaki-Sakellariou 1985, especially table of types: 292–312; Higgins 1980: 64–8, 75–82 (76–82 on relief-beads); Harden 1981: 39–49, pls.II–VI, especially on relief-beads. Sargnon 1987 has many illustrations but must be used with caution. Demakopoulou 1996 contains a wide selection of types and by far the finest colour illustrations. New finds and publications are noted since 1983 in the *Bead Study Trust Newsletter*.
2. Some of the kinds of archaeological evidence available from other societies are simply out of our reach (e.g. those outlined in Alekshin 1983).
3. Lammers (1991: 384), speaking of a much later German context, observes that one horsehair can bear more than 400 grams.
4. The Anglo-Saxons, for example, in their early, still pagan, days left much evidence for the important glass bead trade in their graves. For archaeologists their adoption of Christianity was a misfortune.
5. For more on the opium trade see Majno 1975: 109–11, 144–6; Knapp 1991: 25–6.
6. One of the many intriguing minor characters in the Odyssey is a repulsive woman, 'huge as a mountain peak', the Queen of the Laestrygonians. This otherwise unknown race of gigantic cannibals dwells on a long harbour in a land where Homer's unclear description implies that night meets day, or something of the sort (X: 80–132). This sounds almost like Norway, but there is no evidence that Mycenaeans got that far.
7. A tale in the Odyssey about a Phoenician merchant trying to attract a customer with an amber necklace is inspired by conditions centuries later; the same probably applies to a pestering suitor's offer of one to Penelope (XV, 459–60; XVIII, 295–6).
8. Murray claims that in Middle Kingdom times in Egypt amethyst and dark-coloured stones were worn by the light-skinned upper classes, whereas the darker commoners preferred turquoise-coloured or cornelian beads (1963: 194–5). I cannot evaluate this but note an economic factor: the common blue-green faience beads were cheaper than semi-precious stones.
9. This was the common fate of captured women. A Mesopotamian example concerning priestesses is described by Dalley (1984: 145), whose lively chapter on women (pp.

97–111) illustrates the enviable amount of detail that can be learnt about a society with more developed literacy than the Aegean had. Cf.Eyre 1987: 200–1 and other references to women's work elsewhere in same volume.

10. A Knossian fresco interpreted as depicting a marriage rite shows a necklace with face beads. Called 'negroid' because of their short curly hair, the heads could be of either gender (Higgins 1979: fig.39; Younger 1992: 281).

11. See Warren 1985 for a full and interesting treatment of the significance of various plants in Minoan art and religion as emblems of one or more goddesses. Garlands apparently played an important role, being worn at ceremonies and ritual dances, carried in processions and offered. Women's fertility festivals are known from literary sources in later Crete and must have continued Minoan traditions to some extent. Ivy in Egypt was apparently associated with women and fertility (Hugonot 1994: 79–81). The heart-shaped leaf called 'sacral ivy' by archaeologists is too stylized for sure botanical identification; Dyczek (1990: 141) suggests seeds of the mysterious North African silphium, which enjoyed such a huge market in later Greece and Rome that by late antiquity it was extinct, but this is purest speculation. Both ivy and silphium were known to ancient gynaecologists. If Minoans prized them, was it as emmenagogues rather than as contraceptives or abortifacients? Cf. Riddle 1992: 27–32; Riddle, Estes and Russell 1994.

12. Cf.Andrews 1990: 185 for religious uses of bead necklaces in Egypt.

13. Did they, for example, involve children? As usual, the evidence is hard to get at. Gates examines the few intact children's burials (1992).

14. Kenoyer in a valuable paper (1991: 92) notes that in the Indus Valley large quantities of ornaments shown on figurines are not found in any burials and suggests that valuables or status-markers were passed on to the living and not buried. The Aegean has no such discrepancy.

References

Aegaeum = *Annales d'archéologie égéenne de l'Université de Liège.*
Volumes cited are as follows:
Aegaeum 3 (1989): R. Laffineur (ed.), *Transition: le monde égéen du Bronze moyen au Bronze récent – Actes de la deuxième Rencontre égéenne internationale de l'Université de Liège, 18–20 avril 1988.*
Aegaeum 8 (1992): R. Laffineur and J. L. Crowley (eds), *EIKΩN – Aegean Bronze Age Iconography: Shaping a Methodology. Proceedings of the 4th International Aegean Conference/4e Rencontre égéenne internationale, University of Tasmania, Hobart, Australia 6–9 April 1992.*
Aegaeum 11 (1995): P. Rehak (ed.), *The Role of the Ruler in the Prehistoric Aegean: Proceedings of a Panel Discussion . . . New Orleans, . . . 1992.*
Aegaeum 12 (1995): R. Laffineur and W.-D. Niemeier (eds), *Politeia – Society and State in the Aegean Bronze Age: Proceedings of the 5th International Conference . . . Heidelberg, . . . 1994.*

Alekshin, V.A. (1983), 'Burial Customs as an Archaeological Source', *Current Anthropology*, 24/2: 137–49.

Andrews, C. (1990), *Ancient Egyptian Jewellery*, London: British Museum.

—— (1994), *Amulets of Ancient Egypt*, London: British Museum.

Barber, E.J.W. (1991), *Prehistoric Textiles: The Development of Cloth in the Neolithic and Bronze Ages with Special Reference to the Aegean*, Princeton: Princeton University Press.

—— (1994), *Women's Work – the First 20,000 Years: Women, Cloth, and Society in Early Times*, New York and London: Norton.

Barthélemy de Saizieu, B., and Bouquillon, A. (1993), 'Les Parures en pierre de Mundigak, Afghanistan: collection conservée au Musée Guimet', *Paléorient*, 19/2: 65–94.

Bass, G. F. (1987), 'Oldest known Shipwreck reveals Splendors of the Bronze Age', *National Geographic*, 172/6: 692–733.

Bouzek, J. (1985), *The Aegean, Anatolia and Europe: Cultural Interrelations in the Second Millennium B.C.*, Studies in Mediterranean Archaeology 29, Göteborg and Prague.

—— (1987), 'Macedonian and Thessalian bronzes', *Acta Univ. Carolina Philologica I, Graecolatina Pragensia*, XI: 77–101.

Chadwick, J. (1976), *The Mycenaean World*, Cambridge: Cambridge University Press.

Clark, G. (1986), *Symbols of Excellence: Precious Materials as Expressions of Status*, Cambridge: Cambridge University Press.

Cline, E. H. (1994), *Sailing the Wine-Dark Sea: International Trade and the Late Bronze Age Aegean*, *Brit.Arch.Reports International Series* 591, Oxford.

—— (1995a), '"My brother, my son": Rulership and Trade between the Late Bronze Age Aegean, Egypt and the Near East', *Aegaeum* 11: 143–50.

—— (1995b), 'Tinker, Tailor, Soldier, Sailor: Minoans and Mycenaeans abroad', *Aegaeum* 12: 265–87.

Dalley, S. (1984), *Mari and Karana: Two Old Babylonian Cities*, London and New York: Longman.

Demakopoulou, K. (1988), *The Mycenaean World: Five Centuries of Early Greek Culture 1600–1100 BC*, Athens: Ministry of Culture.

—— (ed.) (1996), *The Aidonia Treasure: Seals and Jewellery of the Aegean Late Bronze Age*, Athens: Ministry of Culture.

Dyczek, P. (1990), 'The so-called Royal Signet-bead from Pylos', *Studia i Prace/Études et Travaux du Centre d'Arch.Médit.de l'Acad.Polonaise des Sciences*, Warsaw, 30/15: 140–8.

Evely, R.D.G. (1993), *Minoan Crafts: Tools and Techniques – an Introduction*, vol.I, *Studies in Mediterranean Archaeology* 92/1, Göteborg.

Eyre, C. J. (1987), 'Work and the Organisation of Work in the New Kingdom', in M.A. Powell (ed.), *Labor in the Ancient Near East, American Oriental Series* 68, New Haven: American Oriental Soc: 167–221.

Francis, P. (1988), 'When is a Bead not a Bead?' *Ornament*, 11/3: 33, 66–9, 71–6.

—— (1992), 'Heirloom Beads in southeast Asia', *Bead Study Trust Newsletter*, 20: 3.

Gale, N.H. (ed.) (1991), *Bronze Age Trade in the Mediterranean: Papers Presented at the Conference held at . . . Oxford . . . 1989*, Studies in Medit.Arch.90. Jonsered: Åström.

Gates, C. (1989), 'Iconography at the Crossroads: The Aegina Treasure', *Aegaeum* 3: 215–25.

—— (1992), 'Art for Children in Mycenaean Greece', *Aegaeum* 8: 161–71.

Gillis, C. (1995), 'Trade in the Late Bronze Age', in C. Gillis, C. Risberg & B. Sjöberg (eds), *Trade and Production in Premonetary Greece: Aspects of Trade – Proceedings of the Third International Workshop, Athens 1993*, Studies in Medit.Arch.and Literature Pocket-book 134, Jonsered: Åström: 61–86.

Harden, D. B. (1981), *Catalogue of Greek and Roman Glass in the British Museum*, vol.I: *Core- and Rod-formed Vessels and Pendants and Mycenaean Cast Objects*, London: British Museum.

Harding, A.F. (1984), *The Mycenaeans and Europe*, London: Academic Press.

Heltzer, M. (1996), *Crafts Organization in the West (Syria, Phoenicia, Palestine), ca.1500–331 BCE, Alt-Orientalische Forschungen* 23/2.

Higgins, R. (1979), *The Aegina Treasure: an Archaeological Mystery*, London: British Museum.

—— (1980), *Greek and Roman Jewellery*, 2nd ed.revised, London: Methuen.

Hughes-Brock, H. (1983), in W.A. McDonald, W.D.E. Coulson & J. Rosser (eds), *Excavations at Nichoria in Southwest Greece*, vol.III: *Dark Age and Byzantine Occupation*, Minneapolis: University of Minnesota.

—— (1985), 'Amber and the Mycenaeans', in J. M. Todd (ed.), *Studies in Baltic Amber (Journal of Baltic Studies*, XVI, special issue): 257–67.

—— (1992), in W.A. McDonald & N. C. Wilkie (eds), *Excavations at Nichoria in Southwest Greece*, vol.II: *The Bronze Age Occupation*, Minneapolis: University of Minnesota.

—— (1993), 'Amber in the Aegean in the Late Bronze Age: Some Problems and Perspectives', in C.W. Beck & J. Bouzek (eds), *Amber in Archaeology: Proceedings of the Second International Conference . . ., Liblice 1990*, Prague: Acad. of Scis.: 219–29.

—— (1995), 'Seals and Beads: Their Shapes and Materials Compared', in J.-C. Poursat (ed.), *Sceaux minoens et mycéniens: IVe symposium international . . . 1992, Clermont-Ferrand, Corpus der Minoischen und Mykenischen Siegel* Beiheft 5, Berlin: 105–16.

—— (forthcoming), 'Amber and other Travellers: Supposition, Speculation, Sentiment, Scepticism', in acts of 1995 Council of Europe Bronze Age Congress *The Aegean and Europe during the second millennium BC*, Athens.

Hugonot, J.-C. (1994), 'Le Liseron et le lierre dans l'Égypte ancienne', *Göttinger Miszellen*, 142: 73–81.

Iakovidis, S. (1977), 'On the use of Mycenaean "buttons"', *Annual of the British School at Athens*, 72: 113–19.

Immerwahr, S. A. (1971), *The Athenian Agora*, vol.XIII: *The Neolithic and Bronze Ages*, Princeton: American School of Classical Studies.

Kenoyer, J. M. (1991), 'Ornament Styles of the Indus Valley Tradition: Evidence from recent Excavations at Harappa, Pakistan', *Paléorient*, 17/2: 79–98.

Kenoyer, J.M., Vidale, M., & Bhan, K.K. (1991), 'Contemporary Stone Beadmaking in Khambat, India: Patterns of Craft Specialization and Organization of Production as Reflected in the Archaeological Record', *World Archaeology*, 23/1 (special issue *Craft Production and Specialization*, ed. J. Graham-Campbell): 44–63.

Kilian-Dirlmeier, I. (1979), *Anhänger in Griechenland von der mykenischen bis zur spätgeometrischen Zeit, Prähistorische Bronzefunde* XI:2, Munich: Beck.

——— (1980), 'Zum Halsschmuck mykenischer Idole', *Jahresbericht des Instituts für Vorgeschichte der Universität Frankfurt a.M. 1978–79.*

Knapp, A. B. (1991), 'Spice, Drugs, Grain and Grog: Organic Identifications in Bronze Age East Mediterranean Trade', in Gale 1991: 21–68.

Laffineur, R. (1995), 'Craftsmen and Craftsmanship in Mycenaean Greece: For a Multimedia Approach', *Aegaeum* 12: 189–99.

Lammers, D. (1991), 'Ein schieberartiger Knochen-"Anhänger" von der Heuneburg, Kr.Sigmaringen', *Archäologisches Korrespondenzblatt*, 21: 383–5.

Lesko, B. S. (ed.) (1989), *Women's Earliest Records from Ancient Egypt and Western Asia: Proceedings of the Conference on Women in the Ancient Near East, Brown University, Providence, RI, 1987*, Atlanta: Scholars Press.

Lewartowski, K. (1995), 'Mycenaean Social Structure: A View from Simple Graves', *Aegaeum* 12: 103–14.

Majno, G. (1975), *The Healing Hand: Man and Wound in the Ancient World*, Cambridge, Mass.: Harvard University Press.

Moran, Wm. L. (ed.) (1992), *The Amarna Letters*, Baltimore: Johns Hopkins.

Müller-Karpe, H. (1985), *Frauen des 13.Jahrhunderts v.Chr., Kulturgeschichte der Antiken Welt* 26, Mainz: von Zabern.

Murray, M. A. (1963), *My First Hundred Years*, London: Wm.Kimber.

Peregrine, P. (1991), 'Some political Aspects of Craft Specialization', *World Archaeology*, 23/1 (special issue *Craft Production and Specialization*, ed. J. Graham-Campbell): 1–11.

Riddle, J. M. (1992), *Contraception and Abortion from the Ancient World to the Renaissance*, Cambridge, Mass.: Harvard University Press.

———, Estes, J.W. & Russell, J.C. (1994), 'Ever since Eve . . . Birth Control in the Ancient World', *Archaeology*, 47/2: 29–35 with ensuing correspondence *Archaeology*, 47/4: 8–10.

Robins, G. (1989), 'Some Images of Women in New Kingdom Art and Literature', in Lesko 1989: 105–21.

Sargnon, O. (1987), *Les Bijoux préhelléniques*, Paris: Geuthner.

Sherratt, A. & S. (1991), 'From Luxuries to Commodities: The Nature of Mediterranean Bronze Age Trading Systems', in Gale 1991: 351–86.

Stocks, D. A. (1989), 'Ancient Factory Mass-production Techniques: Indications of large-scale Stone Bead Manufacture during the Egyptian New Kingdom Period', *Antiquity*, 63/240: 526–31.

Symeonoglou, S. (1973), *Kadmeia I: Mycenaean Finds from Thebes, Greece: Excavation at 14 Oedipus St., Studies in Mediterranean Archaeology* 35, Göteborg.

Vermeule, E. T. (1964 and later editions), *Greece in the Bronze Age*, Chicago: University of Chicago.

Voutsaki, S. (1994), 'Social and political Processes in the Mycenaean Argolid: The Evidence from the Mortuary Practices', *Aegaeum* 12: 55–66.

——— (1995), 'Value and Exchange in pre-monetary Societies: Anthropological Debates and Aegean Archaeology', in Gillis et al. (eds) (see Gillis above): 7–17.

Ward, Wm.A. (1989), 'Non-royal Women and their Occupations in the Middle Kingdom', in Lesko 1989: 33–46.

Warren, P. (1975), *The Aegean Civilisations*, Oxford: Elsevier-Phaidon.

—— (1985), 'The Fresco of the Garlands from Knossos', in *L'iconographie minoenne (Bulletin de Correspondance Hellénique supplément XI)*: 187–208.

Wrede, H. (1975), 'Lunulae im Halsschmuck', in *Wandlungen: Studien zur antiken und neueren Kunst Ernst Homann-Wedeking gewidmet*, Institut für Klassische Archäologie der Universität München: 243–54.

Wright, J. C. (1995), 'From Chief to King in Mycenaean society', *Aegaeum* 11: 63–80.

Xenaki-Sakellariou, A. (1985), *Oi Thalamotoi Taphoi ton Mykenon Anaskaphes Chrestou Tsounta (1887–1898) – Les tombes à chambre de Mycènes, fouilles de Chr.Tsountas (1887–1898)*, Paris: Boccard.

Younger, J. G. (1979), 'Semi-precious Stones to the Aegean', *Archaeological News*, Tallahassee, Florida, 8/2–3: 40–4.

—— (1992), 'Representations of Minoan-Mycenaean Jewelry', *Aegaeum* 8: 257–92.

12

An Archaeological Investigation into Ancient Chinese Beads

Cecilia Braghin

Introduction

The study of beads in ancient China poses interesting questions that have so far remained unsolved. The poor archaeological evidence on the one hand, together with the scant interest shown by Chinese scholars on the other, are the principal reasons why no extensive study has been done so far in the field.[1]

If we attempt to pursue a comparative study of beads in China and in the Western world clear differences become apparent. Beads were fashioned from coloured stones and shining metals among many ancient civilizations in the West such as the Mesopotamian, the Egyptian, the Greek and the Roman. By contrast this phenomenon does not seem to have been present in early China. The Chinese cherished jade from Neolithic times and disregarded, it seems almost deliberately, other precious materials and particularly gold. This situation has led many scholars to compare and contrast the importance of jade in China with the role of gold in the Western world, and to see reflected in the choice of two different materials different aesthetical attitudes and cultural values.

In China jade has always been valued for its physical attributes: the translucence and chromatic unevenness of the texture, the toughness, which makes it so durable, and the pleasing tactile quality. The Chinese must have attached special meanings to these attributes from a very early stage, meanings that we have lost as far as the Neolithic period is concerned, but that we can reconstruct as regards the historic period. A famous passage attributed to Confucius (thought to have lived during the Spring and Autumn period, 770–476 BC) takes jade as a metaphor of the highest moral values advocated by his doctrine. The physical qualities of the stone are associated with the moral virtues of the 'just man', such as benevolence, righteousness, good faith. Objects made of jade were meant to display and to communicate these virtues.

Further meanings were attached to jade by religious Daoism, which developed from the Eastern Han period (AD 25–220). Jade was believed to be a representation on earth of the realm of Heaven, and to be endowed with the power of imparting immortality.

In virtue of its intrinsic qualities and associated meanings jade was reputed a special stone, the most treasured for ceremonial and ritual objects, which allowed man to communicate with the spiritual world, and for ornamental objects, which emblematically stated the power of their owners.

As far as beads are concerned, jade was almost the sole media employed during the Neolithic and Shang periods. It was only by the Western Zhou period that the exclusive use of jade was challenged by other precious materials, such as turquoise, cornelian and faience and, slightly later, rock crystal and glass. This phenomenon will be discussed in detail later in this chapter.

We have noticed so far a clear difference between China and the Western world concerning the choice of materials for beads. Another evident contrast appears as regards the scale of production and distribution. On the basis of the archaeological material collected so far,[2] it would appear that beads in China are not found in great quantity nor is their occurrence uniform as regards geographical or chronological distribution in the Neolithic and early historic period.[3]

This situation would lead us to pose several questions: were beads a popular means of adornment in ancient China as they were in the West? What meanings did the Chinese attach to them? To what extent do these meanings correspond or differ from their Western counterparts? A full-scale investigation into the meanings, typologies and manufacturing techniques of beads in ancient China is far beyond the scope of this work and the actual stage of my research, but would deserve further attention. My aim here is to examine the existing data in order to reconstruct the history of beads in Neolithic and early historic China from an archaeological perspective and explore what they tell us about the status and gender of their owners.

Excavated beads come almost exclusively from tombs; very few were found in sacrificial pits and none in association with settlements. They were probably ornaments worn and cherished by the dead person in life, which were eventually buried in the tomb either to represent his or her private belongings or to indicate the owner's power and wealth, or both.

Beads found in tombs can occur in fairly large quantity, often on the neck or chest portion of the body. In this circumstance they can be reconstructed into necklaces with some degree of confidence. Some tombs, however, possibly of people of lower rank, display only stray finds of beads and in this case it is difficult to interpret their function and meaning. Archaeological contexts of the latter type will not be taken into consideration in this chapter.

The next two sections will be devoted to the Neolithic and Shang periods and will show briefly the localized and scant archaeological evidence of beads, while the fourth section will discuss in more detail the change which occurred by the Zhou period, from which period complex necklaces made up of jade, cornelian, turquoise and faience beads are found in tombs (the map in Figure 12.1 shows the chief archaeological sites dated to these periods). Two excavated tombs will be analysed, purposely selected because they contained inscribed ritual vessels which identify the social status, rank and gender of their owners. This will offer a unique opportunity to study the occurrence of beads in relation to the people who wore them and to speculate about their social-symbolic function.

The Early Occurrence of Beads in the Liangzhu Culture (3000–2000 BC)

Jade was the precious material par excellence in Neolithic China, skilfully worked and turned into a variety of ritual and ornamental objects. 'Jade' is a general term used to identify two types of minerals: nephrite and jadeite. In ancient China only nephrite was employed, a very hard (6,5 in the Mohs scale), translucent stone, whose colour can range from yellow-brown to spinach-green and to an oily mutton-fat white, the most appreciated. However, some softer stones, expecially bowenite, are termed *yu* or jade by the Chinese. Some of the ancient pieces, especially those from the north, may be of bowenite.

Two major cultures are known to have used jade extensively in the Neolithic period in China: the Hongshan culture, which flourished from around 3500 to 2500 BC in the northeast, present-day southern Liaoning, northern Hebei and south-eastern Mongolia provinces, and the Liangzhu culture, which developed from 3000 to 2000 BC along the southern coast in present-day southern Jiangsu and Northern Zhejiang provinces and the Shanghai area. In both cultures jade seems to have played a paramount role, as can be seen from the tomb furnishing: the Hongshan burials are equipped only with jade, and this shows how it was esteemed above all materials and how it was possibly thought to be effective in burial rituals. Several types of objects have been excavated, many of which are provided with holes and are therefore interpreted as ornaments to be hung on strings, but there is very little evidence of beads.

By contrast the interest in beads seems to have occurred in the Liangzhu culture, where a single tomb can yield up to several hundred jade artefacts, especially discs and tubes, variously interpreted by scholars as ritual items. Tombs with rich finds of jade and pottery were probably those of a social élite who supervised and managed the material resources of the community.

Nephrite is a hard material, which cannot be cut or carved but only ground and polished, implying an extremely time- and energy-consuming manufacturing process, especially in this period when metal was not known and so could not provide effective tools. Despite these difficulties, Liangzhu jades are extremely fine, both in respect of their shape and in respect of their surface decoration. Beads found in groups and reconstructed into necklaces by archaeologists tend to be

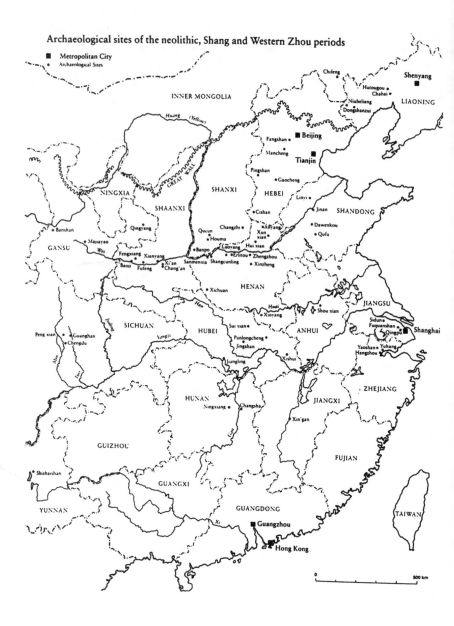

Figure 12.1 Map of China showing the major archaeological sites of the Neolithic, Shang and Western Zhou periods. After Rawson, J. (1995), *Chinese Jade from the Neolithic to the Qing*, London: British Museum Press.

uniform in size and shape and show a good mastery of the drilling technique. They are possibly the result of a well-organized and supervised production scheme, where different people specialized in specific tasks.

Beads represent a substantial part of the overall repertoire of burial jades, and this suggests that they were considered important and valuable objects. Unfortunately we lack any direct written source or indirect pictorial evidence which could throw light on who produced these beads, who wore them and what meanings they conveyed.

What we can say is that, because of the preciousness, the scarcity of the material and the cost of craftmanship, jade could only be afforded by a social élite, and so tombs furnished with jade are likely to belong to socially important people.

We can argue that beads placed in burials could have been worn in life as a manifestation of the power of the owner, but we can only speculate as to their possible symbolic or protective function. This fascination for beads in Liangzhu culture deserves further study, most particularly to understand why it was confined to such a localized area and why it seems to have ended almost abruptly and not stimulated later development.

The Minor Role Played by Beads in the Shang Period (c.1500–1050 BC)

Beads are relatively rare in archaeological sites of the Shang period and this scarcity seems to reflect a situation in which production and consumption of beads were not particularly popular. Jade beads are found in southern China (Jiangxi and Hubei provinces), rarely in central China (Henan province) and almost never in western and northern China. Even Lady Fu Hao, one of the consorts of the Shang king Wu Ding, who was buried around 1200 BC with more than four hundred bronzes, more than seven hundred jades and with several exotic objects traded or raided from cultural areas to the north and the south of the Yellow River basin, possessed only thirty-three jade beads, twenty-six cornelian beads and six turquoise beads.[4] The fact that these beads were placed in the tomb outside the coffin also reflects the relatively low esteem in which they were held.

The cornelian and turquoise beads are rather rare in this period and quite possibly were imported from outside Shang China.[5] The jade beads look typologically similar to the Neolithic Liangzhu specimens. The majority of them are cylindrical and undecorated, very much like their Liangzhu counterparts. It could be argued that, rather than being Shang products, they could well be earlier beads passed on from generation to generation or rediscovered and collected. Jade is a very durable material, so it is not unusual to find jades of earlier date in tombs. Archaeologists have already identified Neolithic jades in the Fu Hao repertoire. This fact might explain why in this period excavated beads are so scarce in number and why they tend to occur in the southern part of China, where the Liangzhu culture developed and where it is more likely that jades were rediscovered. If this is not the case, then we have to think of a situation where only restricted and localized centres of production were making jade beads, possibly as by-products, since they do not show the technical sophistication of other contemporary objects. We do not know whether such beads were worn as personal ornaments, but if we accept the hypothesis that they were earlier pieces, they might have just been collected and treasured as antiques. In three instances beads were found within a *you* type of bronze ritual vessel (Bagley 1987: 372–7), a situation which is quite unique and which makes me wonder if the choice of placing beads inside a valuable bronze container was dictated by the willingness to cherish a treasure or by some kind of ritual practice.

These are just a few considerations drawn on the basis of an archaeological survey which is far from being exhaustive, and which will need to be substantiated by future archaeological material.

A last point of discussion I would like to make is about the attitude towards decoration which characterizes the Shang culture. The art of the Shang shows a great interest in decoration, exploited not only for aesthetic reasons but also as a means of social differentiation. This can be clearly seen in the context of bronze vessels, used in life for performing rituals to the ancestors and buried with their owner at his or her death. The higher the social status, the more numerous, highly decorated and typologically complex were the bronze vessels which equipped the tomb.

What intrigues me, at this stage, is to understand why the Shang very much cherished decoration on their ritual objects but did not particularly stress body decoration. I would suggest that they might have considered other categories of objects as more effective in performing a social-symbolic function. They cherished bronze vessels and valued them as tokens of the family clan and of social prestige. They also had a strong interest in clothes. We know from written sources[6] that in the Shang period members of the royal family and high officials made use of an extensive and varied wardrobe according to ceremonial circumstances, and that colour and decoration of the fabric were symbolically exploited to make visually clear the power and rank of the wearer.

The Re-emergence of Beads in the Western Zhou Period (c.1050–771 BC)

It is with the Zhou Dynasty, which overthrew the Shang in about 1050 BC, that we see a renewed interest in beads and in precious stones, reflecting a more general change in customs and taste brought about by the new ruling family.

The Zhou are thought to have originated from the areas west to the Shang strongholds, possibly Shanxi or even Gansu and Shaanxi provinces, and did not necessarily share features of the Shang culture, at least until they defeated them and assimilated their ritual practices and material culture in order to legitimate their power to rule the country. In virtue of their 'Western' origin, they might have enjoyed contacts with the nomadic tribes of north-western China and could have derived from them the custom of wearing beads. Archaeological excavations show, in fact, that in Bronze Age central Asia there was already an advanced production of jewellery, made of materials often unknown to contemporary China (gold, for instance).

To what extent, therefore, can we relate this re-emergence of bead necklaces to past traditions? I am not very convinced there is any link at all. In the Shang period the interest in beads almost died out and the Neolithic heritage seems too far away. The situation itself suggests a new and independent tradition: the occurrence of beads does not seem to be localized any longer, but seems to be rather more widespread, at least among the territories under the Zhou political control. There is also a move away from an exclusive interest in jade, which characterized the Neolithic and Shang cultures, towards a fascination for other coloured and exotic materials.

I would argue that this is the first instance where precious stones other than jade acquire some importance in themselves and are employed in virtue of their own specific value (primarily aesthetic but also possibly symbolic or magic). Turquoise, for example, had been used in China since Neolithic times, either as an alternative to jade for small carvings or simply as a decorative element in conjunction with other media. This is the first time it is used substantially in its own right. The same can be said of cornelian beads, which cannot be related to any significant previous tradition. The case of faience beads is even more complex and will be discussed later in the chapter.

The three tombs I am going to introduce represent an exceptional opportunity of discussion for several reasons: they were found intact, and so can be analysed from an overall perspective; they also contained inscribed bronze vessels which tell us the identity of the owners and allow us to relate the finds of beads to their rank and gender.

One tomb has been excavated at the Liulihe site, near the town of Fangshan in Hebei province, about 40 km south of Beijing. From the bronze inscriptions we know it belonged to a Marquis of the Yan state named Yan Hou. The other two tombs are located in Shaanxi province, at the village of Baoji Rujiazhuang, not far from the capital Xi'an, and belonged respectively to a Count named Bo who was buried with a concubine, and to his wife, named Jing Ji.

The Yan state was ruled by a relative of the Zhou family, appointed to these northern territories in order to keep them under control. Thus, even at such a great distance, the people buried in the two sites were sharing the same cultural background.

The Marquis of Yan was buried in the early Western Zhou period (eleventh century BC), with a rich set of bronze vessels (twenty-two in number), placed in order along the northern side of the pit outside the coffin. A necklace made up of turquoise, cornelian and jade beads was excavated from inside the coffin, having been placed on the chest of the corpse (Figure 12.2). The composition of the necklace is worthy of notice: the majority of the cornelian beads are discoid but there are a few which display a peculiar bamboo shape (biconical with slightly concave profile). On the whole, there is not much uniformity in shapes and technical quality, especially among the turquoise beads, which can be cylindrical but often of very irregular shape (some beads are just pebbles left in the raw state). As for the jade components of the string, they are not precisely beads, but rather pendants of various shapes: a conical element, a *bi* disc, two bovine masks, two rabbits, three fishes, one silkworm and five flat plaques of irregular shape.

This situation raises some questions: were these elements originally combined in this way? Or were the jade elements, which do not seem to integrate completely, inserted at a later stage? I suggest the second hypothesis. Some of the jade pieces could well be earlier pieces (the flat plaques with irregular shape could be ancient broken pieces), which for some reason were strung into the necklace. If cornelian and turquoise beads were primarily exploited for aesthetic reasons, in order to create an eye-catching colour contrast, jade pieces were possibly endowed with different symbolic or magical meanings.

We do not know whether such a necklace would have been worn in life by its owner or whether it was specifically manufactured to be buried in his or her tomb. It could be that the cornelian and turquoise beads were used in life and that it was only after the owner had died that the jade elements were added, to make the necklace a more special and more effective object to accompany him in the afterlife.

Several burial sites of the Western Zhou period have been excavated in the Baoji area. Among them are two relevant to our research, those of Zhuyuangou and Rujiazhuang. They both provide evidence of beads, but they show a different situation as regards materials. Turquoise beads were found at the Zhuyuangou site, contemporary to Liulihe, but not at the Rujiazhuang site, which is slightly later and can be approximately dated to the early tenth century BC. Later tombs in Shaanxi province[7] also show no evidence of turquoise beads. I would argue that the custom of wearing turquoise beads quickly declined because it was not culturally rooted in this western area but rather borrowed from the north.[8]

In Shaanxi tombs, however, from the late eleventh to the early tenth centuries BC, beads of faience were found, which were completely unknown in the north. There is much debate among scholars as to the origin and provenance of this

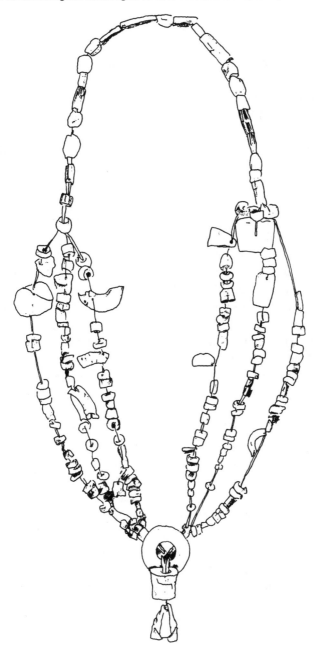

Figure 12.2 Drawing of the necklace belonging to the Marquis of Yan as reconstructed by archaeologists. After Beijing (1995), *Liulihe Xi Zhou Yanguo mudi 1973–1977* (The 1973–1977 excavations at the Western Zhou cemetery at Liulihe), Beijing: Wenwu Chubanshe, plate 48, fig. 2.

material: if faience was made in China, possibly western China, at this stage, this would represent the earliest evidence known so far. But since the evidence is still very limited and since scientific analysis of the material has not been carried out extensively and results are often contradictory,[9] we are not yet in a position to solve this problem. Faience beads were manufactured from the third millenium BC in Mesopotamia and India, where the custom of wearing beads was very deeply rooted. It could be suggested that the interest in beads as well as the exploitation of new materials for beads could have been stimulated by cultural contacts with these western countries.

Faience beads look rather coarse and dull. If they were made in China, this coarseness might be seen as the shortcoming of a manufacturing industry in its formative stage. But it could also indicate that little interest was attributed to the material, employed as a cheaper substitute of jade, as seems to be the case of early glass in China, or possibly of turquoise, as was the custom in the Near East. The glass industry as a whole did not develop to a high degree in ancient China and never became a major artistic tradition. The only exception can be glass beads fashioned as eyes, or 'eye-beads'. They begin to be found in tombs of the Warring States period (475–221 BC), either in stray finds or inlayed into ornamental objects, generally metal belt-hooks. Most of the early examples were imported from the Near East, but some were locally made as well. Unlike monochrome faience beads, it appears that eye-beads were valued as precious and exotic objects, probably in virtue of their visually engaging chromatic texture and their minute surface decoration.[10]

I will now proceed to a detailed analysis of the Rujiazhuang tombs. Observing the sets of ritual vessels owned by the three people, we can clearly see an indication of the rank and social prestige of the owners.[11] Tomb no.1 is a large rectangular pit divided into two chambers; the one on the right was that of the Count while the one on the left was for the concubine. The ritual bronzes were placed outside the coffin on the south-eastern corner of each chamber.

The difference between the two sets is striking: the Count had the largest number of vessels (thirty-seven) and the richest variety of shapes. The majority of pieces are decorated and some are particularly unusual and exotic (Figure 12.3). By contrast the concubine only had nine vessels, of two common types and without any surface decoration (Figure 12.4).

In tomb no. 2, located at the left side of tomb no. 1, the Count's wife was equipped with eighteen vessels (Figure 12.5), among which are some unusual types and several decorated ones, a set larger than that of the concubine but smaller and less elaborate than that of the Count.

Judging their social status as revealed by their bronzes, we immediately perceive a huge contrast: the concubine, even if she was the most important concubine, must have held a very low position in the social hierarchy. Among the women the

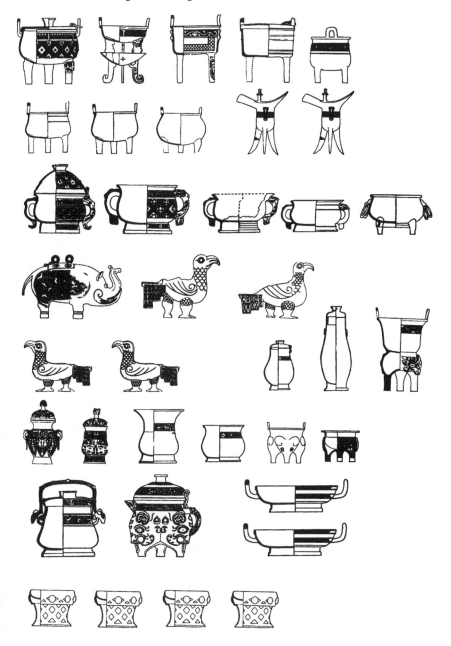

Figure 12.3 Drawing of the set of ritual bronze vessels belonging to the Count found in the right chamber of tomb no 1 at Rujiazhuang, Baoji, near Xi'an. After Lu Liancheng & Hu Zhisheng (1988), *Baoji Yuguo mudi* (Yu State cemetery at Baoji), Beijing: Wenwu Chubanshe.

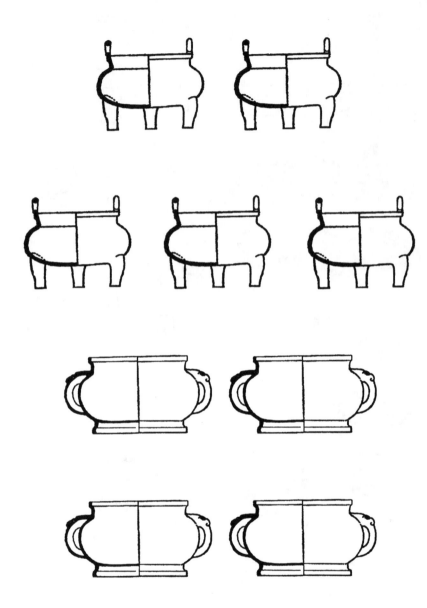

Figure 12.4 Drawing of the set of ritual bronze vessels belonging to the concubine found in the left chamber of tomb no 1 at Rujiazhuang, Baoji, near Xi'an. After Lu Liancheng & Hu Zhisheng (1988), *Baoji Yuguo mudi* (Yu State cemetery at Baoji), Beijing: Wenwu Chubanshe.

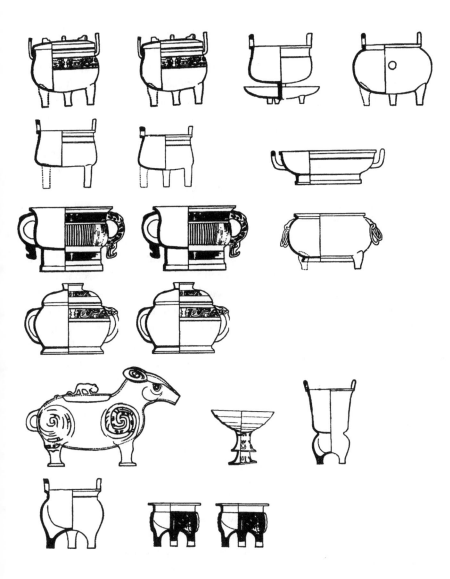

Figure 12.5 Drawing of the set of ritual bronze vessels belonging to the Count's wife Jing Ji found in tomb no 2 at Rujiazhuang, Baoji, near Xi'an. After Lu Liancheng & Hu Zhisheng (1988), *Baoji Yuguo mudi* (Yu State cemetery at Baoji), Beijing: Wenwu Chubanshe.

official wife obviously had more power than the concubine, but they were both subordinated to the privileged role of the man.

What is interesting to notice, however, is that this hierarchy does not fit when we come to compare the necklaces. The man only had one necklace while the concubine had two and the wife three (plus strings of shells on the top of the outer coffin). The Count's necklace was found on the head and is made up of spherical and bamboo-shaped cornelian beads and spherical and cylindrical faience beads, which are arranged in three rows on the front (Figure 12.6). The concubine's strings of beads were located one on the head and one on the belly: the first one combines spherical, cylindrical and rhomboidal faience beads with spherical and bamboo-shaped cornelian beads and a jade *bi* disc in the centre (Figure 12.7). The second string is made up of discoid cornelian beads and two *bi* discs.

The Count's wife's necklaces were found on the head and on the chest. One is made up of cylindrical jade, faience and stone beads and spherical and bamboo-shaped cornelian beads arranged in alternate units. The other two display a more peculiar arrangement: one consists of a string of spherical faience beads with eleven jade silkworm-shaped pendants in the centre (Figure 12.8); the second one is a string of jade shells with small *ge*-shaped, chicken-shaped and fish-shaped pendants inserted. These necklaces are similarly composed and equally articulated. In technical quality there is no evident contrast among the possessions of different owners, unlike the context of bronze vessels. Perhaps this is due to the fact that they were not considered ritual objects, whose number, type and complexity was strictly related to rules in accordance to social status, but were rather personal and ornamental belongings, employed in a more informal way.

Like the example found in the tomb at Liulihe, these necklaces seem to combine precious materials and jade with quite a different purpose. Jade pendants in the shape of animals or plaques are found in great number in all the three tombs, scattered on the head and chest of the body but independently from the strings of beads. Were they endowed with the same meanings as the pendants inserted into the necklaces? It is possible.

In addition to the two sites taken into consideration here, there are a few more of the same period which provide evidence of similar bead necklaces.[12] They are all located in the Yellow River basin (Henan, Shanxi and Shandong provinces), and none comes from further south. It is curious to notice that the geographical occurrence of beads in the Western Zhou period is almost the reverse of the Neolithic situation. This would suggest one more time that the re-emergence of beads and necklaces in the Western Zhou period had no connections with the Neolithic Liangzhu tradition. If future excavations do not prove to contradict this view, we could relate the custom of wearing coloured beads specifically to the Zhou people and suggest that their use conveyed the specific meaning derived from their western limb.

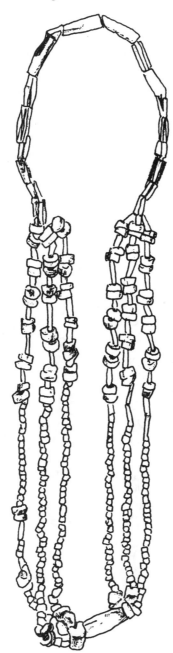

Figure 12.6 Drawing of the necklace belonging to the Count as reconstructed by archaeologists. After Lu Liancheng & Hu Zhisheng (1988), *Baoji Yuguo mudi* (Yu State cemetery at Baoji), Beijing: Wenwu Chubanshe, vol. 2, plate 177, fig. 3.

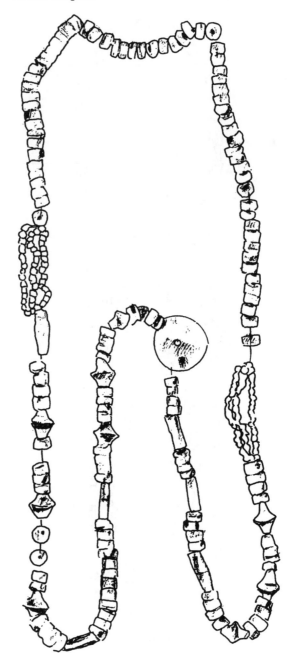

Figure 12.7 Drawing of the necklace belonging to the concubine as reconstructed by archaeologists. After Lu Liancheng & Hu Zhisheng (1988), *Baoji Yuguo mudi* (Yu State cemetery at Baoji), Beijing: Wenwu Chubanshe, vol. 2, plate 177, fig. 1.

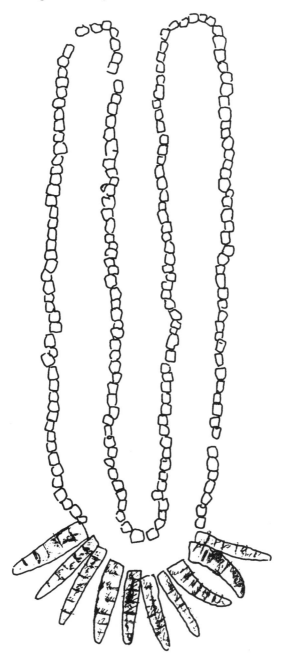

Figure 12.8 Drawing of the necklace belonging to the Count's wife as reconstructed by archaeologists. After Lu Liancheng & Hu Zhisheng (1988), *Baoji Yuguo mudi* (Yu State cemetery at Baoji), Beijing: Wenwu Chubanshe, vol. 2, plate 206, fig. 2.

Conclusion

The history of beads in ancient China is a fascinating topic of research, which is at present a real puzzle. Jade beads had a great start in the Neolithic period within the Liangzhu culture, when they represent a substantial part of the over-all repertoire of jade artefacts and seem to have been considered valuable objects. Gradually they went out of fashion and possibly even out of production in the Shang period. By the Western Zhou period beads of different materials came into use and established a custom which was to last into the Eastern Zhou (770–221 BC) and Han periods (220 BC–AD 220). The reasons for these twists and turns are not clear and deserve further study.

Notes

1. I suspect Chinese scholars are mainly looking at beads as mundane and superfluous objects and so they give priority to other categories of artefacts in their studies. An interest in early Chinese personal ornaments, however, is now arising, particularly in the West, where a few exhibitions and related publications have been produced.
2. A proper campaign of archaeological excavation has only taken place since the establishment of the People's Republic of China in 1949 and the work in the field has been particularly prolific in the last twenty years, during which period several major excavations have been undertaken. It is thanks to the passionate work of Chinese archaeologists that we are now reconstructing in more and more detail the life and culture of ancient China.
3. I am taking into consideration here the time which runs approximately from the 4th millennium BC, when the major jade-yielding Neolithic cultures developed, to the Western Zhou period, which ends in 770 BC.
4. Beijing (1980), *Yinxu Fu Hao mu* (The Tomb of Fu Hao at Yinxu).
5. Turquoise beads could have come from the people living along the northern border of China, who extensively employed this material in their ornaments and weaponry. Turquoise beads were found in a Shang period tomb at the Liujiahe site in Pinggu county, Hebei province, where a non-Chinese warrior lady was buried. (See the report of the excavation in *Wenwu*, 11, 1–8). Cornelian beads are extremely rare in Shang China and could have also been imported from Central Asia, where cornelian had been used for jewellery since much earlier times.
6. The sources to which I refer are the so-called oracle bone inscriptions, carved on turtle's carapaces and cattle's scapulas and used for divination purposes. They represent so far the earliest evidence of a fully developed Chinese writing system and are an invaluable source of information about the religious system of thought and the social and political

life of the Shang people. Another important written document is the *Shijing*, a collection of poems edited by Confucian scholars between c. 1000 and 600 BC, which is thought to incorporate material of an earlier date.

7. See for example the tomb no. 1 at Qiangjia, in Fufeng county, reported in *Wenbo*, no. 4, 5–20.

8. Consider the Shang period tomb of a non-Chinese warrior lady buried at Liujiahe, in Pinggu county, Northern Hebei province. Her tomb provided golden ornaments and turquoise beads. See the report of the excavation in *Wenwu*, no. 11, 1–8.

9. For a more detailed discussion on the chemical structure of these beads and their possible origin see the articles by Zhang Fukan and Wang Shixiong in Brill & Martin 1991.

10. For a more detailed discussion of early Chinese glass and eye-beads see An Jiayao 1987 and Glover & Henderson 1994.

11. For a wider discussion of this phenomenon see Rawson 1993.

12. Among the sites I have studied so far are that of Tianma, Qucun in Shanxi province, that of Lugucheng, Qufu in Shandong province and those of Pingdingshan and Shangcunling, Sanmenxia in Henan province.

References

Alchin, B. (1975), 'The Agate and Carnelian Industry of Western India and Pakistan', *South Asian Archaeology*, 91–105.

An Jiayao (1987), *Early Chinese Glassware* (trans. Henderson, M.), London: The Oriental Ceramics Society Translations, no. 12.

Asian Art Museum of San Francisco (1992), *Beauty, Wealth and Power: Jewels and Ornaments of Asia*, Seattle and London: University of Washington Press.

Bagley, R.W. (1987), *Shang Ritual Bronzes in the Arthur M. Sackler Collections*, Washington, D.C., and Cambridge, Mass.: Harvard University Press.

Barnes, R. & Eicher, J.B. (eds) (1992), *Dress and Gender: Making and Meaning in Cultural Contexts*, New York and Oxford: Berg.

Basa, K.K. (1992), 'Early Glass Beads in India', *South Asian Studies*, no. 8, 91–104.

Beck, H.C. (1928), 'Classification and Nomenclature of Beads and Pendants', *Archaeologia*, vol. 2, no. 27.

—— & Seligman, C.G. (1932), 'Early Chinese Beads of Foreign Type', *Proceedings of the First International Congress of Prehistory and Protohistoric Sciences*, London.

Beijing (1980), *Yinxu Fu Hao mu* (The Tomb of Lady Hao at Yinxu), Beijing: Wenwu Chubanshe.

—— (1995), *Liulihe Xi Zhou Yanguo mudi 1973–1977* (The 1973–1977 Excavations at the Western Zhou Cemetery at Liulihe), Beijing: Wenwu Chubanshe.

Beijing Institute of Cultural Relics (1977), 'Beijing Pingguxian fajue Shangdai muzang' (A Shang Period Tomb Excavated in Pinggu County near Beijing), *Wenwu*, no. 11, 1–8.

Beijing Institute of Cultural Relics and Beijing University, Archaeology Department (1996), '1995 nian Liulihe yizhi muzangqu fajue baogao' (Report on the 1995 Season of Excavation of the Cemetery at Liulihe), *Wenwu*, no. 6, 16–27.

Berger, P. (1997), 'Vanity of Vanities: Adorning the Body in Life and in Death', *Orientations*, vol. 28, no. 3, 63–9.

Calabrese, O. (1986), 'Uomini e Gioielli', *Gioielli: Moda, Magia, Sentimento*, Milano: Mazzotta.

Chang Kwang-chih (1980), *Shang Civilization*, New Haven and London: Yale University Press.

—— (1986), *The Archaeology of Ancient China*, 4th edn, New Haven and London: Yale University Press.

Cultural Bureau of Fufeng County (1987), 'Shaanxi Fufeng Qiangjia yi hao Xi Zhou mu' (Tomb no. 1 of the Western Zhou Period at Qiangjia, Fufeng County, Shaanxi Province), *Wenbo*, no. 4, 5–20.

Douglas, M. (1991), *Purity and Danger: an Analysis of the Concepts of Pollution and Taboo*, London and New York: Routledge.

Dubin, L.S. (1987), *The History of Beads from 30,000 to the Present*, London: Thames & Hudson.

Erikson, J.M. (1969), *The Universal Bead*, New York: Norton & Company.

Eskenazi (1993), *Early Chinese Art from Tombs and Temples*, London.

Flugel, C.J. (1992), *Psicologia dell'Abbigliamento*, orig.ed. 1930, Milano: Franco Angeli Editore.

Francis, P. (1982a), 'When India was Bead Maker to the World', *Ornament*, vol. 6, no. 2, 33–4 and 56–7.

—— (1982b), *Indian Agate Beads*, New York: Lapis Route Books.

Glover, I. & Henderson, J. (1994), 'Early Glass in South and South East Asia and China', in R. Scott & J. Guy (eds), *South East Asia & China: Art, Interaction & Commerce, Colloquies on Art & Archaeology in Asia*, no. 17, London: Percival David Foundation of Chinese Art, 141–70.

Gombrich, E.H. (1979), *The Sense of Order*, Oxford: Phaidon Press.

Grahame, C. (1986), *Symbols of Excellence*, Cambridge: Cambridge University Press.

Hsu Cho-yun and Linduff, K.M. (1988) *Western Zhou Civilization*, New Haven and London: Yale University Press.

Keightley, D.N. (1978), *Sources of Shang History: The Oracle-Bone Inscriptions of Bronze Age China*, Berkeley, Los Angeles and London: Yale University Press.

—— (1990), 'Early Civilization in China: Reflections on how it became Chinese', in P.S. Ropp (ed.), *Heritage of China*, Berkeley: University of California Press, 22–8.

Liu, R.K. (1995), 'Ancient Chinese Ornaments: Zhou to Han', *Ornament*, vol. 19, no. 1, 46–53.

Lu Liancheng & Hu Zhisheng (1988), *Baoji Yuguo mudi* (Yu State Cemetery at Baoji), Beijing: Wenwu Chubanshe.

Müller-Karpe, H. (1985), *Fraven def 13° Jahkhunderts v. Chr., Kultur Jeschacht der Antiqen Welt*, no 27, Meinz: von Zabern.

Ogden, J. (1992), *Ancient Jewellery*, London and Berkeley: British Museum Press and University of California Press.

Pirazzoli-t'Serstevens, M. (ed.) (1996), *L'Arte della Cina*, 2 vols, Torino: Utet.

Rawson, J. (1990), *Western Zhou Ritual Bronzes in the Arthur M. Sackler Collections*, 2 vols, Washington, D.C., and Cambridge, Mass.: Harvard University Press.

—— (1992–93), 'Contact between Southern China and Henan during the Shang Period', *Transactions of the Oriental Ceramic Society*, no. 57, 1–24.

—— (1993), 'Ancient Chinese Ritual Bronzes: the Evidence from Tombs and Hoards of the Shang (c. 1500–1050 BC) and Western Zhou (c. 1050–771 BC) Periods', *Antiquity*, vol. 67, no. 257, 805–23.

—— (1995), *Chinese Jade from the Neolithic to the Qing*, London: British Museum Press.

—— (ed.) (1996), *Mysteries of Ancient China: New Discoveries from the Early Dynasties*, London: British Museum Press.

Seeger, A. (1975), 'The Meaning of Body Ornaments', *Ethnology*, no. 14, 211–24.

Shaughnessy, E.L. (1991), *Sources of Western Zhou History: Inscribed Bronze Vessels*, Berkeley, Los Angeles and London: Yale University Press.

So, J.F. & Bunker, E.C. (1995), *Traders and Raiders on China's Northern Frontier*, Seattle and London: Smithsonian Institution and University of Washington Press.

Strathern, M. (1979), 'The Self in Self-Decoration', *Oceania*, vol. 49, no. 9, 241–57.

Tait, H. (1991), *Seven Thousand Years of Jewellery*, New York: Abradale Press.

Untracht, O. (1982), *Jewellery Concepts and Technology*, New York: Doubleday & Company.

Wang Shixiong (1991), 'Some Glasses from Zhou Dynasty Tombs in Fufeng County and Baoji, Shaanxi', in R.B. Brill & J.H. Martin (eds), *Scientific Research into Early Chinese Glass*, New York: Corning Museum of Glass, 151–6.

White, J.M. & Bunker, E.C. (1994), *Adornment for Eternity: Status and Rank in Chinese Ornament*, Denver and Hong Kong: Denver Art Museum and The Woods Publishing Company.

Wu Hung (1995), *Monumentality in Early Chinese Art and Architecture*, Stanford: Stanford University Press.

Zhang Fukang (1991), 'Scientific Studies of Early Glasses Excavated in China', in R.B. Brill & J.H. Martin (eds), *Scientific Research into Early Chinese Glass*, New York: Corning Museum of Glass, 157–66.

Zhejiang Provincial Institute of Archaeology (1989), *Liangzhu wenhua yuqi* (Jades of the Liangzhu Culture), Beijing: Wenwu Chubanshe.

Zhou Xibao (1984), *Zhongguo gudai fushi shi* (The History of Ancient Chinese Costume), Beijing: Zhongguo Xiju Chubanshe.

Zhou Xun and Gao Chunming (1991), *Zhongguo lidai funü zhuangshi* (Chinese Women's Adornments of All Periods), Shanghai: Xuelin Chubanshe.

Appendix A

What Beads Mean to Craft Producers Supported by Oxfam

Carol Wills

The vehicle broke down on the dusty, dirt road north of Isiola in northern Kenya. I was on my way to visit Samburu women making bead necklaces for a living. It had rained the previous day for the first time in three years (20 October 1994). The rural people are pastoralists whose traditional way of life has been threatened by the long drought in which 40 to 50 per cent of the livestock have died. Many people are dependent upon relief. Foreign tourists visit Isiola and the desert beyond to see both the wildlife and the tribal people in traditional dress. Few local people benefit from the tourism. There are six large tourist hotels near Isiola which generally employ people from other parts of Kenya. The handicraft shops near the hotels mostly belong to outsiders who pay the tourist bus drivers a handsome fee to stop at their shops.

The project I was trying to visit for the charity Oxfam was started in 1990/91 to try to find markets for the beads made by local people. There are thirty members most of whom are illiterate women heads of household. (Other members are traditional blacksmiths who make metal jewellery.) In 1992 they opened a small stall together on the main road just outside Isiola, and three young men work as hawkers. They have registered themselves as a Non-Governmental Organization called APPEAL (Assistance to Pastoral People for Education and Livelihood).

We never reached the women bead necklace makers out in the desert beyond Isiola, but a group of Samburu warriors and women came to look at us sitting in the broken down vehicle. The warriors – who rarely have to perform as warriors anymore – are supported by the community for seven years and spend their time, it would appear, doing their hair in the most elaborate styles, colouring it with red ochre (which keeps away the lice) and adorning it with arrangements of beads (and sometimes buttons as well). The women, in contrast, tend to shave their heads and adorn themselves with hundreds of strands of small glass beads in many colours which sit like great, stiff collars around their necks.

The beads they try to sell to make a living are less grand, usually one strand necklaces of coloured glass beads interspersed with metal. Sometimes they use

295

amber beads (brought down by traders from Ethiopia) and malachite. Oxfam is going to help the women develop designs for sale in the Oxfam shops and catalogues in the UK.

Oxfam undertakes this type of work as part of its Fair Trade programme in support of poor people who face all kinds of disadvantages but who are working to overcome them through their own efforts. The general pattern of trade tends to benefit the trader, leaving the producer vulnerable to exploitation. What Oxfam calls Fair Trade is all about giving the producer a better deal and strengthening their hand in a trading relationship.

The Oxfam Fair Trade programme pays fair prices, provides advances on orders, and shares its profits with producers. It also provides services which may include design and product development, marketing, business skills improvement, technical assistance, help with costing and pricing, and identification of locally available financial services. Producers are people who are especially vulnerable such as women heads of household, indigenous people, people with disabilities, refugees, urban slum dwellers, and seasonally employed agricultural workers.

Oxfam currently (in 1995) work with 293 producer groups in thirty countries in Africa, Asia and Latin America. The retail value of our Fair Trade activity is just under £10 million. During 1995 Oxfam sold 231 lines of jewellery accounting for (roughly) about 4 per cent of sales. This is expected to grow. Market research tells us that the size of the UK market for fashion jewellery in 1992 was £97.8 million with 63.5 per cent of jewellery being imported (20 per cent from India, the Philippines and Thailand).

Among Oxfam's current lines which incorporate beads are:

- glass beads, large and small, produced by a cooperative group of men and women in Agra in India (the men make the beads and the women string them as necklaces).
- clay beads from Peru made by rural people with a tradition of bead making going back hundreds of years.
- necklaces of tiny, black, glass beads (often supporting a silver pendant) made by the Tuareg people of Niger whom we reach through the Union Régionale des Cooperatives which has an effective and worthwhile craft promotion department providing a marketing service to women's groups. (The 'silver' beads and pendants are traditionally made by melting down old coins. I have seen this being done also in Akha villages in the hills of North Thailand. The commercial jewellery workshops now set up to produce copies of tribal jewellery use sheet metal instead.)
- glass bead necklaces made by women at the Gypsy Bead Centre in Madras. Gypsy Beads is a unit of the South India Scheduled Tribes Welfare Association established to assist with the social and economic development of nomadic tribespeople of Tamil Nadu.

- necklaces of coloured stones (with some metal) made by people in a rehabilitation project for the hearing impaired in Calcutta.
- necklaces of lapis and turquoise with gilt made by men and women at the Bombolulu Coast Workshop for People with Disabilities, Mombasa, Kenya.
- necklaces and earrings of clay, papier mâché and wooden beads made by men and women at the Jacaranda Workshop in Nairobi, Kenya.
- necklaces of wooden beads made by women in Manila, Philippines, whose husbands are casual daily labourers with no employment security.
- assorted collars of small, coloured, glass beads made by people in the townships of South Africa as part of an employment creation scheme.
- multi-strands of black and white glass beads made by young school and university 'drop-outs' (dropped out because the family can no longer afford to pay the fees) in Java, Indonesia.
- small glass and, sometimes plastic, bead earrings, collars, necklaces and belts made by the T'Boli people of Mindanao in the southern Philippines. The T'Boli are tribal people living around Lake Sebu who have been dispossessed systematically of the land on which they depend to make their living. They are being squeezed by lowlanders who want the fertile land for farming and by speculators who want the mountain land for its wood and for the gold that may be under the ground. 80 per cent are now landless. They have traditional craft skills – such as weaving, basket making, lost wax brass casting, and jewellery making – which are enabling them now to make products which can be sold for money to buy all the things they need to live. The T'Boli put a high value on their large glass beads (usually old beads which are passed down from generation to generation) and do not wish to sell them. They have found a way to copy them at low cost. They soften coloured plastic such as combs, rulers and ballpoint pens, and then roll the malleable substance into beads which, when hardened, are made up into traditional necklaces (but with a singular difference!).

Oxfam has a great variety of beads from a great variety of groups. What we try to do is work with people in the best way possible in the circumstances. Stringing beads can provide a means of earning money for women and men with a low level of skill; it can be done at home as well as at a workplace (and so women are able to fit it in with domestic responsibilities); it does not require special equipment; the investment needed is low; it can be done alone or in a group. In a group it is possible to talk while working, and so people are able to exchange news, share information, discuss problems, and find solutions together. Bringing people together in a group also allows savings and credit schemes to be set up which is very important for the development of sustainable livelihoods for people. Stringing beads will never earn anyone very much money. But if a little money can be set aside on a regular basis, this can lead to the development of other enterprises.

Oxfam has many examples on record of women using their savings to buy livestock in order to generate more income through the sale of eggs, milk or curd; to dig out and stock fishponds as a community endeavour; to buy rickshaws for their husbands; to train their husbands in a new skill which will enable them to earn more; to buy sewing machines to establish small sewing businesses (for example making sari blouses); or to set up tea shops or small grocery stores. The T'Boli people have set up a tree nursery with the dividend they have received from the profit made by Oxfam on the sale of their products. Earnings are almost always used to educate children and buy more food for the family.

Apart from all this, people seem to enjoy making products which are going to be used for adornment. Many people like wearing jewellery of all kinds which enhances their appearance, and beads are used for hair ornaments, earrings, necklaces and chokers, pendants, bracelets, belts and anklets; and for decoration on garments. If you enjoy wearing something yourself, but also make something similar to sell, you more easily understand how the products are going to be used and, in my experience, that is a source of satisfaction to the makers.

The whole purpose of Oxfam's work in this area is deliberately to promote the social, economic and environmental well-being of the producers, as well as to make a profit. Our profits are small. We aim for 2 per cent net and do not always achieve this. When we do make a profit, this does not go into our general funds but is earmarked for dividends for the producers. We are not setting about our work in the traditional business way with the prime purpose of profit maximization. If we were doing that we would concentrate on buying highly marketable product from easily accessible, and relatively few, sources. We would probably buy from wholesalers to avoid all the risks involved in importing. For Oxfam it is essential to have a direct relationship with the producers and to work with them, providing them with support according to their own perceived needs, and helping them to find markets for their products.

Appendix B

Don't get your Necklaces in a Twist! Often-used Specialist Bead Terms and their Definitions for Researchers and Collectors

Stefany Tomalin

We can only guess when the first 'bead' was threaded and put around that first neck. It may have been a garland of perishable flowers or seeds, and thousands of years before the earliest pierced shells and teeth that have survived in burials. But now that systematic professional research is being undertaken, data becomes available that will show more accurately than ever the earliest history of our subject, and there is less and less excuse for us, whether scholars, designers, collectors, traders, journalists, or addicts, to continue to be imprecise with our terminology.

We are usually attracted to beads because they satisfy a human hunger for decoration, as small meaningful treasures they may have amuletic or talismanic properties, and since the earliest times, long before money, they must have visibly displayed wealth and fulfilled acquisitive impulses even among early nomadic peoples. It's not so different today, as our range of ways of self-adornment are constantly extended to new limits by the demands for so-called 'novelty' by the fashion industry. Indeed, the jewellery we wear need not consist only of the most costly gemstones and gold; beads adapt to such a great variety of 'looks' and threading methods. Those we love the most can be repeatedly recycled – incorporated into new arrangements and forms.

My purpose is to clarify some of the most often misunderstood terminology concerning beads.

Beadwork

Any technique where small regular round or tubular beads are used as units to build up or embellish a decorative textile construction with one or more threads or wire:

299

The processes for producing beadwork of any complexity are based on such common fibre techniques as sewing, looping, and weaving . . . In creating beadwork the artist either applies beads to a surface or unites them in a free-standing structure. Beadwork is either fabricated on a supporting framework, such as a loom, or worked off-loom, with needle and thread (Moss & Scherer 1992).

Names for more familiar types of beadwork worked with a fine beading needle and thread, include: daisy chain, bead lace, bead netting, and *peyote* stitch.

Beadweaving is worked onto a warp, using a specific weaving technique with beading needle and thread. Usually strips are produced.

Beads generally used for beadwork are known as embroidery beads, *rocailles*, seed beads and bugles.

Knitting with beads, crochet and tambour work are techniques that require beads to be already strung on a thread and passed down one at a time between each stitch.

Bead embroidery uses beads added ornamentally onto an existing textile, also with needle and thread, or a tambour hook, either singly in strict horizontal and vertical rows following a squared-up pattern such as for cross-stich, or in many imaginative and 'free' ways, varying in stitch size and density of beads, colours, and sizes.

Tassels, fringes or even bead curtains can also come under the category of beadwork, but straight threaded beads of any size, with or without knots between, single or multistranded, do not.

Too many craft writers use the terms 'beadwork' or 'beading' (which by itself means nothing), when they mean bead threading or working with beads.

Terms for Necklaces

A string of beads of the same material may be **graduated**, the largest bead at the front, then beads arranged symmetrically in diminishing sizes towards the back. The term **multistrand** describes any necklace with a number of strands that travel the whole length, whether thickly bunched or arranged to lie flat, one strand next to the other, and perhaps kept evenly spaced with the use of **spacers** – bars with a row of holes through which each strand passes.

Short or small necklaces: **necklet, choker** (this can either be single, or a broad strip of parallel strands or beadwork to fit closely around the throat), **collar** (usually made to lie flat around the neck, often also constructed with a beadwork technique).

Sautoirs or muff chains are very long strands, generally at least 36 in. (90 cm) – instructions in old needlework magazines use these names dating back to the times when muffs were in use. This length can also be worn bandolier fashion, diagonally.

A '**dally**' is a pendant necklace with flirtatious associations.

Parure is a complete matching set of jewellery, which may include necklaces, bracelets, earrings, and brooches, or the term is sometimes used for a single neck-hung ornament that is elaborate enough to cover most of the bosom or chest, also known as a 'pectoral'.

Worry Beads and Prayer Beads

In Greece and much of the Middle East today, Christian and Muslim men alike carry a short strand of beads with a tassel, called *rombologion* in Greece, which derives from Islamic and Christian prayer bead traditions. Originating, it is believed, with the Hindu *mala*, still also in use today, and equally part of the Buddhist and Tibetan practices, counting beads helps the reciting of prayers. The Christian **paternoster** , or **rosary** and the Muslim *tasbiah* have the same function.

Other jewellery items predominantly made of beads usually include: bracelet, anklet or ankle bracelet, waist beads worn next to the skin, girdles or belts, earrings, headband and various hair ornaments.

Specialist Terms for Components, or 'Findings'

Fastenings: **clasp, catch, bolt ring, snap, screw clasp, barrel, hook and eye**. The term **spacer** means a bar shaped component with a row of holes to separate parallel strands and keep a multistrand necklace spread out evenly. The term is not correctly used when describing the small beads put between larger more precious or interesting beads.

Bullion, gimp, purl, necklet ends, french wire (and hence the misnomer *bouillon*) are terms for the small coils of fine wire used to cover the exposed thread at either end of a necklace as a protective sleeve where it goes through the fastener loop before being knotted to finish.

Crimps, crimping beads, french crimps and **callottes** are different types of metal attachments to secure the end of a strand of beads quickly and cheaply to the fastener by squeezing them shut or bending flat with pliers, to cover up or minimize the need for a tidy knot.

Threading Materials

For the tiniest beads, seed pearls and coral, the strongest natural fibres used to be recommended, such as **silk** or **linen**. Our choice today includes tough man-made yarns such as multifilament spun nylon, *kevlar* and dental floss, which are all proper threads that can be knotted. Strong, but not nearly so fine, are: nylon monofilament fishing line, **gut, sinew, horsehair, raffia, leather thonging, braids cords** and **macrame ropes**, 'tigertail', a form of nylon coated steel wire cable, and fine chain.

Beads

Beads can be **natural substances** with natural holes, such as worn down shells often found on the beach, the small flints with hollow middles called 'witch stones' found in parts of southern England, or the small fossilized crinoid segments with natural holes found on the north east coast, called 'St Cuthbert's beads'. More often existing substances are carved, with a hole that is 'drilled' or 'bored'.

Carving is one form of cutting to shape, so is the grinding of facets, or turning on a lathe to get a rounded form. Many natural substances of organic origin are easily carved: **wood, amber, coral, jet, shell, ivory, bone,** the exception being pearls which are drilled to make beads.

The Japanese *ojime* sliding beads, and *netsuke* toggles to attach a purse to the sash in traditional formal dress, represent some of the finest miniature carved masterpieces ever made, and often bear the signature of the sculptor.

In addition to pearls, amber, coral and jet, the gemstones in constant demand are, **turquoise, lapis and amethyst, then jade, rosequartz and moonstone**, followed by **tiger's eye and garnet**. There are many more varieties of quartzes, agates and jaspers and other groups of gemstones with less well-known names which are also popular, and the lay person can be confused by their similarities.

As gemstones have a high intrinsic value, they are often imitated, and even the serious bead researcher may be misled. Your gemstone could be identified and assessed by experts, and enquiries to the Gemmological Association and Gem Testing Laboratory of Great Britain, can provide helpful booklists; also gemmology can be studied at every level in their classes.

Some famous, rare and very highly prized gemstone beads are the 'etched agates', ancient beads of cornelian or other natural colour agate, artificially embellished with lines of white resembling the *batik* technique. Very specifically black or brown barrel shapes with formalized designs of white lines and circles are known as *tzi* or *dzi*, beads of the Himalayan area, and are valued heirlooms.

A large proportion of beads are modelled into shape, made either of soft resins which may retain a scent, or the many forms of ceramic pastes, with a genealogy going back to the brilliantly coloured *faience* of dynastic Egypt where the earliest quantity production seems to have begun. The copper and soda-rich clays of Egypt gave a brilliant turquoise blue glaze to the small shapes with one firing.

Inexpensive decorated ceramic beads are widely made today by hand, in Africa, India, China and South America, as well as by designer/makers in Europe and USA.

A new modelling material making its mark is a **polymer 'clay'** obtainable in many colours which hardens permanently by baking, and can be worked in fine accurate detail. Hobbyists and children can use it as easily as some of the most accomplished artists who have chosen to make exquisite one-of-a-kind beads. Brand names include 'Fimo', 'Sculpey', 'Formello' and 'Cernit'.

Metal beads and dangling pendants add a shiny allure, suggestive of wealth, and have always constituted a large part of the bead repertoire. Metals can be cast in moulds, shaped from sheet or wire with hammering and soldering, and make the base for Chinese cloisonné enamel.

Glass is the substance from which more beads were and are made than any other material, even in today's industrial mass production. It could be classed as a substitute or synthetic, and often fills that function, but the skill it demands at the highest level shows imagination and artistry in bead making which far outstrips the attraction of gemstones, in my opinion. Glazes, fused or melted glass 'pastes' and ground enamels, the forerunners of true glass, were already found in Egypt and the Middle East before approx. 2,400 BC when glass began to be used as a material in its own right, worked in a hot state, and melted into moulds.

Bead Making Techniques

Fused Powder Glass (*Pate de Verre*)
Hot worked glass: Blown and drawn tubes.

Blown bubbles stretched while viscous into long tubes can be cut into many sections to make donut, barrel or tubular glass beads in quantity, such as *rocailles* **or 'bugles'** for beadwork.

Hot worked glass can be either **furnace** – or **lampwork,** that is, by working with molten coloured glass in a flame or other heat source to build up and decorate the beads, one at a time. This requires considerable skills.

Millefiori is a very popular form of floral decorative motif on Venetian glass beads in particular, consisting of a previously made rod or 'cane' with an elaborate design built up in its cross-section. When the 'cane' is heated and stretched, the pattern becomes miniaturized without loss of detail. Many tiny slices can be made and melted onto the surface of a bead, allowing matching and repeating motifs.

Glass beads resemble natural crystal when they have ground and polished facets.

Some names of traditional handmade glass beads known in this country to lacemakers who use them on their bobbin spangles: **Jug beads, Kitty Fisher's Eyes, Squarecuts.**

Another well-known glass bead is the **Chevron**, among the most loved and collected of Venetian beads, made and traded for over 500 years. A large barrel-shaped drawn glass bead with an intricate cross-section, bevelled or rounded at either end to reveal the pattern as zigzags. The most popular is in a blue-white-red colour combination.

Trade Beads is a general expression associated with cylindrical *millefiori* beads made in large quantities for trade in particular into Africa. They were sometimes called *Goulamin* beads by the '60s hippies who brought them back from Morocco. They are no longer made.

Eye-Beads describe the most prolific of amuletic beads carrying an eye design to avert the evil eye. They are often in turquoise blue glass, though they are also made of many other materials including carved wood, stone, bone, and so on.

Glass beads are made today in quantity in Italy, India, China, Japan, Indonesia and the Czech Republic. Studio glass artists in USA, Europe and Japan make one-of-a-kind masterpieces.

Plastic is another extensively used category of bead material. Although it is often used to imitate more expensive substances, modern plastics allow an amazing range of creative novelty, and plastic jewellery, including beads, is an inexhaustible item for collectors.

Fakes are also worth collecting as they show so much ingenuity and sometimes the fake is rarer than what it tries to resemble.

Manufacturers' Sample Cards are used by serious bead researchers, since they are often among our best clues about periods and origins.

The selected bibliography lists generally available source books on aspects of beads:

Beck, H. (1981), *Classification and Nomenclature of Beads and Pendants*, Shumway.

Carey, M. (1986), *Beads and Beadwork of East and South Africa*, Aylesbury: Shire.

—— (1991), *Beads and Beadwork of West and Central Africa*, Aylesbury: Shire.

Clabburn, P. (1980), *Beadwork*, Aylesbury: Shire.

Dubin, L. S. (1987), *The History of Beads*, London: Thames and Hudson.

Edwards, J. (1966), *Bead Embroidery*, London: Batsford.

Farneti Cera, D. (ed. Abrams 1992), *Jewels of Fantasy*, Milan/New York.

Francis, Jr., P. (1994), *Beads of the World*, Pennsylvania: Schiffer.

Guido, M. (1978), *Glass Beads of Prehistoric and Roman Periods*, London: Thames & Hudson.

Higgins, R.A. (1961), *Greek and Roman Jewellery*, London: Methuen.

Jargstorf, S. (1993), *Baubles, Buttons and Beads*, Pennsylvania: Schiffer.

—— (1995), *Glass Beads from Europe*, Pennsylvania: Schiffer.

—— (1991), *Glass in Jewelry*, Pennsylvania: Schiffer.

Kinsey, R. O. (1991), *Ojime, Magical Jewels of Japan*, New York: Abrams.

Liu, R. (1995), 'Collectible Beads,' *Ornament*, California.

Mack, J. (ed.) (1986), *Ethnic Jewellery*, London: British Museum.

Maxwell-Hyslop, K.R. (1971), *Western Asiatic Jewellery*, London: Methuen.

Moss, K. & Scherer, A. (1992), *The New Beadwork*, New York: Abrams.

Ogden, J. (1982), *Jewellery of the Ancient World*, London: Trefoil.

Tomalin, S. (1997), *The Bead Jewellery Book*, Newton Abbot Devon: David & Charles.

—— (1988), *Beads!*, Newton Abbot Devon: David & Charles.

Van der Sleen, W.G. (1973), *A Handbook on Beads*, Liège Belgium: Librairie Halbart.

Wilkins, E. (1969), *The Rose Garden Game*, London: Gollancz.

Wilkinson, A. (1971), *Ancient Egyptian Jewellery*, London: Methuen.

Useful addresses:

UK:

Bead Society of Great Britain
Membership Secretary, Dr. Carol Morris
1, Cosburn Lane
Burwell
Cambridgeshire CB5 OED
Subscription (£7–10 0verseas) bring 5 newsletters per annum,
workshops, meetings and annual bead bazaar.

Bead Study Trust
Secretary, Ms M.E. Hutchinson
29 Elliscombe Road
London SE7 7PF

Gemmological Association and Gem Testing Laboratory of Great Britain
27 Graville Street
London EC1N 8SU

USA:

For up-to-date addresses of Bead Societies, consult:

The Bead Directory
PO Box 10103
Oakland
CA 94610
USA

Ornament Magazine
PO Box 2349
San Marcos
CA 92079
USA

List of Contributors

Cecilia Braghin graduated from the Faculty of Oriental Languages and Literatures, University of Venice in 1994 with a thesis on typology and functions of ancient Chinese jade personal ornaments. She then obtained a Master in Chinese Art and Archaeology at the School of Oriental and African Studies, University of London in 1995. At present she is undertaking a PhD in Chinese Archaeology at the University of Oxford under the supervision of Dr Jessica Rawson. Her research is devoted to ancient beads and the symbolic use of precious materials in ancient China.

Margret Carey began her career as an archaeologist, then became an assistant keeper in the British Museum's Department of Ethnography (now the Museum of Mankind, London) from 1953 till the birth of her elder daughter in 1961. She has worked as an assistant in the ethnographical section of the Horniman Museum, London, and is currently a special assistant at the Museum of Mankind, where she curated an exhibition on the Bemba people of Zambia in 1983. Her special areas of interest are the beadwork of Africa, and the art of eastern and southern Africa. She has contributed to the *Encyclopaedia Britannica*. She has written and edited books on African art, including *Masks and Figures from Eastern and Southern Africa*, and *Myths and Legends of Africa* (both Hamlyn) and she has contributed to the Newsletters of The Bead Study Trust (of which she is a Trustee), and The Bead Society of Great Britain.

Penny Dransart is lecturer in archaeology at the University of Wales, Lampeter. Her research focuses on the herding of llamas and alpacas in the Andes and on textiles woven from camelid fibre. She is co-editor of *Basketmakers: Meaning and Form in Native American Baskets* (1992) and editor of *Andean Art* (1995). Other publications include chapters in *Dress and Gender* (Berg 1992) and *Creating Context in Andean Cultures* (Oxford University Press 1997).

Joanne B. Eicher, Regents' Professor at the University of Minnesota in the department of Design, Housing and Apparel, specializes in dress as non verbal communication. Editor of *Dress and Ethnicity* and co-editor of *Dress and Gender* and *Dress and Identity*, she has produced a video on *Owuarusun*, a spectacular Kalabari masquerade event in the early 1990s.

Helen Bradley Foster holds dual M.A. degrees, one in American Studies and another in Ancient Studies; she received her Ph.D. in Folklore and Folklife from the University of Pennsylvania. Foster teaches African American Art and American Folk Art at the University of Minnesota, and American Studies at the College of Visual Arts, St. Paul. She is the author of numerous publications on material culture.

Helen Hughes-Brock works on beads and engraved seals from the Mycenaean and Minoan civilizations of Bronze Age Greece and Crete (third and second millenia BC). She has contributed to excavation reports and written articles on Bronze Age amber and other bead subjects. She has been a Trustee of the Bead Study Trust and is a major contributor to the *Bead Study Trust Newsletter.*

Monica Janowski carried out fieldwork in the Kelabit Highlands, Sarawak, Malaysia in 1986–8 and 1992–3. After completing her doctorate in 1991, she held an Evans Fellowship at the Department of Social Anthropology at the University of Cambridge for three years. She currently has a post at the Natural Resources Institute, University of Greenwich. She has published a number of articles on the Kelabit. During fieldwork, she made collections of Kelabit artefacts for the Museum of Mankind and for the Sarawak Museum, and is working on a publication relating to these.

Lynn A. Meisch received her Ph.D. in anthropology from Stanford University in 1997, and joined the faculty of Saint Mary's College of California, Moraga, as an assistant professor of anthropology. She has conducted fieldwork in Colombia, Ecuador, Peru and Bolivia since 1973 and published on such topics as *artesanías*, traditional Andean textiles, costume and ethnicity, globalization, tourism, the indigenous rights movement, and the prevention of intractable ethnic violence in Ecuador.

Ann O'Hear lectured at Kwara State College of Technology, Ilorin, Nigeria from 1976 to 1985, and is now at Niagara University. She has published widely on the social and economic history and historiography of Ilorin. Her monograph, *Power Relations in Nigeria: Ilorin Slaves and their Successors*, was published in 1997.

Lidia D. Sciama is a member of the Oxford Centre for Cross-Cultural Research on Women. She has conducted fieldwork in Venice and the islands of the northern lagoon. Among her publications are: 'The Problem of Privacy in Mediterranean Anthropology,' in S. Ardener (ed.), *Women and Space*, Croom Helm, 1981; Berg 1993; 'Kinship and Residence on a Venetian Island,' *International Journal of Moral and Social Studies*, Oxford. Summer 1986; 'Lacemaking in Venetian Culture,' in R. Barnes and J. Eicher (eds), *Dress and Gender*, Berg 1992; 'The Venice Regatta:

From Ritual to Sport,' in J. McClancy (ed.), *The Social Anthropology of Sport*, Berg 1996.

Stefany Tomalin is a founder member of the Bead Society of Great Britain: she is designer, collector, author and retailer of antique and unusual loose beads and bead jewellery.

Francesca Trivellato was born in Padua (Italy) in 1970. She graduated from the University of Venice in 1995 with a thesis on the Venetian glass manufacturing and guild organization in the seventeenth century. She is currently expanding this research topic for her dissertation. She studied at the University of California at Berkeley in 1992/93 and was a Fulbright student at Brown University in 1996/97.

Laurie A. Wilkie received her doctorate in Archaeology from UCLA in 1994, and is currently an Assistant Professor of Anthropology at the University of California, Berkeley. Wilkie's research interests include the anthropological study of ethnicity, gender and race relations through contemporary and archaeological material culture in the southern and western United States, and in the Caribbean.

Carol Wills is the director of the International Federation for Alternative Trade, a global network of Fair Trade Organizations. Formerly she worked for Oxfam for 14 years. She is currently working for an M.Sc. in Responsibility in Business Practice, a new interdisciplinary course at the University of Bath Business School.

Index